The
Baccalaureate

Also available in the *Future of Education From 14+* series:

Access, Participation and Higher Education edited by Annette Hayton and
  Anna Paczuska
Apprenticeship edited by Patrick Ainley and Helen Rainbird
Beyond A Levels by Ann Hodgson and Ken Spours
New Labour's New Educational Agenda by Ann Hodgson and Ken Spours
Policies, Politics and the Future of Lifelong Learning by Ann Hodgson
Tackling Disaffection and Social Exclusion edited by Annette Hayton
Young People's Perspectives on Education, Training and Employment by
  Lorna Unwin and Jerry Wellington

Available from all good bookshops. To obtain further information, please
contact the publisher at the address below:

Kogan Page Limited
120 Pentonville Road
London N1 9JN
Tel: +44 (0)20 7278 0433
Fax: +44 (0)20 7837 6348
www.kogan-page.co.uk

THE FUTURE OF EDUCATION FROM 14+

The Baccalaureate

A Model for Curriculum Reform

Edited by
Graham Phillips and Tim Pound

KOGAN
PAGE

London and Sterling, VA

First published in Great Britain and the United States in 2003 by Kogan Page
Limited

Apart from any fair dealing for the purposes of research or private study, or
criticism or review, as permitted under the Copyright, Designs and Patents Act
1988, this publication may only be reproduced, stored or transmitted, in any
form or by any means, with the prior permission in writing of the publishers,
or in the case of reprographic reproduction in accordance with the terms and
licences issued by the CLA. Enquiries concerning reproduction outside these
terms should be sent to the publishers at the undermentioned addresses:

120 Pentonville Road
London N1 9JN
UK
www.kogan-page.co.uk

22883 Quicksilver Drive
Sterling VA 20166–2012
USA

© Graham Phillips, Tim Pound and the individual contributors, 2003

The right of Graham Phillips, Tim Pound and the individual contributors to
be identified as the authors of this work has been asserted by them in
accordance with the Copyright, Designs and Patents Act 1988.

ISBN 0 7494 3837 1

British Library Cataloguing-in-Publication Data

A CIP record for this book is available from the British Library.

Library of Congress Cataloging-in-Publication Data

The baccalaureate : a model for curriculum reform / edited by Graham
Phillips and Tim Pound.
  p. cm.
Includes bibliographical references and index.
  ISBN 0-7494-3837-1
  1. Education, Secondary--Great Britain--Curricula. 2. Vocational
education--Great Britain--Curricula. 3. Curriculum change--Great
Britain. I. Phillips, Graham, 1939- II. Pound, Tim, 1949-
  LB1629.5.G7B33 2003
  373.19′0941--dc21

                                        2003005590

Typeset by Saxon Graphics Ltd, Derby
Printed and bound in Great Britain by Biddles Ltd, Guildford and King's Lynn
www.biddles.co.uk

Contents

Notes on the contributors

Graham Able is the Master of Dulwich College. He was one of the initial Co-Chairs of the joint GSA/HMC Education/Academic Policy Committee. He is Chairman of HMC (the Headmasters' and Headmistresses' Conference) for 2003. His earlier career was spent teaching in the independent sector.

Robert Adams is Head of Research for the Welsh Joint Education Committee (WJEC), the schools examinations board for Wales, and the base for other all-Wales educational activities. He has held the post for 17 years, during which time he has been engaged in a number of curriculum initiatives, including the Records of Achievement National Project in Wales. Before his appointment he worked for the Somerset TVEI Project, developing a modular curriculum and its assessment systems. He was part of the WJEC team that wrote the tender, which was accepted by the Welsh Assembly, for the pilot of the Welsh Baccalaureate Qualification.

Phil Butler is Assistant Principal for Quality at City College Birmingham. From 1996 he led the development in the UK of the International Associate Degree Program with City Colleges of Chicago. From 1998 he led the group of colleges working with FEDA (now LSDA) on developing the College Diploma for the UK. He has a comprehensive background for innovative curriculum development and the improvement in quality in further education. In his early career he taught in colleges in Manchester, before moving to the Midlands.

James Cambridge is a research officer with the Centre for the Study of Education in an International Context (CEIC) at the University of Bath. He has 25 years experience of practice as a biology educator in the United Kingdom, the Middle East and southern Africa. His current professional interests include science education, international education and the organizational cultures of international schools.

John David was formerly Head of Radyr Comprehensive School in Cardiff. His previous posts included Director of Sixth Form at Singapore International School, Deputy Head of Atlantic College and of Whitchurch High School. At Atlantic College he was involved in the development work leading up to the replacement of A levels by the International Baccalaureate (IB). In Singapore he prepared the staff and the sixth form for the introduction of this qualification. Recently he has worked as an educational consultant with the Institute of Welsh Affairs (IWA), and was a member of the team that developed the Welsh Baccalaureate.

Michèle Deane is a Senior Lecturer in Education in the Centre for Research in Education and Development in Teacher Education at the Open University. Previously she worked as a Staff Tutor in Education (PCGE) at the Open University in the south west and as a Lecturer in Education at the University of Bath. In her early career, she taught in schools in the south west of England and was advisory teacher for modern languages in the former County of Avon.

Dr Mary Hayden is a Senior Lecturer in the Department of Education at the University of Bath, where she is also Head of the International Education Research Group and Director of the Centre for the Study of Education in an International Context (CEIC). Mary Hayden worked for the International Baccalaureate Organization and for the research section of the University of London Examinations and Assessment Council (ULEAC) prior to moving to Bath, where her research interests are located in the field of international schools and international education, as well as in assessment and evaluation. Currently she directs the internal evaluation dimension of the Welsh Assembly Government's Welsh Baccalaureate Qualification pilot project, for which the University of Bath has responsibility, working closely with the Welsh Joint Education Committee (WJEC).

Dr Ian Hill is Deputy Director General of the International Baccalaureate Organization (IBO), based in Geneva. Prior to joining the IBO in 1993 he was director of the International School of Sophia Antipolis, a bilingual IB Diploma school in the south of France. From 1986 to 1989 he was senior private secretary/advisor to the Minister for Education in the state of Tasmania, and represented the Australian government on the IBO Council of Foundation. In Australia he has held positions as a senior administrator in government schools; a university lecturer in education, and team member of an Australian national programme for curriculum development at secondary school level.

Dr Ann Hodgson has worked as a teacher, lecturer, editor, civil servant and LEA advisor, joining the Institute of Education in 1993. She is currently a Senior Lecturer and Research Tutor in the School of Lifelong Education and International Development at the University of London's Institute of Education. Her recent research includes 'Broadening the Advanced Level Curriculum: Institutional responses to *Qualifying for Success*', funded by the Nuffield Foundation, international comparative work on financing lifelong learning, and a number of smaller scale research and development projects on post-16 reforms and the issue of part-time work among full-time students. Her recent books include *Beyond A Levels: Reforming 14–19 curriculum and qualifications* (Kogan Page, 2003) co-authored with Ken Spours, *Policies, Politics and the Future of Lifelong Learning* (Kogan Page, 2000); *Where are the Resources for Lifelong Learning?* (OECD,

2000), co-authored with Andy Green and Gareth Williams; and *New Labour's Educational Agenda: Issues and policies for education and training from 14+* (Kogan Page, 1999), co-authored with Ken Spours.

Colin Jenkins recently retired as Principal of the United World College of the Atlantic. He was earlier involved in the transition that followed Atlantic College's decision to drop GCE A levels and adopt the (then unknown) International Baccalaureate Diploma (IB). He has been closely associated with the IB's development as a member of its Curriculum Board, and with specific curricular developments in environmental education and global education. For three years he was Deputy Director General and Director of Examinations of the International Baccalaureate Organization, and later became Vice-Chairman of its Executive Committee. Currently he is directing an IB project to assess reactions by UK universities and higher education to the academic content of the diploma. Since 1996 he has been part of an initiative developing a proposal for a Welsh Baccalaureate for the Institute of Welsh Affairs.

Geoff Lucas is General Secretary of the Headmasters' and Headmistresses' Conference (HMC), representing some of the UK's leading independent schools. From 1989 to September 2000 (when he joined HMC) he held various senior posts at the National Curriculum Council, the School Curriculum and Assessment Authority and the Qualifications and Curriculum Authority. As Assistant Chief Executive at SCAA, he was seconded to work with Lord Dearing as team leader for his *Review of Qualifications for 16–19 Year Olds*. At QCA he was Head of Corporate Policy until July 1999. He then led the project team that worked on phase 1 of the Graduation Certificate. In his early career he taught in schools and higher education in the Midlands and north of England.

Françoise Martin-van der Haegen is deputy director of the IUFM of Poitou-Charentes. She is in charge of teacher in-service training for primary and secondary school teachers. Previously she was Deputy Director at the IUFM of Pays de la Loire, where she looked after initial teacher training for 10 years.

Sue Peacock OBE was until recently Head of Research and Development at EMTA, the National Training Organization for Engineering Manufacture, where she was responsible for the development of occupational standards, qualifications and training systems, notably modern apprenticeships. She is a member of one of the two national statutory committees of the Learning and Skills Council, the Young People's Learning Committee, and is a member of the Modern Apprenticeship Board. She is a longstanding member of MANTRA, the committee responsible for the approval of modern apprenticeship frameworks.

Graham Phillips is a Visiting Fellow at the Westminster Institute of Education, Oxford Brookes University. He was formerly the founding Principal of The Henley College, where he introduced the International

Baccalaureate to the 16+ curriculum. He has previously held visiting fellowships at the Universities of Warwick and Oxford.

Dr Tim Pound is currently a Senior Lecturer in Education at the Westminster Institute of Education, Oxford Brookes University. He taught English for a number of years in sixth form colleges before moving to Oxford to begin research for a doctorate in the field of post-compulsory education. He was recently involved in a Socrates-funded project which examined the teaching of literature in the upper secondary curriculum in schools across the EU. His publications include articles on the teaching of English, the A level system and the post-16 curriculum.

Dr Ken Spours is a Senior Lecturer in the School of Lifelong Education and International Development at the University of London Institute of Education. In 1990 he co-authored the influential IPPR document *A British 'Baccalauréat'*, and since then he has been involved in a variety of research projects during the 1990s, on 14–19 education and more recently on *Curriculum 2000*. His recent publications include, co-authored with Ann Hodgson, *Beyond A Levels: Reforming 14–19 curriculum and qualifications* (Kogan Page, 2003), *Dearing and Beyond: 14–19 qualifications, frameworks and systems* (Kogan Page, 1997) and *New Labour's Educational Agenda: Issues and policies for education and training from 14+* (Kogan Page, 1999). He has also published numerous papers and journal articles on qualifications reform.

Jonathan Stewart is Director of Sixth Form Studies and Assistant Headteacher at George Abbot School, an 11–18 comprehensive in Guildford, Surrey. He also works as an Associate Consultant 14–19 for Surrey LEA. Jonathan is currently Consortium Manager for the Surrey Sixth Form Graduation Certificate which is now being followed by sixth form students in 16 Surrey schools. Over the past two years he has been a member of the QCA Graduation Practitioners Group. As an English and drama teacher, Jonathan previously taught in schools in Dorset, Hampshire and Surrey.

Professor Jeff Thompson CBE is Professor of Education at the University of Bath and Academic Director for the International Baccalaureate Organization (IBO), for which he also directs the IB Research Unit. In addition to deploying various roles within the university and the IBO over a number of years, he has had major involvement in a range of national education projects including the development of the National Curriculum for England and Wales, for which he chaired the Science Working Group. Jeff Thompson is currently chair of the Examinations Appeals Board for England, Wales and Northern Ireland. His research interests are linked to the field of international education, in both national and international contexts, and particularly to curriculum issues within that context.

Series editors' foreword

The publication of a book on baccalaureates could hardly be more timely. For the first occasion, it appears that the government in England is open to suggestions about a more holistic approach to curriculum and qualifications for 14–19 year olds and the word 'baccalaureate' has actually appeared in a government policy document. There is a sense of excitement and anticipation about radical long-term change, but also an anxiety about how the process of reform will be conducted and what it will mean for learners and teachers.

Since the introduction of *Curriculum 2000* and particularly since the A level crisis in August 2002, there has been a great deal of discussion in the Media about the possibility of introducing a baccalaureate to replace A levels. Much of this reporting has assumed that we will simply be copying the International Baccalaureate or the French Baccalaureate. This landmark publication takes a much broader view. Its intention is to inform public and policy debate on curriculum and qualifications reform in the upper secondary phase.

Following the publication of *14–19: Opportunity and Excellence*, the Government's response to its Green Paper consultation process on 14–19 education, Mike Tomlinson, former Chief Inspector of OFSTED, was asked by the Secretary of State, Charles Clarke, to chair a Working Group for 14–19 Reform. The Working Group, whose task is to make recommendations for longer-term change in this area, has three main strands of work – the development of coherent learning programmes for 14–19-year olds, the improvement of assessment arrangements for this age group and suggestions for the creation of a unified framework of qualifications. While it is within this final strand of work that discussions on possible baccalaureate models are most likely to occur, the other two strands of work are also inevitably going to be heavily influenced by discussions on baccalaureate-type awards. The time for a major national debate on baccalaureates has finally arrived and this book provides an excellent starting point.

Now that the term 'baccalaureate' is out in the open and in the policy debate, five important questions immediately spring to mind.

What do we mean by the term baccalaureate and what are the strengths and weaknesses of existing models?

What baccalaureate features or models might be appropriate for the English context and how might the needs of different types of learners be met within a single system of awards?

What can baccalaureates offer to address long-standing weaknesses in the English education and training system (eg low status vocational qualifications and lack of breadth in post-compulsory general education)?

How do we move from current curriculum and qualifications arrangements for 14–19-year olds to a new system? Is it a question of simply replacing GCSEs, A levels and vocational awards with the new system or are there strengths upon which we can build?

What might be the practical implications of introducing a baccalaureate system and how might we avoid some of the mistakes associated with recent curriculum and qualifications reform processes in England?

In *The Baccalaureate: A model for curriculum reform*, Graham Phillips and Tim Pound draw on the expertise of a range of eminent national and international researchers, practitioners and policy-makers to address these questions. The first seven chapters explore the concept through the lenses of historical and policy analysis, conceptual mapping, international comparison and accounts of current practice in the use of baccalaureates and associated grouped awards. The final chapter argues for a fully inclusive baccalaureate system for the English context and suggests some broad principles to underpin its architecture and reform process.

What this book captures is a sense of a possible new and coherent approach to curriculum and qualifications from 14+ in England. At the same time it does not underestimate the amount of debate and discussion that will need to take place before we can arrive at the right model for curriculum reform. In skilfully striking this balance, it offers an informative and stimulating discussion of the role that baccalaureates might play in curriculum reform and some lessons that might be learnt from national and international experience in this area.

This book, carefully crafted by Graham Phillips and Tim Pound to meet a real need at a particular time in the policy process in England, should be compulsory reading for the Tomlinson Working Group on 14–19 Reform and others involved in local and national developments in this area. However, we believe that it will also have an enduring place in the broader international literature on the upper secondary curriculum. We are pleased to end our term as Series Editors of the *Future of Education from 14+* with a book that we are sure will make an important contribution to debate on education reform both in this country and beyond.

Ann Hodgson and Ken Spours
Series Editors

'With a baccalaureate firmly on the agenda, I warmly recommend this collection for all those who want to contribute to shaping the way ahead.'

Lord Dearing

'This important book breaks new ground, and will undoubtedly make a significant contribution to the current debate on the future of 14–19 education and training in this country.'

David Melville, Vice-Chancellor of the University of Kent and a member of the Tomlinson Inquiry into 14–19 Qualifications

'This book could not have come at a more appropriate time, as the government is reviewing the 14–19 phase of education as a priority. An essential part of that review concerns the system of qualifications. This book – providing both an historical and a comparative perspective and also providing actual case studies – is essential reading for that review. As the excellent introductory chapter claims, the book contributes to the debate by presenting the case for radical and holistic reform. As such, it is rooted in a public debate which has been with us for a long time. But it brings a critical edge to that debate in order to show the best way forward.'

Richard Pring, Professor of Educational Studies, University of Oxford

Introduction

Graham Phillips and Tim Pound

This book has two aims. First, it presents a critical evaluation of a number of existing baccalaureate models; and second, it presents the case for major reform of the 14–19 curriculum.

Since A levels were introduced in 1949, attempts to reform the system have been incremental and piecemeal. For example, although the *Curriculum 2000* reforms aimed to promote greater subject breadth at Advanced level and to raise the status of vocational education and training, in reality the changes that have taken place have been largely nominal. A levels were replaced by AS and A2; AVCEs (or Vocational A levels) replaced GNVQs; Advanced Extension awards replaced S level papers, and a new Key Skills qualification was introduced. These revisions have done little to allay the growing criticism of the current state of post-compulsory provision but have, in fact, intensified the debate on how the system can best be reformed.

This book contributes to this debate by presenting the case for radical and holistic reform. It argues for the development of a new unified system of qualifications based on a baccalaureate model. Such a single unified system would, we believe, address systemic weaknesses in the current framework in order to meet the learning needs of young people in a way that also responds to the social policy requirements of an advanced economy in the 21st century. Systemic weaknesses in current provision include premature specialization, the hierarchical division between academic and vocational education, and a failure to meet the issues of coherence and inclusion.

The key advantages of adopting a baccalaureate model are that in comparison to the existing qualifications framework, it offers greater breadth, coherence, inclusivity, progression and internationalism.

Breadth

The effects of premature specialization and the desirability of studying a broader range of subjects are well known and have been widely documented:

1

the Higginson (DES, 1988) and Dearing (1996) Reports are but two examples. Typically, students following a baccalaureate model study some five or six subjects.

Baccalaureate curricular models usually combine a compulsory core with options. In doing so they aim to strike a suitable balance between approaches that allow freedom for individual learners to pursue their own interests and those that are highly prescriptive. A framework that includes prescription as well as freedom of choice serves two specific purposes. First, it ensures that the curriculum is more responsive to individual needs, rather than forcing the individual to accept a set curriculum; and second, it combines breadth with depth of study.

Coherence

For many learners the current AS/A2 curriculum has been criticized on the grounds that it lacks coherence because it is made up of subjects that do not necessarily relate to each other. Indeed, we would argue that such subject fragmentation is not a true curriculum. The alternative model is a grouped award which recognizes the interdependence of subjects in terms of knowledge, skills and understanding. Such an award usually includes an element of a focused/core curriculum. Examples of this include the French baccalaureates as well as vocational courses in the UK, of which arguably the best examples are the BTEC National and First awards. The International Baccalaureate includes a compulsory theory of knowledge course which integrates the component elements of the Diploma programme.

Inclusion

The current system continues to be dominated by the effects of selection and exclusion. The consequences of this have been well documented in the report *A British 'Baccalauréat'* published by the Institute for Public Policy Research in 1990 (Finegold *et al*). Nowhere is this more apparent than in the twin-track approach to academic and vocational education, with only limited opportunities for transfer between the two. The resulting 'qualifications' hierarchy, partly reinforced by societal influences, promotes the academic in favour of the vocational, the pure/theoretical over the applied, and 'those who think over those who do'. An important objective of a new curriculum framework should, therefore, be to raise the status of vocational education – something recent reforms have failed to do. The best way to achieve this, we believe, would be to remove the distinctions between academic and vocational study through the establishment of a unified system and a common framework of qualifications.

However, this is a tall order and the difficulties of such a task should not be underestimated.

Progression

A reformed curriculum structure would include clear routes/pathways from one level to another, with defined outcomes at each level, leading to further/higher education and training opportunities and employment.

The Higginson Report drew attention to a deep-rooted philosophical and practical faultline in 14–19 education, where learning is interrupted by a series of hurdles: each stage is designed only for those who demonstrate the ability to go on to the next stage, and to fail those who are unable to do so. An alternative view – and it is one that is held by most advanced countries – is that each stage should be designed for the majority of those who take it, and the following stage then starts from where the previous stage ends.

The absence of clear routes of progression tends to reinforce failure and militates against the notion of ladders of opportunity. This period of transition has been compared to a game of snakes and ladders (Coles, 1995) – where there are more snakes than ladders. Clearly these progression routes should extend across both 14–19 education and training opportunities, and on to higher education and employment.

Internationalism

A new qualifications framework should prepare young people for a globalized and interdependent world. An international dimension should not only aim to increase knowledge and awareness of other cultures but, in doing so, promote international understanding: to quote the prospectus of the United World College of the Atlantic, 'We cannot save the world but we can produce people who want to save the world'. It could also be used to achieve greater transferability of qualifications across national boundaries.

A major policy aim of curriculum reform in the UK is to raise the staying-on/participation rates in further and higher education. Currently the UK lies twentieth out of the 24 Organisation for Economic Cooperation and Development (OECD) member countries for staying on at 17, and twenty-second out of 24 countries for staying on at 18. Clearly the wastage of potential – these are, after all, drop-out rates as well – is considerable.

It is also current UK government policy to increase the higher education participation rate to 50 per cent of those under 30 by 2010, notably by increasing the proportion from lower socio-economic groups. This dramatic increase can clearly only be achieved by radical changes to the pre-higher education system. Or, to put it another way, *more* has to mean *different* – and this demands a new curriculum, for a new population, for a new century.

This book thus argues the case for reform, as well as exploring the direction that the reform process might take. The opening chapters provide a context against which the implementation of existing and proposed baccalaureate frameworks can be critically evaluated. Chapter 1 adopts a historical perspective. It examines the extent to which a belief in the academic rigour and dependability of A levels has proved to be a potent force in undermining repeated attempts to introduce a broader and more inclusive qualifications system in England and Wales. Chapter 2 examines the nature of a baccalaureate qualifications framework and proposes a classification framework/ typology of baccalaureate-style curricula across the world. Chapter 3 provides a detailed insight into the structure and implementation of one of the most widely-known and respected baccalaureate curriculum models, the International Baccalaureate (IB) Diploma Programme. This international focus is sustained throughout Chapter 4, which looks at the evolution and significance of the French baccalaureates, including the recent development of the technical baccalaureate (*baccalauréat technologique*) and the vocational baccalaureate (*baccalauréat professionel*).

The potential of a baccalaureate model to provide a unifying framework for general and vocational courses is a central issue in Chapter 5, which explores the rival merits of two competing versions of the Welsh Baccalaureate, the second of which is about to be piloted in a number of schools and colleges. The contents of this chapter also provide an interesting case study of a social policy initiative in response to devolved government in the UK.

The final chapters examine a number of current national initiatives. These anticipate the need for more radical reforms to the English system following the problems associated with *Curriculum 2000* and the publication in 2002 of the Government's Green Paper *14–19: Extending opportunities, raising standards* proposing a new Matriculation Diploma. Chapter 6 provides a theoretical overview of the 'Graduation Certificate' and discusses its relationship to other baccalaureate-style qualifications. Chapter 7 includes four perspectives on reform by representatives of the maintained, independent and college sectors, together with that of employers. Finally, Chapter 8 argues the case for a planned, long-term approach to reform with the development of an English Baccalaureate system at three levels – Foundation, Intermediate and Advanced. This radical new model aims to achieve breadth, balance, social inclusion and coherence across the 14–19 curriculum.

References

Coles, B (1995) *Youth and Social Policy*, UCL Press, London

Dearing, Sir R (1996) *Review of Qualifications for 16–19 Year Olds*, SCAA, London

Department of Education and Science (DES) (1988) *Advancing A levels: Report of a Committee Appointed by the Secretary of State for Education and Science and the Secretary of State for Wales*, HMSO, London

Department for Education and Skills (DfES) (2002) *14–19: Extending opportunities, raising standards*, consultation document, HMSO, London

Finegold, D, Keep, E, Miliband, D, Raffe, D, Spours, K and Young, M (1990) *A British 'Baccalauréat': Ending the division between education and training*, Institute for Public Policy Research (IPPR), London

1

The resistance to reform: from Crowther to *Curriculum 2000*

Tim Pound

Introduction

A levels have proved to be remarkably resilient. Despite incremental changes to their structure and modes of assessment, their original function – essentially that of selection and exclusion – has remained substantially unaltered throughout their unprecedented 50-year history. Recently modularized and reformulated into two distinct stages, A levels continue to cast an elitist shadow over their vocational counterparts, and to define the standards against which alternative qualifications are invariably judged.

That they have retained their reputation for academic excellence in the rapidly developing context of post-compulsory education and training, however, arguably says as much about the English aversion to change as it does about the intrinsic merits of an exclusively academic curriculum. The fact that A levels have become the pedagogical equivalent of the 'gold standard', and that they have attracted rich, metaphorical labels such as 'the jewel in the crown' of the post-compulsory curriculum, clearly suggests the extent of the ideological support they have generated. More specifically, it may also explain why attempts to abolish them have been greeted in some quarters as emotively as a prospective negative referendum vote on the future of the monarchy.

One of the more obvious reasons for the establishment of this equation between A level qualifications and academic rigour undoubtedly stems from their original function as the principal rite of passage for university entry. When they were first introduced more than half a century ago, A level syllabuses – like those of their immediate antecedents, the School and Higher School Certificates – were dominated by university examining boards, with vested interests in both maintaining academic standards and, perhaps more importantly, ensuring the continuing viability of the three-year honours degree. In the absence of any vocational alternative, A level qualifications also became reliable indicators of an individual candidate's employment potential, often putting even those sixth formers who had failed to secure the grades for university entry at a considerable advantage over the vast majority of the age group who had left school at 15 or 16. Their status was further enhanced by the fact that around 25 per cent of those who sat A levels failed their terminal examinations, and thus had nothing to show for two years' study in the sixth form: this was a real, but less defensible, confirmation of their academic rigour.

The cumulative cost of preserving such elitist qualifications, in terms of failure and exclusion, has been considerable. But equally, success has come at a price, most obviously in the form of narrow and intense academic specialization with an exclusive bias towards either the arts or the sciences. This left the privileged minority leaving the grammar and independent schools across the country ill-equipped to deal with much beyond the anticipated route that the examinations had prepared them for – the single-subject degree course. As critics of the A level system have been quick to point out, the inherent weakness in such qualifications is their singularity – in other words, the fact that 'there is no such thing as the A level curriculum' (Young and Leney, 1997).

The choice of A level subjects has always remained voluntary and largely a matter of personal preference, and while traditionally specific combinations have been selected in response to university entrance requirements, students have never been compelled to study subjects that fail to match their perceived academic strengths and interests. Any attempt, then, to evaluate the A level system from the perspective of concepts like an 'over-arching framework', 'minimum core requirements' or the mandatory selection of subjects from a number of discrete, epistemic domains, is therefore wholly inappropriate, since A levels have always managed to resist the imposition of such prescriptive labelling.

The proven capacity of the A level system to withstand repeated attempts to subsume it under a broader and more balanced curriculum and examinations framework provides the principal focus of this opening, context-setting chapter. While subsequent contributors to the book variously examine a range of baccalaureate-style qualifications and frameworks – each with the potential to exert a positive influence on the future development of a more inclusive and coherent English system – this chapter chronicles the wasted opportunities that have given rise to the inequity and curricular fragmentation which characterize the current state of 14–19 educational provision. It will begin by re-focusing attention on the Crowther Report, and in doing so, it will reaffirm the fact that concerns over the specialized nature of A level qualifications – and consequently, the comparative absence of breadth in the post-compulsory curriculum – began to surface almost from the moment of their very inception. For as the Crowther Committee discovered during the mid-1950s, when it considered, amongst other issues, the function of A levels in the post-compulsory curriculum, here was a systemic weakness that would prove not only impossible to ignore, but also extremely difficult to vindicate.

Crowther and the concept of subject-mindedness

When the Crowther Committee was first convened in 1956, barely five years had passed since the first A level certificates were awarded, and yet criticism of what was perceived as an excessively specialized academic curriculum, and its relevance to the country's future economic and social needs, had already begun to manifest itself. Such concerns were implicitly acknowledged in the framing of Crowther's remit, which had been to:

> consider, in relation to the changing social and industrial needs of our society, the education of boys and girls between the ages of 15–18, and in particular, to consider the balance at various levels of general and specialised studies between these ages and to examine the interrelationships of the various stages of education.
>
> (Ministry of Education, 1959: xxvii)

To its credit, the response of the Crowther Committee to the issue of raising levels of national productivity and social prosperity was quite far-reaching, involving a number of policy recommendations to widen access to post-compulsory education. A four-fold expansion of the participation rates for 17-year-olds in full-time education was proposed, taking the figure to a projected 50 per cent of the age group by 1980. This was to be achieved through the raising of the school-leaving age to 16; the development of 'local examinations' for pupils 'for whom external examinations below the level of the GCE may serve a useful purpose' (Ministry of Education, 1959: 88), effectively the Certificate of Secondary Education (CSE) in embryonic form (*ibid*: 83); and also through the expansion of the FE sector and the introduction of the 'Junior College' – a blueprint for sixth-form and tertiary colleges – possessing, in the words of the Report, the 'adult atmosphere of the technical college' while offering 'a much wider range of curriculum with terms of reference nearer to those of a school' (*ibid*: 422).

However, when it turned its attention to a consideration of the upper-secondary curriculum – and in particular, the issue of A levels and academic specialization – the Crowther Committee displayed a stunning degree of complacency, a marked deference towards tradition and, in places, an untenable sense of logic. Arguing, on the one hand, that it was extremely unlikely that any student could be 'really at home in the higher reaches of more than one or two subjects', the Committee decided that what was at stake was 'not whether specialization is desirable or unavoidable', but rather, 'when it should begin' (Ministry of Education, 1959: 258). Yet on the other hand, comparisons with the United States and Scotland forced the Committee to concede that in both countries, students successfully followed a 'much wider spread of subjects' (*ibid*: 258). Similarly, a consideration of European systems proved to be equally disconcerting, forcing the Committee to accept that 'On the continent of Europe, there is no question of dropping altogether the study of languages or history or mathematics or science' (*ibid*: 258).

None the less, despite the endorsement of breadth implicit in these international comparisons – and despite conceding the fact that specialization in England could well act 'as a constricting frame and not a liberating agent' (*ibid*: 260) – the Crowther Report proceeded to assert that by the age of 16, academically-minded pupils in England inclined towards 'subject-mindedness' (*ibid*: 262). In the absence of any empirical evidence to support its claims, the report was moved to conclude that the 'mark of the good and keen Sixth Former' was someone who has 'looked forward to being a science specialist, or a classic [sic], or a historian' (*ibid*: 223).

Academic specialization was not only established as an innate yet peculiarly English phenomenon, it was also described in a language redolent of a more genteel, post-Romantic age which befitted its mid-19th-century cultural and pedagogical origins. For example, subject-mindedness was likened to a 'spring from which the disinterested pursuit of knowledge swells' (Ministry of Education, 1959: 223), and those who entered the sixth form were defined as an 'intellectual aristocracy' and 'adults capable of a reverence for knowledge, beginners in a lifelong quest for truth' (*ibid*: 259).

As critics of Crowther's defence of academic specialization have pointed out (Pound, 1995), the kind of language used here appears more indebted to the spirit of a liberal-humanist, philosophical tradition than to a mood of post-war optimism and reform. Moreover, the decidedly Arnoldian, anti-utilitarian tone of such pronouncements is further reflected in the belief that courses of study that might prove 'vocationally useful in later life' should be avoided in favour of those that guaranteed an introduction to 'the fundamental process of thought and the greatest achievements of the human mind' (Ministry of Education, 1959: 263).

Perhaps the one consolation for those who opposed narrow specialization lay in the Crowther Report's insistence that subject-mindedness was, after all, only a transient condition, mysteriously emerging during what was then designated the '15–18' phase, but afterwards susceptible to both correction and improvement through a process of self-discipline and further study. As the Committee put it: 'If a boy turns that intellectual corner, as he often does at the end of his Sixth Form time, we can be sure that, narrow as his education may have been during the last few years, he will take steps to widen it as well as deepen it' (*ibid*: 263).

Arguably, the simple truth beneath this increasingly desperate and convoluted defence of academic specialization was that by retaining A levels in their contemporary form, the continuing viability of the equally specialized three-year undergraduate degree was ensured. Even the Crowther Committee itself, in one of its less guarded moments, argued that at very least, specialization 'saves time in the total educational process from the infants' school to the postgraduate course' (*ibid*: 260–61). The extent to which this mundane consideration would prove a decisive, albeit underlying, factor in subsequent decisions to reject proposals to broaden A level studies ought not to be underestimated.

What is surely extraordinary about the legacy of the Crowther Report's pronouncements on the future of the post-compulsory curriculum is not simply the extent of its devotion to an ostensibly Victorian paradigm of general education, but the way in which the kind of deference exhibited by its authors towards a narrow, traditional concept of academic excellence has remained such a potent obstacle to curricular reform in England. As a contemporary *Times Educational Supplement* editorial put it, those who compiled the report seemed 'prisoners of conservative headmasterdom and dons ignorant and uninterested in educational matters' (15 January 1960). And it concluded sardonically:

> The trouble in England is that we boast about our very deficiencies. We think we're terribly clever, in the sixth form and universities, to produce first degree scientists only 21 years old. In fact, this scholastic efficiency is being bought at the sacrifice of proper education.
>
> (*TES*, 15 June 1960)

Of those educationists who criticized the Crowther Committee's complacency over academic specialization, perhaps the most persistent was A D C Peterson, who had recently been appointed Director of Education at the University of Oxford. Dismayed by the Crowther Report's empirical shortcomings, Peterson was determined to prove that the concept of 'subject-mindedness' had no real basis in observable fact. With the support of the Gulbenkian Foundation, Peterson embarked on an enquiry into the issue of subject choice in the sixth form, publishing his findings in a brief report entitled *Arts and Science Sides in the Sixth Form* (1960). What his limited study eventually confirmed was that A level choice was almost wholly determined by university entrance requirements, and that given the freedom to follow their own academic interests, students would, in fact, opt for a broader range of subjects. Having thus exposed the Crowther Report's deliberations on 'subject-mindedness' as blatantly misguided, Peterson proceeded to argue the case for introducing a four-subject A level framework to promote greater curricular breadth. Yet although his proposals attracted a considerable amount of interest (Pound, 1998), in practice they failed to secure widespread support both in the schools and, more crucially, within the universities.

As we shall see in Chapter 3, however, what subsequently arose out of Peterson's critique of the narrow, specialized nature of the sixth-form curriculum was the development of what would become one of the most acclaimed, broad-based alternatives to A levels currently on offer – the International Baccalaureate (IB). The irony of this seminal initiative emerging in the wake of an official report which gave a ringing endorsement to the virtues of academic specialization should not be overlooked.

The quest for breadth in the post-Crowther years

Between the early 1960s and the mid-1980s a whole raft of initiatives to broaden the academic route was launched, but each continued to prove unacceptable to the two principal stakeholders in the A level system – the schools and the universities. As we shall see, what is notable about a number of these proposed reforms is their close affinity to the innovative, academic framework of the IB Diploma, developed in Geneva and introduced in 1968 with a six-subject curriculum at 'Higher' and 'Standard' level. In England, however, although the quest to introduce curricular breadth continued unabated, the culture of academic specialization proved virtually impossible to dislodge.

In 1962, for example, the Committee of Vice-Chancellors and Principals, acknowledging the low levels of general education among first-year undergraduates, argued that university entrance requirements should be based upon a combination of two specialist subjects, supported by ungraded passes in three 'general' papers, including one in the recently-introduced 'Use of English' examination, and another in a foreign language. Despite being rejected by the Secondary Schools Examinations Council on the grounds that such measures would increase the examination burden on sixth-formers (1962), as Peterson himself remarked, such proposals amounted to 'the first real break in the stranglehold of premature and one-sided specialisation' (*Observer*, 7 May 1962).

Similarly, when the Robbins Report appeared in 1963, with its much-vaunted recommendation for a significant expansion in the number of universities to cope with a projected doubling of the undergraduate population between 1963 and 1980, it was forced to acknowledge the damaging effects of premature specialization. Rejecting the case for extending the length of first degrees from three to four years, the Report nonetheless lamented the fact that 'too many entrants cannot express themselves clearly in English, have an inadequate understanding of elementary mathematical principles and have made no significant progress in any modern language' (Committee on Higher Education, 1963: 76).

Within three years the first of a series of proposals for reforming the post-compulsory curriculum was published by the newly-established Schools Council (1966). Noting that the sixth-form population had virtually doubled in the seven years between 1958 and 1965, it accepted, first, that a significant proportion of the current cohort were students 'whose needs may best be met by some alternative to 'A' level courses'; and second, that the traditional academic curriculum should become broader (Schools Council, 1966: iii). In proposing a new framework involving a combination of 'major' and 'minor' qualifications, both occupying two years of full-time study and complemented by a programme of general studies, the Schools Council document referred directly to the two opposing positions in the recent debate about the post-compulsory curriculum.

What it hoped was to 'reconcile the Crowther reaffirmation of the principle of study in depth' with that of 'the Peterson plea for a wider range of examinable studies' (*ibid*: 12).

Criticized for ignoring the needs of a growing number of students whose interests extended beyond traditional academic courses, however, the 'major/minor' framework was soon superseded by a new set of proposals in which sixth-formers would take a core of two A levels supplemented by a number of 'elective' courses, internally assessed and externally moderated. On this occasion, however, the Schools Council's efforts were denounced for effectively putting the needs of the less academically minded – the so-called 'new sixth formers' – above those of their more academic peers (Schools Council, 1967: 4). Moreover, the universities expressed their misgivings about the prospect of leaving the assessment of electives in the hands of the schools, while concerns were also raised about the impact of the new, intermediate 'elective' examinations – succinctly, would the status and significance of A levels become enhanced further through the introduction of lower-level qualifications? (Kingdon, 1991: 61). Given such objections, the idea of electives was quietly dropped.

Clearly determined to find an acceptable solution to the problem of narrow specialization, in the very year that the IB was first piloted in England, the Schools Council produced yet another provisional framework for curricular reform, on this occasion in conjunction with the Standing Conference on University Entrance (SCUE). What emerged from these joint deliberations were the 'Qualifying and Further' proposals (Q and F), with a maximum of five 'Q' or 'Qualifying' examinations taken after one year in the sixth form, followed by three 'Further' examinations in the second year (SCUE/SC JWP, 1969). A year earlier in 1968, the Council for Scientific Policy under the chairmanship of Lord Dainton had urged the universities in an influential report to 'reconsider their entry requirements with a view to encouraging a broad span of studies in the sixth forms' (Council for Scientific Policy, 1968: 93), but what was radical about the proposed 'Qualifying' examinations was not simply their encouragement of breadth, but once again an assessment pattern which included a coursework element in addition to terminally marked examinations. Despite some reservations about a possible lowering of academic standards, SCUE, no doubt reassured by the promise of an absolute reliance on conventional three-hour papers at 'F' level, gave their conditional support to the 'Q and F' proposals. But this time it was the schools that vetoed the idea of a five-subject curriculum, arguing that the proposed qualification framework was too challenging for students of average ability, and furthermore, did not cater for the needs of those looking for an alternative to the purely academic route.

Three years later, however, proposals for the introduction of a new, more vocationally-oriented qualification, the Certificate of Extended Education (CEE) were published (Schools Council: 1972). Devised for the 'sixth-form pupil for whom the examinations at present available are inappropriate' (*ibid*: 88), this ill-fated award not only went some way towards addressing the needs of the 'new sixth-former' but also set a precedent in that the Schools Council now felt it appropriate to consider what it defined as 'The FE Alternative' and thus 16–19 provision as a whole. This initiative was further reinforced by the development of 'Alternative O Level' (AO) syllabuses which, apart from heralding the introduction of new subject areas such as electronics, computing and drama, were also conceived as a means of broadening the academic curriculum and bridging the divide between CSE/O level and A level study (Kingdon, 1991: 64).

It was in the wake of these developments that the Schools Council made what amounted to its final attempt to break the stranglehold of academic specialization, on this occasion with its 'Normal' and 'Further' ('N' and 'F') qualifications framework (SCUE/SC JWP, 1973). Finally shaped in collaboration with SCUE, these proposals were initially based upon a five-subject curriculum across both levels in order to put an end to academic specialization. Following pressure from the universities, however, it was decided to raise the standard of 'F' level courses to 'a depth of conceptual understanding suitable for those who will be capable of taking an honours degree in the subject and equal to that at present required for an A level' (Schools Council, 1973: 74).

As a result of such interventions, a potentially broader curricular framework, with close similarities to the IB, had finally evolved into a two-tier system in which the 'N' level had become devalued even before it had a chance of being introduced. In such circumstances, the response of the universities and the examining boards was a foregone conclusion, with the former arguing that drastic changes to the current system could only be justified if the standard of the proposed 'F' level were more precisely defined, while the latter feared that a four-year degree would be the inevitable consequence of adopting such a system. It was therefore hardly surprising that when the then Secretary of State for Education, Mark Carlisle, in announcing his intention to reject the 'N' and 'F' proposals, acknowledged that while A levels failed to 'meet the needs of all sixth-formers', they none the less embodied 'established, recognized and widely-respected standards' and remained 'the best guarantee for the continuation and success of three-year degree courses' (Hansard, 1979–80: 1087).

Thus a further six years of consultation and debate had foundered over the issue of breadth and academic standards, once again leaving A levels virtually unscathed. As Peterson had pointedly remarked earlier in the decade, successful resistance to reform could usually be attributed to the pervasive influence of those he defined as the 'silent conservatives', whom he collectively accused of wishing to 'preserve the sixth-form curriculum for many years more, as a sort of museum piece, the one unchanging element in a rapidly changing world' (*Guardian*, 15 May 1973). No doubt reassured by the election of a political party more attuned to their views, those who opposed change presumably took considerable comfort from the fact that with the demise of a Labour government, the future of the A level system looked increasingly secure.

The growth of vocational alternatives

However, in the very year in which the 'N' and 'F' proposals were swiftly abandoned by the incoming Conservative government under the leadership of Margaret Thatcher, the publication of what would prove to be a seminal report appeared to offer some hope to those who had argued that reform of the post-compulsory curriculum was long overdue. This groundbreaking report, entitled *A Basis for Choice* and published by the Further Education Curriculum Review and Development Unit (FEU), argued the case for developing general and specific one-year vocational courses for students who wanted some kind of 'public recognition for attainment equivalent to that achieved by the academic route' (FEU, 1979: 24). What was significant about this document was that in outlining the structure of what would later emerge as the Certificate of Pre-Vocational Education (CPVE) – first introduced in 1984 – it was arguably one of the first to extend its frame of reference to embrace both education and training. In fact, against a background in which a growing number of sixth forms were offering pre-vocational qualifications validated by such bodies as the Royal Society of Arts (RSA) and the City and Guilds London Institute (CGLI), while further education colleges were increasingly involved in A level provision, this seemed an appropriate response to the gradual blurring of boundaries between types of institutions and the courses they offered.

However, if the borders between academic and vocational qualifications appeared on the verge of being eroded (DES, 1980: 8), the coexistence of the FEU with the Schools Council was also symptomatic of the continuing divide between the two routes – and as some have argued, its very presence was perceived as an obstacle to curricular unification (Holt, 1980: 55–56). For example, while the FEU argued the case for a rationalization of vocational provision and a more integrated approach to post-compulsory education and training, the Schools Council focused its attention on broadening the academic route in its proposals for the development of an 'intermediate' examination pitched between O and A level in order to 'confirm the appropriateness of A level as a foundation for higher education' (Schools Council, 1980: 21). These new qualifications, subsequently entitled 'Advanced Supplementary' (AS) levels, were finally introduced in 1987 and restricted to full-time A level students, their function being 'to broaden without diluting academic standards the curriculum for these students' (DES, 1984: 4).

Despite receiving representations from those who argued for a more inclusive approach towards the examinations framework, the government thus appeared intent on strengthening the academic route by endorsing a qualification that would ultimately fail to establish itself as a credible means of encouraging academic breadth. As Macfarlane (1993) notes, after three years of being launched, not only were participation rates for AS level courses low, but 'for every student who was using an AS course to provide a contrast to an A level programme, three were doing so to complement it' (*ibid*: 27). Moreover, although the introduction of AS levels was supported in principle by SCUE, the absence of any formal guidance or prescription regulating subject choice for university entry inevitably resulted in the majority of students playing safe by opting for a conventional combination of three A levels. The introduction of the new qualifications, as Smithers and Robinson aptly put it, thus amounted to little more than the government 'tinkering at the edges' of a system which in reality needed fundamental reform (*TES*, 11 March 1988).

The Higginson Report and its aftermath

The extent of the Conservative government's reluctance to embrace reform was further evinced in the framing of the remit given to the Higginson Committee as it began to gather evidence on the principles governing the framing of A level syllabuses and their assessment. What was stressed from the outset was 'the Government's commitment to retain the General Certificate of Education (GCE) Advanced Level examinations as an essential means for setting standards of excellence' (DES, 1988: 39).

Yet in spite of the unequivocal wording of this caveat, the Higginson Committee none the less proceeded to stretch the bounds of its remit by unexpectedly recommending a radical overhaul of the A level system. Its proposal for the introduction of a five-subject framework to broaden the academic curriculum – summarized in the memorable phrase 'leaner, tougher' syllabuses (DES, 1988: 19) – was a direct consequence of the repeated criticism it had encountered over the intensely specialized nature of the A level experience during its consultation with a selection of all the acknowledged users and end-users of the A level system. Perhaps not unexpectedly, the narrow A level qualifications framework was yet again unfavourably compared with the broader, post-16 provision of the country's leading, economic competitors, prompting the Committee to point out that:

> Time after time the plea was made that the UK should follow the example of other developed countries. These countries provide educational breadth for the 16–19 age group; they recognise the national economic benefits arising from a broadly educated and adaptable workforce. We believe that we should follow suit.
>
> (DES, 1988: 8)

In addition to its radical proposals for increasing academic breadth, the Higginson Committee advocated the development of 'common cores' for all

A level subjects and recommended that further research be conducted on the introduction of modular syllabuses, both to increase the flexibility of learning patterns and to accredit the incremental achievements of individual students. It also argued that a modular A level framework would facilitate the establishment of equivalence between academic and vocational pathways, an idea that would be explored more fully in a report published by the newly-founded School Examinations and Assessment Council (SEAC) during the course of the following year.

Once again, however, a series of proposals that threatened to dilute the high, academic standards embedded in the A level system found itself abruptly consigned to the dank pit of curriculum history. Although the rejection of its proposals took the Higginson Committee by surprise (since its principal recommendations had attracted considerable support), the government's response was defended on the grounds that the recent introduction of AS levels would, in itself, add breadth to the A level framework; and that since the schools were already coping with a sea-change at 16+ with the decision to merge CSE and O level examinations into the new General Certificate of Education (GCSE), any additional disruption should be avoided. Beyond this, however, lay what appeared to be an unshakeable commitment to the standard of academic excellence that the A level system had always been able to guarantee. As the then Prime Minister, Margaret Thatcher, observed in her response to a question about whether she would maintain her support for the retention of A level qualifications, 'It is absolutely vital that we continue to regard the deep study of some single subjects as important during the years from 16–18, particularly for people going to university' (Hansard, 1987–88: 434).

Just why the preservation of academic specialization, at the expense of both breadth and achievement in vocational pathways, was 'absolutely vital' remained unexplored. Yet its defence, in a language redolent of the text of the Crowther Report, provides a powerful indictment of the elitist bias underpinning its dominating position in the post-compulsory curriculum.

Steps towards unification: the concept of a core curriculum

Although the Higginson proposals were summarily rejected, the argument in favour of broadening A levels and raising the status of vocational education and training could not be dismissed so easily. Tacitly acknowledging the groundswell of opinion in support of reform, by late 1989 the then Secretary of State for Education, John MacGregor, had written to SEAC requesting guidance on the development of core skills at 16+. 'Specialisation at A level, and the maintenance of rigorous standards', MacGregor had insisted, '... is vitally important. But it must not, and need not, be at the expense of developing broader skills, knowledge and understanding which will be needed in the twenty-first century' (NCC, 1990: 4).

In response to MacGregor's request, SEAC identified six core skill categories: communication, problem-solving, personal skills (defined as evaluating one's own performance, managing one's own learning and working as part of a team), numeracy, information technology and modern language competence. Although SEAC proceeded to argue that core skills should be 'embedded in every A and AS syllabus wherever possible and be a requirement of syllabus design' (SEAC, 1990: 8), these recommendations were eventually rejected, first by the examining boards because of difficulties over teaching and assessment; and second by the government, which continued to stand firm against any proposals to dilute the academic content of A level syllabuses.

Thus, despite its optimistic belief that core skills would provide 'the basis for a structure which will eventually integrate education and training for all post-16 students' (SEAC, 1990: 20), the SEAC proposals came up against a familiar stumbling block – the 'gold standard' of the A level syllabus. On the other hand, what was deemed unsuitable for the academic route soon proved appropriate for vocational pathways, since core skills rapidly became established as an integral part of the new General National Vocational Qualification (GNVQ) first outlined in the 1991 White Paper, *Education and Training for the 21st Century*.

From the outset, GNVQs were perceived as a kind of compromise between their more job-specific counterparts, NVQs, and A and AS level qualifications. They were to cover 'broad occupational areas' while offering students 'opportunities to develop the relevant knowledge and understanding, and to gain an appreciation of how to apply them at work' (DES, 1991: 19). Moreover, they were to be 'of equal standing with academic qualifications at the same level', while simultaneously linked to NVQs, in order that 'young people can progress quickly and effectively from one to the other' (*ibid*: 19). The fact that the White Paper acknowledged that A level syllabuses needed to evolve, while affirming that they should do so 'without undermining the consistency of high standards' (*ibid*: 20), implied that the form of this 'progress' or transfer would be confined largely to vocational routes, which subsequently proved to be the case.

Given that one of the central aims of the White Paper was, in the words of the then Prime Minister, John Major, to 'promote equal esteem for academic and vocational qualifications, and clearer and more accessible paths between them' (DES, 1991: 3), the introduction of GNVQs alongside an existing academic qualification that had been so fulsomely endorsed in its current form did not augur well for the future establishment of parity of esteem. Neither did the decision to develop an overarching award, the Advanced Diploma, to acknowledge achievements in all three proposed routes, despite the rhetorical urgency of the government's promise to introduce it 'at the earliest practicable date' (DES, 1991: 25).

The fact remained that while A levels continued to provide the benchmark for high academic standards, GNVQs were bound to struggle to achieve the status of a viable alternative. As Hodgson and Spours argue, rather than raising the status of vocational education and training, the effect of the White Paper was 'to formalize the academic/vocational division' (1997: 11) within the qualifications framework, by demonstrating the government's explicit aim of restricting access to A levels through the development of a clear vocational alternative for those who wished to participate in full-time post-16 study – namely GNVQs.

Developing breadth and balance: a British Baccalaureate

One of the most radical proposals for reforming the post-compulsory curriculum – and one that is central to the concerns of this book – came in the form of a 1990 Report published by the Institute for Public Policy Research entitled *A British 'Baccalauréat': Ending the division between education and training* (Finegold *et al,* 1990). The authors of the report took issue with what they saw as the inherent weakness of contemporary strategies for bridging the gap between academic and vocational routes post-16, which they collectively summarized as seeking to 'reform the divided system rather than replace it'. And they continued, 'While most current policy proposals take as given the separation of academic from other studies, we take the abolition of this separation as the starting point for reform. The interests of a fairer society and the demands of a modern economy both point to the need for a more unified and inclusive system of education and training' (*ibid*: 4).

Given the rejection of the comparatively modest recommendations embodied in the Higginson Report, this was indeed a bold platform for reform. However, in the context of the late 1980s, following a series of curricular developments such as the merging of GCE O levels and CSEs; the introduction of the Technical and Vocational Education Initiative (TVEI) and its impact on efforts to broaden A level study through links with more traditionally work-based areas of study, together with the changing pattern of assessment at A level through the growth of coursework and the regional piloting of modularization, in many respects this was a logical development. At its core, however, as the above quotation makes emphatically clear, was the need to re-structure the organization of post-compulsory education and training by making it more responsive to the changing economic climate – and perhaps more importantly, to issues of social inclusion.

What emerged was a series of far-reaching proposals designed to widen participation and based around a unified, modular qualifications framework divided into three levels. First was a 'Foundation' stage for all students above the age of 16, including those involved in work-based training. Such an award, it was argued, 'would replace the current jungle of one year full-time provision including GCSE, the BTEC First Award, various CGLI awards and CPVE' (Finegold *et al*, 1990: 25). Second was an 'Advanced' stage, equivalent to a 'British Baccalauréat', and designed to replace A levels together with 'all existing vocational awards below HNC' (*ibid*: 25). Beyond this a third 'Higher' stage was envisaged, and this was intended to embrace undergraduate study and more advanced vocational awards.

Given the focus of the Report, it was the second of the three stages, the 'Advanced Diploma', that was the subject of the most detailed attention. In order to provide maximum flexibility in terms of student choice, together with a balance between specialization and curricular breadth, the modular framework of the proposed award was to be subdivided into what were called three 'domains' of study, each one offering a range of academic and vocational courses. These domains were delineated as follows:

1. **Domain A: Social and Human Sciences** This domain would include history and social science modules as well as applied areas such as health, caring and business studies.
2. **Domain B: Natural Sciences and Technology** This domain would include maths, the natural sciences and engineering as well as more skills-based modules.
3. **Domain C: Arts, Languages and Literature** This domain would include performing and visual arts and design, as well as languages, literature and media studies.

(Finegold *et al*, 1990: 27)

Within the three domains three different types of module were to be offered. 'Core' modules were seen as a means of providing access to an agreed body of knowledge and skills appropriate to students at this level, while 'specialist' modules, covering both theoretical and applied subject areas, would enable students to pursue specific topics in more depth. Finally, 'work/community-based' modules were to be incorporated into the framework of the diploma in order to accredit employment experience and work training, and to ensure that students were encouraged to broaden the range of their activities and interests. To satisfy the requirements of the diploma, it was suggested that students would be required to select a minimum number of each type of module across the three domains of study.

Perhaps the greatest strength of these proposals lay in the creation of a unified qualifications system, and thus the abolition of the separate tracks that effectively preserved the rigid distinction between academic and vocational routes post-16. Within the proposed framework, the degree of rigour and specialization traditionally associated with advanced level study would not only be retained, but also, in theory at least, more systematically conferred upon redesigned practical or applied courses (which, the report conceded, in their current form continued to suffer from low standards and a narrow, job-specific focus). Moreover, by insisting on a balance between 'core' and 'specialist' modules, the report ensured that curricular breadth could be achieved without the sacrifice of depth, and further enriched through the recognition of work or community-based experience. Given such an outline, it was hardly surprising that the authors of the report likened their proposed model to the International Baccalaureate.

Moreover, beyond these detailed suggestions for a radical remapping of the landscape of post-compulsory education and training lay a number of related, strategic ideas for implementing the proposed changes. For example, there was the development of a three-tier qualifications system embracing Foundation, Advanced and Higher levels of achievement, which Dearing would adopt in his influential 1996 review. Also the view that such a framework would result in the GCSE becoming 'increasingly redundant as a 16-plus examination' (Finegold *et al*, 1990: 26) and its ultimate absorption within a 14–19 continuum adumbrated more recent government pronouncements on examinations at 16+ (DfES, 2002). Finally there were the report's recommendations for the creation of a Joint Qualifications Board (Finegold *et al*, 1990: 12) to regulate the new system and coordinate the development of new modular courses within an overarching framework. As we shall see, this prescient idea would be taken up by Dearing in his proposals for the establishment of a single national awarding body and for regional examining boards to merge with their vocational counterparts.

The pre-Dearing context: further proposals for a unified curriculum

Between the publication of this seminal IPPR Report and the Dearing Review in 1996, however, a number of other proposals for reforming the post-compulsory curriculum appeared in print, many of which echoed the IPPR Report's belief that only through radically reforming the current system could the nation meet the education and training needs of the new millennium. For example, in 1991 the Royal Society published a report proposing the introduction of a new, unified framework combining academic and vocational pathways, aiming to end the division between the two tracks by raising the status of vocational education and training. Entitled *Beyond GCSE* and compiled by a Working Group of the Royal Society's Education Committee which included Higginson, the report traversed familiar ground, pointing out that comparisons with other countries revealed the alarmingly high proportion of 16-year-olds who left education at 16 compared with the country's leading European competitors. Urgent action was called for to raise participation and achievement and to 'equip students with the flexibility to adapt to the changing needs of society throughout their lifetime' (Royal Society, 1991: 7).

The specific proposals for reform centred on the development of an Advanced Diploma, normally awarded after two years, and an Advanced

Certificate, equivalent to one year of full-time study and training. In the words of the report itself, 'The revised system is based on a single integrated system of academic and vocational education taught through a modular framework with study drawn from three domains: social, economic and industrial domain; scientific, mathematical and technological domain; and creative language and aesthetic domain' (Royal Society, 1991: 7).

Such a framework, the report proceeded to argue, would not only provide students with a considerable degree of flexibility – in terms of subject choice and depth of study – but would also facilitate the mixing of academic and vocational courses and the transfer between both tracks. This would be facilitated further through the integration of a common core of key skills into all programmes of study, reinforced by work placements in either industry, commerce or the community, which the Working Group saw as an 'essential feature for post-16 programmes of study' (*ibid*: 28).

Like those of the 1990 IPPR Report, the recommendations embodied in *Beyond GCSE* were thus shaped by the desire to maximize individual achievement and to make the English system more responsive the country's social, economic and technological needs. 'A post-16 system which takes us into the 21st century', the Working Group concluded, '... must encourage breadth of study. The system should ensure the study of both communication (including a foreign language) skills and science and mathematics for all students in a broad and balanced curriculum. Breadth of study will develop a clearer understanding of the issues which face society' (Royal Society, 1991: 23).

Support for such a baccalaureate-type qualification gained further momentum with the publication in 1993 of *Learning to Succeed: A radical look at education today and a strategy for the future*, compiled by the National Commission on Education, established in 1991 under the chairmanship of Sir Claus Moser. This was a wide-ranging document which addressed a number of key educational issues, but in terms of the post-compulsory curriculum, its main proposals for reform once again centred around the development of modular courses to replace A levels and the current range of vocational courses, leading to the award of a General Education Diploma (GED) at two levels – Ordinary at 16 and Advanced at 18. Despite the indicative age levels, the Commission's commitment to the principle of lifelong learning ensured that in practice, no age limits would be imposed to restrict access and participation, while a process of credit accumulation was seen as the most effective means of encouraging greater participation through flexible learning patterns. The only stipulation was that achievement should be measured across a range of subject domains and that a balance should be struck between breadth and depth of study.

In a further report published in 1995, affirming the importance of core skills and the merging of SCAA and NCVQ as a means of establishing parity of esteem between academic and vocational study, the Commission asserted that the development of the GED would not only provide 'a unified framework for learning' but would create 'a variety of pathways leading to higher education, advanced technical and vocational study, work-based training and employment' (National Commission on Education, 1995).

The recognition that separate assessment authorities for academic and vocational learning merely exacerbated the division between the two pathways also prompted the Confederation of British Industry (CBI) to add its voice to calls for a unified body with responsibility for post-16 provision as a whole. In a report entitled *Routes for Success*, published in 1993, the CBI also lent its support to a unified qualifications framework, arguing that if such a system were implemented, 'then parity of esteem between the academic and the vocational would be a reality' (CBI, 1993: 16). To provide a theoretical basis for such reforms, the CBI document identified a number of principles, and proceeded to suggest that they should:

- be defined in terms of outcomes, or competence;
- offer scope to accumulate credit;
- enable individuals to transfer to different routes, academic or vocational;
- develop core, transferable skills;
- prepare for entry to employment and higher education.

(CBI, 1993: 16)

Underpinning these principles was the desire to make standards and assessment objectives more explicit; for A level subject cores to become integrated with those of GNVQs; and in particular, for core skills to become 'an outcome of all learning' (CBI, 1993: 17). The intention behind such proposals was the by now familiar one of increasing participation rates through the establishment of a more integrated and inclusive system, responsive to national needs and once again ratified by the introduction of an overarching qualification, in this case a Careership Certificate. But if the proposed title of the award failed to grip the imagination, the CBI's marketing credentials were more forcefully brought to bear on the issue of delineating what it considered to be an essential strategic measure necessary for the successful implementation of its proposals – succinctly, the abandonment of existing qualifications terminology. 'As a priority', the report insisted, 'fresh thought needs to be given to the titles of A/AS Levels, GNVQs and NVQs. Given the individual's need for maximum choice it may be preferable to focus on routes – the occupational, vocational and academic – and to highlight the scope for flexibility' (CBI, 1993: 18).

This was undoubtedly a moot point, and one which, as we have seen, successive governments had refused to confront directly. As Young has argued, such titles, and the divisions they represent, are implicit in 'the vocabulary of a society deeply rooted in its past' (1993: 216) and therefore a fundamental cause of the continuing divide rather than a means of bridging it. In recognizing the continuing presence of A levels – and the qualifications that evolved under their shadow – as a stumbling block to radical reform, *Routes for Success* provided a further contribution to the growing chorus of support for replacing a divided system with a unified framework.

North of the border, however, the impetus for reform began to move beyond the level of rhetoric, as the policies announced in the 1994 Scottish Office report, *Higher Still: Opportunity for all*, amply testify. Rejecting the Howie Committee's proposals (Scottish Office Education Dept, 1992) for a twin-track system of academic and vocational routes on the grounds that each 'would not be held in equal regard' (Scottish Office, 1994: 7), the Scottish Office announced its intention to establish a unified and coherent curriculum framework covering five levels, and incorporating new, two-year Advanced Highers and extended study time to cover the teaching of a core skills programme. What was also significant about this radical set of measures was the explicit shift of focus away from the conventional parameters defining post-compulsory education towards the concept of a more inclusive 14–19 curricular framework, in which students would be presented with 'the opportunity to take whatever mix of "academic" and "vocational" education seems most appropriate to their needs and aspirations, but without the difference in status which can arise from separate awards systems' (Scottish Office, 1994: 22).

An additional feature of the reforms was that they were to be incremental, with existing modularized qualifications providing the initial basis of accreditation across the proposed levels. Despite the absence of prescribed or compulsory units of study, and the exclusion of work-based training from the qualifications framework, the *Higher Still* reforms represented a decisive step towards the establishment of a unified system – and thus in one sense, have proved to be much more closely aligned to the British Baccalaureate proposals than any subsequent developments in England.

In fact, the English reluctance to embrace anything other than evolutionary or incremental reform was further highlighted by developments in Wales, with the emergence of a radical set of proposals for the development of a Welsh Baccalaureate (Jenkins and David, 1996), a curriculum initiative explored more fully in both its original and current versions in Chapter 5. While other reports calling for the introduction of a unified system of qualifications in England continued to appear (Richardson *et al*, 1995), the publication of the Dearing Report in 1996, with its proposals for a national framework of qualifications incorporating three distinct tracks or 'pathways' – academic, applied education and vocational training – temporarily halted the momentum towards the development of a unified examinations and assessment system.

The Dearing Report and its legacy

In many respects, the Dearing Report can be seen as laying the foundations for closer unification. Essentially a prime example of the English predilection for compromise, its proposals for a national qualifications framework providing equivalence at four levels between academic and vocational awards, its support for the introduction of a reformulated AS level to be pitched midway between the GCSE and full A level standard, its plans for harmonizing the assessment process between A levels and GNVQs, and finally, its endorsement of a merger between academic and vocational awarding bodies, all seem to sit uneasily alongside Dearing's principal remit of 'maintaining the rigour of A levels'. Equally, an official report which recommended the establishment of national targets for achievement linked to overarching qualifications to recognize success either within or across the three tracks, while simultaneously relying on existing awards to do so, effectively appeased both conservatives and reformers alike.

The underlying conservative bias of the Dearing review was thrown into sharp relief by the publication of a Labour Party document on curriculum reform entitled *Aiming Higher* (1996), which appeared in the very month that the Dearing Committee published its findings. Criticizing successive Conservative governments for their failure to 'bring greater coherence and purpose to post-16 studies' and for their 'piecemeal and uncoordinated' approach to the issue of reform (Labour Party, 1996: 2), the Labour Party committed itself to the establishment of greater breadth at A level, improving standards of vocational study and training, and introducing a modular credit framework to encourage transfer between academic and vocational routes. Additionally, the document outlined Labour's plans for the merging of SCAA and NCVQ, together with the development of an overarching certificate both to recognize achievement and ostensibly to pave the way for the staged introduction of a unified curriculum in which all learners would 'undertake core and specialist studies' complemented by 'community-based' experience as a preparation for citizenship and adult working life (*ibid*: 18). But beyond this vision of a baccalaureate-style programme lay a further, and arguably more radical, commitment – that of raising levels of participation and motivation by reducing the emphasis on the traditional divide at 16+. This was to be achieved through the development of what the Labour Party document referred to as 'a coherent 14–19+ curriculum' (*ibid*: 17) in which vocational options were to be offered to 'disaffected' students (*ibid*: 18) at Key Stage 4 of the National Curriculum.

Following its election victory in 1997, however, the Labour Party has tended to adopt a decidedly more cautious attitude to reform. As Hodgson and Spours argue in Chapter 8, the radical edge of the *Aiming Higher* proposals has largely been dissipated and replaced by a more overtly pragmatic approach, involving incremental changes to broaden A level studies and to raise the status of vocational qualifications. These systemic changes emerged as result of the consultation process initiated by the publication of *Qualifying for Success* (DfEE, 1997), and resulted in the *Curriculum 2000* reforms which saw the reformulation of A level syllabuses into the new

Advanced Subsidiary (AS) and the A2; the proposed introduction of a higher award, the Advanced Extension (AE) paper; and the further evolution of the GNVQ into the Advanced Vocational Certificate of Education (AVCE).

Given the implications of such revisions, in terms of their impact on schools and colleges across the country, it was hardly surprising that the introduction of an overarching award received relatively scant attention. Subsequent official papers, however, including *Schools: Achieving success* (DfES, 2001) and the more recent Green Paper *14–19: Extending opportunities, raising standards* (DfES, 2002) with its proposals for a core of 'common learning' and a Matriculation Diploma to accredit existing qualifications at three levels – Intermediate, Advanced and Higher – have clearly succeeded in refocusing attention on the merits of a unifying award in bringing a belated sense of clarity, cohesion and inclusivity to the 14–19 curriculum and qualifications framework.

Following the widespread and persistent criticism of the *Curriculum 2000* reforms – succinctly, their failure to promote breadth, balance and inclusivity in the English system – the question which surely remains is not whether a baccalaureate-style framework is desirable, but when, and how quickly, we should proceed with its implementation.

References

Committee on Higher Education (1963) *Higher Education: Report of the Committee appointed by the Prime Minister under the chairmanship of Lord Robbins*, HMSO, London

Confederation of British Industry (CBI) (1993) *Routes for Success: Careership, a strategy for all 16–19 learning*, CBI, London

Council for Scientific Policy (Great Britain) (1968) *Enquiry into the Flow of Candidates in Science and Technology into Higher Education*, HMSO, London

Dearing, R (1996) *Review of Qualifications for 16–19 Year Olds: Full Report*, SCAA, London

Department of Education and Science (DES) (1980) *Secondary Examinations Post-16: A programme of improvement*, HMSO, London

DES (1984) *AS Levels: Proposals for the Secretaries of State for Education and Science and Wales for a Broader Curriculum for A levels*, HMSO, London

DES (1988) *Advancing A levels: Report of a Committee appointed by the Secretary of State for Education and Science and the Secretary of State for Wales*, HMSO, London

DES (1991) *Education and Training for the 21st Century: Presented to Parliament by the Secretaries of State for Education and Science, Employment and Wales*, HMSO, London

Department for Education and Employment (DfEE) (1997) *Qualifying for Success: A consultative paper on the future of post-16 qualifications*, DfEE, London

Department for Education and Skills (DfES) (2001) *Schools: Achieving success*, Stationery Office, London

DfES (2002) *14–19: Extending opportunities, raising standards*, Consultation document presented to Parliament by the Secretary of State for the Department of Education and Skills, Stationery Office, London

Finegold, D, Keep, E, Miliband, D, Raffe, D, Spours, K and Young, M (1990) *A British 'Baccalauréat': Ending the division between education and training*, Institute for Public Policy Research, London

Further Education Curriculum Review and Development Unit (1979) *A Basis for Choice: Post-16 pre-employment courses*, Further Education Curriculum Review and Development Unit, London

Great Britain. Parliament. House of Commons (1979–80) *Parliamentary Debates* (Hansard), Fifth Series, Volume 969, HMSO, London

Great Britain. Parliament. House of Commons (1987–88) *Parliamentary Debates* (Hansard), Sixth Series, Volume 134, HMSO, London

Hodgson, A and Spours, K (1997) *Dearing and Beyond: 14–19 qualifications, frameworks and systems,* Kogan Page, London

Holt, M (1980) *The Tertiary Sector: Education 16–19 in schools and colleges*, Hodder and Stoughton, London

Jenkins, C and David, J (1996) *The Welsh Baccalaureate*, Institute of Welsh Affairs, Cardiff

Kingdon, M (1991) *The Reform of Advanced Level*, Hodder and Stoughton, London

Labour Party (1996) *Aiming Higher: Labour's proposals for the reform of the 14–19 curriculum*, Labour Party, London

Macfarlane, E (1993) *Education 16–19: In transition*, Routledge, London

Ministry of Education (1959) *15–18: A report of the Central Advisory Council for Education (England)* (the Crowther Report), HMSO, London

National Commission on Education (NCE) (1993) *Learning to Succeed: A radical look at education today and a strategy for the future,* Report of the Paul Hamlyn Foundation National Commission on Education, Heinemann, London

NCE (1995) *Learning to Succeed: After 16. A report from the Paul Hamlyn Foundation*, NCE, London

National Curriculum Council (NCC) (1990) *Core Skills 16–19: A response to the Secretary of State*, NCC, York

Peterson, A (1960) *Arts and Science Sides in the Sixth Form: A report to the Gulbenkian Foundation*, Abbey Press, Abingdon

Pound, T (1995) *The Function of A Level English Literature in the 16–19 Curriculum*, D.Phil. thesis, Department of Educational Studies, University of Oxford

Pound, T (1998) *Forty Years On: The issue of breadth in the post-16 curriculum*, Oxford Review of Education, 24, 2

Richardson, W, Keep, E, Miliband, D, Raffe, D, Spours, K and Young, M (1995) *Learning for the Future: Interim report*, Post-16 Education Centre, University of London and Centre for Education and Industry, University of Warwick

Royal Society (1991) *Beyond GCSE: A report by a working group of the Royal Society's Education Committee*, Royal Society, London

Secondary School Examination Council (1962) *Sixth Form Studies and University Entrance Requirements: Sixth Report of the Secondary School Examination Council*, HMSO, London

Schools Council (1966) *Sixth Form: Curriculum and examinations*, Working Paper no 5, HMSO, London

Schools Council (1967) *Some Further Proposals for Sixth Form Work*, Working Paper no 7, HMSO, London

Schools Council (1972) *16–19: Growth and response: 1. Curricular bases*, Working Paper 45, Evans/Methuen, London

Schools Council (1973) *16–19: Growth and response: 2. Examination structure*, Working Paper 46, Evans/Methuen, London

Scottish Office (1994) *Higher Still: Opportunity for all*, HMSO, Edinburgh

Scottish Office Education Department (1992) *Upper Secondary Education in Scotland: A report of the Committee to Review Curriculum and Examinations in the Fifth and Sixth Years of Secondary Education in Scotland*, HMSO, Edinburgh

SCUE/SC JWP (1973) *Preparation for Degree Courses*, Working Paper 47, Evans/Methuen, London

Standing Conference on University Entrance and the Schools Council Joint Working Party on Sixth Form Curriculum and Examinations (SCUE/SC JWP) (1969) *Proposals for the Curriculum and Examinations in the Sixth Form*, HMSO, London

Young, M (1993) A curriculum for the 21st century? Towards a new basis for overcoming academic/vocational divisions, *British Journal of Educational Studies*, **41** (3), pp 203–22

Young, M and Leney, T (1997) From A levels to an advanced curriculum of the future, in *Dearing and Beyond: 14–19 qualifications, frameworks and systems*, ed A Hodgson and K Spours, pp 40–56, Kogan Page, London

2

Towards a structural typology for baccalaureate-style curricula

Jeff Thompson, Mary Hayden and James Cambridge

Defining a baccalaureate

The basis on which a reform of educational qualifications at the upper secondary level of schooling should be undertaken has been a subject of intense debate over many years throughout the world, including England and Wales, where it could be claimed that debate is currently at its most intense. Such debate has been fuelled by criticisms that the existing Advanced Level arrangements form 'a highly selective, narrow and elective curriculum' (Young and Leney, 1997: 43), and numerous proposals have been made for reform. Many of the proposals have themselves been criticized, however, as being 'incremental' rather than 'fundamental', and have been easily resisted by the more conservative opponents of changes to the status quo. Among the recommendations for reform in this context have been the Higginson Report (DES, 1988) which proposed a five subject grouped award, *A British 'Baccalauréat'* (Finegold *et al*, 1990) which put forward a unified framework bringing together general and vocational education with core, specialist and work/community modules, and the report of the National Commission on Education (1993) which suggested a grouped award comprising a range of subjects including a compulsory core and a nominated major area of study. More recently, the Green Paper published in February 2002 proposed the introduction of a Matriculation Diploma in England to mark the end of the 14–19 phase of education (DfES, 2002), while in 2001 the National Assembly for Wales initiated work on the development and piloting of what is known as a Welsh Baccalaureate Qualification for the post-16 sector (WBQ, 2002), discussed in detail in Chapter 5.

These initiatives have a number of features in common, including an approach to the curriculum which encourages breadth as well as providing structure through a model of compulsory core plus options. Although such a curriculum framework has, in some cases, been described as a baccalaureate model, the precise meaning of the term 'baccalaureate' is not necessarily shared by all who use it. One early definition of the term baccalaureate, or its French version *baccalauréat*, was:

> a school leaving examination in French secondary schools which is used for admission to Higher Education. It is more like the German Abitur than the GCE Advanced Level in that it is broadly based rather than specialized, though in recent years a greater degree of specialization has been permitted.
>
> (Gordon and Lawton, 1984: 14)

while a more recent definition proposes that a baccalaureate is:

> an examination qualification determining entrance to Higher Education in most European countries. It is comparable to A-Level or, in Scotland, the Higher Grade of the Scottish Certificate of Education. The broadly-based examination requires acceptable grades in a wide range of subjects such as mathematics, literature, a foreign language, science, history and religious or ethical education. Different countries have their own form of the Baccalaureate. Also the European School movement awards the European Baccalaureate. In certain schools across the globe an International Baccalaureate Diploma is offered.
>
> (Farrell , Kerry and Kerry, 1995)

In the absence of a shared meaning of the term, this chapter is offered as a contribution towards arriving at a clearer understanding of what the nature of a baccalaureate might be. It does so through a search for a classification of the range of interpretations currently given in describing baccalaureate-style curricula, based on a scoping study undertaken to ascertain the most appropriate basis for such a classification.

Various approaches may be adopted for the classification of such curricula in post-16 systems, one of which is based on the values and aims underlying the descriptions of curricula by the various agencies responsible for their generation and implementation.

Approaching a classification through values and aims

Le Métais (1997) argues that values 'are concerns about what ought to be. A value is a belief which need not rely upon facts or evidence, although a value position can be supported or challenged by knowledge propositions.' Particular aims, structures and working methods are influenced by value positions. Le Métais further argues that aims may be expressed as objectives, goals and targets: 'educational aims may be intrinsic (eg to contribute to lifelong education) or instrumental (eg preparing young people for work and contributing to the national economy). They may focus on developing individual qualities and capacities, or promote citizenship and a sense of community or safeguarding a cultural heritage (or literacy).'

National differences are discussed by Le Métais under five category headings, including the expression of values and aims. According to the degree of detail with which national values are expressed, countries cited in the International Review of Curriculum and Assessment Frameworks project (INCA, 2002) may be categorized in three broad groups. Among countries with a commitment to pluralism and devolved authority (eg Canada, England and Wales, Hungary, Netherlands, the United States), Le Métais argues that minimal reference is made to values in education legislation. In other countries (including Australia, New Zealand, Spain), general statements on values are made at national level but the details are determined by the authorities with devolved responsibilities. Countries with highly centralized systems (eg Japan, Republic of Korea, Singapore) tend to express very detailed aims and clear educational and social values. Educational aims are expressed by national systems in numerous categories including artistic, cultural, developmental, economic, environmental, personal, political, social, moral or religious, and physical. 'The way in which issues of national identity are expressed in educational aims', Le Métais (1997) argues, 'reflects a number of broader values including freedom, respect for the individual, social cohesion and the preservation of cultural heritage.' These aims may be achieved in education systems by:

- active promotion of multi-cultural knowledge, skills and understanding for all;
- parity of provision;
- support for minority groups; and
- compensatory programmes for those perceived as disadvantaged in terms of national culture or language.

Further research is clearly required in order to establish whether the details of these aspects of the curricula of different national systems are expressed unambiguously enough in terms of specifications for distinctions to be drawn between them as a basis for a useful classification. This approach has not been pursued further here.

Approaching a classification through inputs and outcomes

A second approach to curriculum classification could be to determine whether curricula are specified by inputs, such as class contact hours or syllabus content, or as measurable learning outcomes expressing what the learner can achieve (Young, 1998). So far, 'unitization' through the adoption of an outcomes-based approach has been used in England and Wales, mainly in the assessment of skills in vocational education, but it has been proposed that 'there should be a common approach to the definition of achievement used for all qualification routes and all kinds of achievements', and that 'discussion of the content and characteristics of qualifications is more fruitful if it is related to the units of achievement of which they are comprised' (Stanton, 1997).

The syllabus details of academic subjects may be expressed as lists of topics to be covered by the class; these, it is argued, may be interpreted as input data. On the other hand the syllabus may be expressed in terms of statements of what the student is expected to perform; that is as an outcome specification. Syllabus content of subjects in the International Baccalaureate (IB) Diploma Programme, for example, is expressed in terms of outcomes, as illustrated in the following example relating to biology:

> The assessment statements (AS) form an examinations syllabus, not a teaching syllabus. They are intended to prescribe to examiners what can be assessed by means of the written examinations. Each one is classified according to the IB assessment objectives... using appropriate action verbs. The former are relevant for the examinations and for balance within the syllabus, whilst the latter are important to give guidance to students (and teachers) as to the depth. These action verbs are categorized and defined.... It is important that students are made aware of the meanings of these action verbs so that they know precisely the intent of examination questions and what will be expected of them in their answers.
>
> (IBO, 1996: 27)

This example represents an explicit statement of assessment policy that renders the issue transparent. Further research is required to establish whether the syllabus details of different national systems are expressed in terms of input or outcome specifications, with a level of transparency that would aid the generation of a classification system based upon them. This task has not been attempted here.

A review of existing baccalaureate-style programmes

In deciding not to pursue further exploration of the classification of baccalaureate-style curricula based on analysis of values and aims or the identification of inputs and outcomes, we have adopted a more pragmatic approach in exploring the explicit structural characteristics of existing programmes, across as wide a selection of baccalaureate-style curricula as seemed appropriate.

The national systems whose programmes have been reviewed as the basis of this approach are all from countries that are economically developed, and include some with more than one official language. Information, mainly from the International Review of Curriculum and Assessment

Frameworks Archive (INCA, 2002), has been drawn upon in relation to France, Germany, Ireland, Japan, Singapore, Sweden and New Zealand. In addition, the review has included a number of programmes of study that may be described as 'non-national' or 'international', in the sense that they may be followed by students based in a variety of different countries but are not specifically identified with any particular national system. Four such programmes for upper secondary students have been included:

- the International Baccalaureate Diploma Programme (IBDP), an international programme of study followed by students in national and international schools around the world;
- the European Baccalaureate (EB), a programme of study followed by students in the 10 European Schools located in six countries of the European Union (Belgium, Netherlands, Germany, Italy, United Kingdom and Luxembourg);
- Cambridge International Examinations (CIE) Advanced International Certificate of Education (AICE), a programme of study followed by students in national and international schools around the world; and
- the AP International Diploma for Overseas Study (APID), a programme of study based on the US College Board Advanced Placement examinations for entry to universities in North America.

Detailed analysis emerging from the review has not been included in this chapter, but may be found in Cambridge, Hayden and Thompson (2001).

Essential characteristics of baccalaureate systems

During the course of the structural analysis undertaken, a number of characteristics associated with the descriptions of baccalaureate systems emerged, as follows.

The baccalaureate as a school-leaving examination

Gordon and Lawton (1984) describe a baccalaureate as a school-leaving examination. While such a description may be considered valid up to a point, as a baccalaureate qualification may involve an examination at the termination of compulsory or post-compulsory education, it does not constitute an exclusive definition (since courses that would not be described as a baccalaureate also lead to school-leaving examinations). It may also be challenged on the basis that it describes a product, rather than a framework giving structure and coherence to an educational experience in the form of a curriculum or programme of study. This is a distinction made by Prost (2000), in pointing out that the French *baccalauréat* is the name for both the high school leaving examination and the qualification obtained. An examination may be considered to be an outcome or product of an educational experience, but a baccalaureate may clearly also be described in curriculum terms, as a framework giving structure and coherence to that experience.

If it is accepted that a curriculum is more than a series of intended learning outcomes, then an examination alone will not be sufficient to constitute a curriculum. In the context of upper secondary education in England and Wales, for instance, it has been argued that:

> A-Levels are subject examinations and the Examining Boards examine subjects, not the curriculum. For the Examining Boards there is no such thing as the A-Level curriculum. The term 'A-Level curriculum' refers to the programmes of study that a school or college can offer and a student can choose, based on A-Level subject examinations. The A-Level curriculum is the responsibility of individual schools and colleges, and for each school and college it is different.
>
> (Young, 1998: 119)

If they are to be more than a series of intended learning outcomes, such programmes of study need to be given structure and coherence and, in some cases, to introduce breadth and balance through enquiring into the promotion of interconnections between subjects and cross-curricularity, and by asking whether attitudes and skills beyond the cognitive domain are encouraged and developed.

Our review suggests, therefore, that one characteristic of a baccalaureate is that it is a programme of study for upper secondary education which may be used as a school-leaving examination.

Admission to higher education

As already noted, it has been suggested that a baccalaureate qualification is used for admission to higher education (Gordon and Lawton, 1984; Farrell, Kerry and Kerry, 1995). To suggest, however, that admission to higher education is the sole purpose of a baccalaureate qualification would be unduly limiting, since education between the ages of 16 and 19 is required for a wider range of opportunities than entry into higher education alone; students may require qualifications for entry into employment, for instance, and as a starting point for lifelong learning. It may be argued, however, that the present use of school examinations for selection purposes in England and Wales results in a prioritization of academic knowledge and understanding over vocational knowledge and understanding, and that this discourages wider participation in education at ages 16–19. In support of this argument, it has been observed that:

> whereas fewer students passed the *Baccalauréat* in France than A-Levels [in England and Wales] until the 1980s, by the end of the decade, twice as many students were achieving one of the new three track French Baccalaureates as

achieve 2 or more A-Levels. In other words, by remaining so exclusive and as a consequence of devaluing other qualifications, A-Levels are part of the reason why levels of post-16 attainment in England are so low. The powerful selective role of A-Levels limits the extent to which they can provide general education to a wide section of each cohort.

(Young, 1998: 121)

The definition of a baccalaureate may thus be revised and expanded to make reference to the possible provision of a broader and more inclusive curriculum that comprises elements not only of academic general education, suitable for those students with aspirations to study in higher education institutions, but also of vocational education. The Irish Leaving Certificates, for instance, have among their stated aims the preparation of students for immediate entry into open society including the world of work. It is generally considered desirable that academic and vocational tracks share parity of esteem. The National Commission on Education (1993) argued for ways towards overcoming the barriers for all those, including adult learners, who seek to improve their educational qualifications up to and including post-16 education. It may therefore also be considered appropriate for a baccalaureate qualification to be a foundation or goal for learning throughout life.

The second characteristic emerging from our review is that a baccalaureate may be used as a qualification for admission to higher education, for entry into employment, and as a foundation for learning throughout life.

Breadth and balance

Encyclopaedism and essentialism

Sources previously cited imply that a baccalaureate is a programme of study that is 'broadly based' (Gordon and Lawton, 1984; Farrell *et al*, 1995) rather than 'specialized'. The selection of a small number of subjects for study at A level in England and Wales, prior to more recent moves towards the introduction of greater breadth such as *Curriculum 2000* (QCA, 1999), has been considered to be a problem by some, as noted by Finegold *et al* who argue that:

> there is now widespread support for the notion that the structure of 'A' levels does not serve the interests of people who take them. Our system of post-16 education – based on two, three or occasionally four 'A' levels – is more specialized than any other in the industrialized world. From the North American system of a graded High School Diploma for all to the divided West German arrangements, pupils pursuing academic studies take a wide range of courses, usually on a modular basis. For students taking the International Baccalaureat [sic] six subjects is the norm. In England and Wales, the focus of one, two or three subjects makes a nonsense of any claim that school prepares students for the variety of challenges they will face during their lifetime.
>
> (Finegold *et al*, 1990:10)

The terms 'breadth' and 'balance' could be considered to refer to the number and types of subjects studied by a learner. Gordon and Lawton (1984) make a cross-reference between their discussion of the term 'baccalaureate' and what they term 'encyclopaedism', which is defined as 'a view of schooling that suggests that up to the compulsory school leaving age all education should be general and should be planned to cover the major kinds of knowledge and experiences. Thus a good education would be a balanced selection from all known forms of human knowledge and experience' (Gordon and Lawton, 1984: 63).

This argument is reinforced by another cross-reference to discussion of the term 'essentialism', one definition of which is expressed as:

> the belief that there is an 'essential' body of knowledge that all pupils (or possibly students in Higher Education) should acquire. It is sometimes not clear whether it is the knowledge which is important or the hard work necessary to attain the knowledge. The term is sometimes employed in comparative education to refer to continental school systems such as the Soviet or the French. The view is sometimes also referred to as *encyclopaedism*, which suggests that where there is a compulsory system of education, then this should be general education up to the compulsory school leaving age. Schemes of specialization and 'options' common in English comprehensive schools will be condemned in terms of their narrowness or lack of breadth.
>
> (Gordon and Lawton, 1984: 65)

Gordon and Lawton's suggestion that 'a good education would be a balanced selection from all known forms of knowledge and experience' has echoes of, for instance, the *Realms of Meaning* of Phenix (1964) and the *Modes of Experience* promoted by Hirst and Peters (1970). Such considerations are also of value to this discussion since they extend the definition of what constitutes the broad and balanced content of a baccalaureate qualification beyond knowledge only (the cognitive domain) to include experiences in other domains. Therefore, it may be proposed not only that a baccalaureate constitutes a curriculum or programme of study for school leavers prior to entry to higher education and employment, but also that such a curriculum embraces a broad and balanced view of the kinds of experiences that develop the knowledge, skills and attitudes appropriate for such students.

Furthermore, reference to the inclusion of 'a wide range of subjects' (Farrell *et al*, 1995) in a baccalaureate programme suggests a view of a broad and balanced curriculum which may assume 'an essential body of knowledge that all pupils... should acquire'. If this is the case, then it may be argued that the concept of a baccalaureate is derived from an essentialist and rational encyclopaedist philosophy of education, leading to the conclusion that the rationale of the baccalaureate qualification is based upon a particular ideology of education which implies that there is a general body of knowledge that all learners should acquire. This notion is opposed by a view that specialization on a more narrow range of school subjects is desirable, and by another view that the personal, moral and spiritual development of the individual is the major aim of education. McLean (1995) argues that the first view is associated with an educational ideology of rational encyclopaedism, the second with classical humanism, and the third with a naturalist philosophy after Rousseau. The rationalist view of content, learning and teaching, according to McLean:

> is associated with a systematic view of the physical worlds. Capacities for logic, deduction and abstraction together with systematization and synthesis should be developed to make sense of the universe and ultimately to change it. The medium is that group of subjects such as languages, mathematics and science through which these qualities can best be trained. But worthwhile knowledge is also external and standardized and the student should cover the encyclopaedic kaleidoscope of all legitimate areas for as long as possible. The private and irrational are excluded. These attributes form almost a mirror-image of nineteenth and twentieth century English humanism.
>
> (McLean, 1995: 30)

What content, then, would need to be found in a programme of study leading to a baccalaureate qualification if breadth and balance are to be assured? Where part of the curriculum is compulsory, that part may be described as the core. Some curricula, such as the French *baccalauréat*, have included a compulsory core of subjects that include the study of the national language, and the national culture and institutions, as exemplified by national history and geography. Many curricula that have a core require continued study of mathematics and science subjects, foreign languages and the humanities at upper secondary level. A frequently adopted approach (such as is found in the International Baccalaureate Diploma Programme) is to group related subjects together and prescribe selection by students of a suite of subjects comprising at least one from each group. Such a strategy might be expected to ensure that breadth is intrinsic to the programme and that the representation of different subject areas in an individual's programme of study is balanced. An alternative approach is to make breadth extrinsic to the spread of subjects in the programme, which may be achieved by allowing free choice of most subjects but also specifying the inclusion of supplementary 'broadening subjects' such as General Studies and 'key skills' subjects in the programmes of those students deemed by their subject choice to require them.

Great expectations have been placed by some upon the inclusion of 'core skills' or 'key skills' in the curriculum. Green comments that:

> critics of overspecialized A-levels... have seen core skills as a way of introducing breadth and balance into the academic curriculum; advocates of competence-based vocational education have seen them as essential for promoting skills transfer and the portability of qualifications... and supporters of the concept of a unified post-16 curriculum have seen them as a potential bridge between the academic and vocational tracks. Just about everyone recognizes

that they are necessary building blocks for student progression to higher levels of education and training.... Some, like Nicholas Tate of the Schools Curriculum and Assessment Authority (SCAA), go even further and see them as a vehicle for reinserting moral values into the curriculum.

(Green, 1997: 88)

The place of key skills in areas such as numeracy, literacy, information and communications technology, and personal communication skills, is articulated differently in various curricula. In some, the key skills are represented as being intrinsic to the programme, with the assumption that they will be developed across the curriculum in the different subject areas. In others the key skills are treated as extrinsic 'add-ons' to the programme of study, frequently as components of the 'broadening subjects', although many curricula make no specific reference to key skills at all.

Academic and vocational dimensions

It is evident that academic programmes leading to continued study at the tertiary level of education are not for all students. Preparation of the learner for the world of work is approached in different ways in different countries. Contrasts exist between the perceived importance and provision of vocational education in different national systems. In some systems (such as the German *Abitur*) a distinction is made between contrasting 'academic' and 'vocational' programmes, but in other systems learners are given the opportunity to follow mixed programmes that bring together these approaches. Historically, in some countries, such as France, the responsibility for vocational education has been placed with the national education system (Prost, 2000), but other systems, such as England and Wales, 'lost sight of the real purpose of work-based learning by demonizing the role of employers, downgrading the concept of vocationalism, falsely elevating the worth of education institutions as sites of learning and underestimating the capacity of young people to develop as learners if they leave education after the compulsory stage' (Unwin, 1997: 76).

The division between 'academic' and 'vocational' dimensions of education has been recognized in England and Wales, and steps taken to address it through recent initiatives including *Curriculum 2000* (QCA, 1999), the Green Paper in England (DfES, 2002) and in Wales the Welsh Baccalaureate (WBQ, 2002), are discussed elsewhere in this volume.

An inclusive baccalaureate qualification that makes claims for breadth and balance might, it is argued, be expected to comprise elements of academic and vocational education supplemented by a programme of education in key skills.

Balance in assessment

The nature, timing and outcomes of assessment of learning also vary between different curricula. In some systems all subjects are assessed, while in others there are non-assessed subjects. This leads to a question concerning the extent to which non-assessed subjects are *de facto* non-subjects in the eyes of students and their teachers. Learning may be assessed by a terminal examination of the entire programme or by modular examinations throughout the course of the programme. Formative or diagnostic assessment is a component of the curriculum in some systems such as France (INCA, 2002). Assessment of learning may take the form of written examinations only, or there may be oral components, as in Germany, for example, and in the European Baccalaureate programme (European Baccalaureate, 2002). In different systems assessment may be school-based, or it may be centralized and common to all students in a country.

Besides being expressed in terms of assessed outcomes, a curriculum may also be specified in terms of inputs. The award of a certificate or diploma may depend upon the number of hours of attendance, or on achievement of a prescribed number of points or credits (as in Japan), or it may depend upon completion of a specified suite of subjects, as might be found in certain group programmes, such as the *Baccalauréat* in France, the *Abitur* in Germany, and the International Baccalaureate Diploma Programme.

In conclusion, breadth and balance in the curriculum may be interpreted in contrasting ways. Breadth may refer to the number of subjects studied, and balance to the different areas of knowledge represented; on this basis, a programme of study comprising only two languages or three science subjects, for instance, would be considered to be lacking in breadth and balance. It may be argued that a broad and balanced curriculum leading to a baccalaureate qualification should include a variety of subjects from different areas of knowledge and experience.

An alternative way of addressing breadth and balance is to consider whether there are certain core or key skills that it is desirable for all individuals to have. These are likely to include skills that are generally applicable across the curriculum, such as those associated with the effective use of information and communications technology, and skills associated with personal communication, literacy and the application of number. A third way of addressing breadth and balance is to incorporate vocational as well as academic dimensions into the curriculum, while yet another way of addressing breadth and balance is to consider the basis on which progress of learners is assessed, whether the assessment be formative or summative, of various domains (such as knowledge, skills and attitudes), or through a variety of assessment modes.

Hence, our review suggests that a further characteristic of a baccalaureate is that it is a programme of study that constitutes a broad and balanced curriculum. Some aspects of breadth and balance in the curriculum may be assured if the composition of the programme of study is prescribed, with such prescriptions likely to include the specification of a compulsory common core element and a range of optional or elective elements, as will be discussed in the next section.

A common experience

Does the need for assurance that the programme of study leading to a baccalaureate qualification demonstrates breadth and balance imply that it must always contain a compulsory core element, offering learners a common experience, in addition to optional or elective elements? The term 'compulsory core element' is used in preference to 'core subjects' in this context because the compulsory core may comprise key skills or cross-curricular components rather than formal academic subjects as such. No distinction is made here between 'optional' and 'elective' elements of the curriculum; both terms identify elements that are not part of the compulsory core and are subject to student choice.

The term 'a common experience' may be interpreted in various ways. It may be used to identify a specific programme of subjects that all students are required to follow without deviation. On the other hand, a less tightly prescriptive definition might identify the common experience with the selection of subjects chosen from different subject groups to make up a programme of study, in which case the shared common experience for students would be identified with the breadth and balance in the overall programme of study engendered by their selection of one subject from each group.

Types of option group

It is evident that there is variation between different curricula in terms of how the optional or elective subjects are arranged into groups and how the common core is constructed. In education systems such as in England and Wales, where there has been free choice of academic subjects, there have been no subject groups. In systems which attempt to promote a broad and balanced curriculum, the selection of options or electives is guided by grouping academic subjects together. Curricula appear to vary according to how they either place optional or elective subjects together into small numbers of large groups or split them into many small divisions.

One approach, as is the practice in Germany (INCA, 2002), is to construct three groups of subjects comprising languages, literature and the arts; social sciences; and mathematics, natural sciences and technology. Every student is required to study subjects selected from each of the groups up to the completion of upper secondary education, including the *Abitur* examination. The Advanced International Certificate of Education (CIE, 2002), meanwhile, requires the study of subjects from three curriculum areas comprising mathematics and sciences (Group A); languages (Group B); and arts and humanities (Group C), while the Leaving Certificate Vocational Programme in Ireland (INCA, 2002) has five subject groups comprising languages, sciences, business, applied science and social sciences.

The academic subjects of the International Baccalaureate (IB) Diploma programme (IBO, 2002) are arranged in six groups comprising language A (the candidate's own language: Group 1); second language (Group 2); individuals and societies (Group 3); experimental sciences (Group 4); mathematics (Group 5); and the arts (Group 6), with the award of the IB Diploma also requiring the completion of an extended essay, a course in the theory of knowledge, and a programme of creativity, action, service (CAS) activities.

In the case of the European Baccalaureate (EB) programme (European Baccalaureate, 2002), all students must typically follow a compulsory group of subjects. For an English-speaking student this would comprise English language and literature, mathematics, philosophy, religion, gym, a second language and history (in a second language). Additional subjects are taken according to the area of specialization of the students. For English-speaking science-oriented students the subjects to be taken are advanced mathematics, physics, chemistry and a third language, whereas for a student specializing in the humanities the subject to be added include advanced English, sociology (in another language), geography (in another language) and a third language. Similar arrangements, but with a different emphasis on the actual languages, apply to students whose 'mother tongue' is other than English.

Subjects of the Advanced Placement International Diploma for Overseas Study (APID) are organized into five areas (APID, 2002), requiring students to select two languages from area I, one science subject from area II, one subject from area III (mathematics) and one or more subject(s) from any other area not selected – areas IV (history and social sciences) and V (art subjects and computer science).

It is evident on the basis of inspection of data from numerous sources that most curricula are defined in terms of traditional subject areas such as mathematics, the physical sciences, the social sciences/humanities and languages. There may be some variation as to whether, for instance, mathematics is grouped with the physical sciences, or information and communications technology, or in a group of its own, or where the expressive arts or technological subjects are placed, or whether literature, first language, modern foreign languages and classical languages are grouped together or separately, but the same recognizable canon of academic subjects appears to be found in the curricula of most national systems.

Types of common core

In some systems (such as Germany) there is no specification for a common core group of subjects, but students pursuing specific academic or vocational tracks may be required to select subjects from particular groups. In other systems (such as Japan and Singapore), particular subjects are specified as compulsory components of the core curriculum common to all students. It may be argued that compulsory core subjects ensure that the breadth and balance of the curriculum are maintained; supporting evidence for this argument may be seen in those curricula in which traditionally recognizable academic subjects (such as mathematics, sciences and languages) form the compulsory common core. A contrasting approach, however, is to specify subjects or areas that enhance cross-curricular themes between subjects and give coherence to the programme of study. Such subjects, it may be argued, form part of a curriculum that facilitates 'interstitial learning' (Thompson, 1998). The extended essay, theory of knowledge, and the creativity, action, service (CAS) components of the IB Diploma Programme, for instance, may be identified with the promotion of cross-curricular coherence and interstitial learning.

The fourth characteristic suggested by our review is that a baccalaureate always contains a compulsory core element offering learners a common experience, in addition to optional or elective elements.

Summary

Based on the foregoing analysis, it is seen that a baccalaureate is associated with some, or all, of the following characteristics, expressed in a form appropriate to the particular context within which they arise:

- It is a curriculum or programme of study for upper secondary education which may be used as a school leaving examination.
- It may be used as a qualification for admission to higher education, for entry into employment, and as a foundation for learning throughout life.
- It is a programme of study which constitutes a broad and balanced curriculum.
- It contains a compulsory core element offering learners a common experience, in addition to optional or elective elements.

Towards a structural typology

Classification of baccalaureate-style curricula in terms of subject choices and combinations offered represents a pragmatic approach to analysis, constructed as it is by reference to published sources such as INCA (2002). Such analysis identifies the importance of two aspects of choice of subject content: the selection of optional or elective subjects from subject groups, and the inclusion of a compulsory common core of subjects.

Arranged orthogonally, these contrasting aspects generate a matrix containing four cells that presents a typology of curricula in two dimensions (see Figure 2.1), where four types of curricula described in the matrix comprise those with:

- selection of optional or elective subjects from subject groups with a compulsory common core (type A);
- free selection of options with a compulsory common core (type B);

	Selection of options from subject groups	Free selection of options
Compulsory common core subjects	Type A	Type B
No compulsory common core	Type C	Type D

Figure 2.1 A general typology of curricula

- selection of optional or elective subjects from subject groups with no compulsory common core (type C);
- free selection of options with no compulsory common core of subjects (type D).

The possibility needs to be acknowledged that a curriculum model may exist which comprises compulsory core subjects only with no options, but in practice this is not found. All post-16 curricula found in the sources reviewed for this chapter appear to contain an element of voluntarism, with at least some optional or elective components selected by students. Expressed diagrammatically, the range of general possibilities is as illustrated in Figure 2.2.

A curriculum with selection of optional or elective subjects from subject groups and with a compulsory common core (type A) may be seen, for instance, in the *première* and *terminale* years of the French *baccalauréat*, during which students are required to study compulsory French and mathematics whilst they pursue specialist subjects. This type of curriculum may also be seen in the IB Diploma Programme, in which students are required to select a balanced range of options from six subject groups and complete a core programme comprising the theory of knowledge (TOK) course, the extended essay and the creativity, action, service (CAS) component. The 16–18 curriculum in Japan also has a type A organization, with students required to study an extensive compulsory core of subjects, while the curriculum in Sweden has some resemblance to this model with all upper secondary programmes consisting of three components: core subjects, subjects specific to one of 17 national programmes of study, and individual options.

A curriculum with free selection of options and a compulsory common core (type B) is found in Singapore, where students have a relatively free choice of subjects, albeit determined by considerations of university entrance requirements, in addition to a compulsory core. A type C curriculum with selection of optional or elective subjects from subject groups with no compulsory common core may be seen in the Leaving Certificate (Established) in Ireland, which requires selection of optional subjects from five groups. This programme may also, however, have some affinity with a

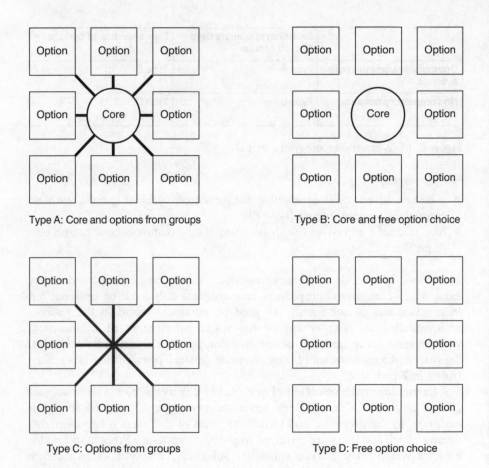

Figure 2.2 A structural typology of curriculum models

type A curriculum on the grounds that *Gaeilge* (Irish) is a compulsory subject. The type C model is also seen in the Cambridge Advanced International Certificate of Education (AICE) in which students are required to select subjects from groups, a requirement which is also a feature of the AP International Diploma of Overseas Study (APID). A curriculum with free selection of options and with no compulsory common core of subjects (type D) may be seen in the New Zealand Qualifications Framework, in the sense that it is not a mandatory programme.

In terms of the summary characteristics identified, it is clear that models A and B represent possibilities for structures applicable to baccalaureate programmes. The observation that such programmes should include a common experience for all students in order to qualify as a true baccalaureate in such a classification would lead us to suggest that models C and D should be treated as quasi-baccalaureate structures.

Conclusion

Through a review of the literature and of current practice in a number of different educational systems, it has been possible to identify a set of model structures all of which lay some claim, in one respect or another, to represent a baccalaureate or quasi-baccalaureate approach to curriculum organization. It is hoped that such a structural typology will be of assistance to those whose tasks involve the design, implementation and evaluation of baccalaureate programmes, and to readers of the following chapters in this volume.

References

APID (2002) *AP Advanced Diploma for Overseas Study* [Online] http://www. collegeboard.com (accessed 21 June, 2002)

Cambridge, J C, Hayden, M C and Thompson, J J (2001) *Towards a Typology for Baccalaureate-style Curricula in Post-16 Education Systems*, unpublished report for the Project Steering Group of the Welsh Baccalaureate Qualification Project (November)

Cambridge International Examinations (2002) *Advanced International Certificate of Education* [Online] http://www.cie.org.uk (accessed 21 June, 2002)

Department of Education and Science (DES) (1988) *Advancing A-levels, Report of the Committee chaired by Professor Gordon Higginson*, HMSO, London

Department for Education and Skills (DfES) (2002) *14–19: Extending opportunities, raising standards*, consultation document, HMSO, London (February)

European Baccalaureate (2002) *The European Baccalaureate* [Online] http://www.eursc.org/SE/htmlEn/intro7.html (accessed 21 June, 2002)

Farrell, M, Kerry, T and Kerry, T (1995) *The Blackwell Handbook of Education*, Blackwell, Oxford

Finegold, D, Keep, E, Miliband, D, Raffe, D, Spours, K and Young, M (1990) *A British 'Baccalauréat': Ending the division between education and training*, Institute for Public Policy Research, London

Gordon, P and Lawton, D (1984) *A Guide to English Educational Terms*, Batsford, London

Green, A (1997) Core skills, general education and unification in post-16 education, in *Dearing and Beyond: 16–19 qualifications, frameworks and systems,* ed A Hodgson and K Spours, pp 88–104, Kogan Page, London

Hirst, P H and Peters, R S (1970) *The Logic of Education*, Routledge and Kegan Paul, London

IBO (1996) *Biology Subject Guide*, International Baccalaureate Organization, Geneva

IBO (2002) *International Baccalaureate Organization* [Online] http://www.ibo.org (accessed 21 June, 2002)

INCA (2002) *The International Review of Curriculum and Assessment Frameworks Archive* [Online] http://www.inca.org.uk (accessed 21 June, 2002)

Le Métais, J (1997) *Values and Aims in Curriculum and Assessment Frameworks* [Online] http://www.inca.org.uk/pdf/values_no_intro_97.pdf (accessed 21 June, 2002)

McLean, M (1995) *Educational Traditions Compared*, David Fulton, London

National Commission on Education (1993) *Learning to Succeed: Report of the Paul Hamlyn Foundation National Commission on Education*, Heinemann, London

Phenix, R (1964) *Realms of Meaning*, McGraw Hill, New York

Prost, A (2000) The creation of the Baccalauréat Professionnel: a case study of decision making in French education, *Journal of Education Policy*, **15** (1), pp 19–31

QCA (1999) *Curriculum Guidance for 2000: Implementing the changes to 16–19 qualifications*, Qualifications and Curriculum Authority, London [Online] http://www.qca.org.uk/ca/14–19/curric2000.asp (accessed 21 June, 2002)

Stanton, G (1997) Unitization: developing a common language for describing achievement, in *Dearing and Beyond: 16–19 qualifications, frameworks and systems,* ed A Hodgson and K Spours, pp 121–34, Kogan Page, London

Thompson, J J (1998) Towards a model for international education, in *International Education: Principles and practice*, ed M C Hayden and J J Thompson, pp 276–90, Kogan Page, London

Unwin, L (1997) Reforming the work-based route: problems and potential for change, in *Dearing and Beyond: 16–19 qualifications, frameworks and systems,* ed A Hodgson and K Spours, pp 75–87, Kogan Page, London

Welsh Baccalaureate Qualification (2002) [Online] http://www.wbq.org.uk (accessed 21 June, 2002)

Young, M (1998) *The Curriculum of the Future*, Falmer, London

Young, M and Leney, T (1997) From A-levels to an advanced curriculum of the future, in *Dearing and Beyond: 16–19 qualifications, frameworks and systems,* ed A Hodgson and K Spours, pp 40–56, Kogan Page, London

3

The International Baccalaureate

Ian Hill

Through comprehensive and balanced curricula coupled with challenging assessments, the International Baccalaureate Organization aims to assist schools in their endeavours to develop the individual talents of young people and teach them to relate the experience of the classroom to the realities of the world outside. Beyond intellectual rigour and high academic standards, strong emphasis is placed on the ideals of international understanding and responsible citizenship, to the end that IB students may become critical and compassionate thinkers, lifelong learners and informed participants in local and world affairs, conscious of the shared humanity that binds all people together while respecting the variety of cultures and attitudes that makes for the richness of life (IB Organization mission statement, 1996).

Introduction

Since the first official examinations in 1970, the IB Diploma Programme has become a widely recognized qualification giving access to higher education and equipping students with the skills they will need for the future. From its headquarters in Geneva and its other major offices in Cardiff, New York, Buenos Aires, and Singapore, the IB Organization (IBO) administers a programme which has provided an important educational service to students displaced around the world, initially in international schools. It has also attracted the attention of a number of governments who find in the structure, pedagogy and philosophy of the IB an interesting model to contemplate during periods of national educational reform. The IBO is regularly involved in projects and consultation with UNESCO, both at its Paris headquarters and with field offices.

After outlining the beginnings of the IB, this chapter explains the IB model with particular attention to breadth and balance in the choice of subject disciplines. The programme objectives are then examined, and from this the reader is taken through a discussion about the student experience – the extent to which the stated objectives are achieved in reality, relying on research evidence and student comment. This is followed by the status of the IB diploma as a qualification for higher education, supported by research on IB student performance in universities.

The penultimate section is about the contribution of the IB Diploma Programme to education and social policies, with particular reference to the IBO's pedagogical and ideological underpinnings, and the way it can influence such policies through its collaboration with governments and UNESCO. A number of recent curriculum and other innovations by the IBO are outlined in the final section.

The origins of the IB

The 1960s was a time when teaching methods came under scrutiny from visionary teachers and educational reformers. The audio-lingual and audio-visual boom produced many new course books for the teaching of foreign languages, emphasizing oral communication and spontaneity as a reaction against the ineffectiveness of the grammar-translation method to produce people who could actually converse in another language. Innovative teachers were attempting to move beyond the presentation of one view of national history to an analysis from different cultural perspectives, while in the sciences an enquiry-based approach with motivating text books (such as the Nuffield Foundation material) was being mooted. A variety of student assessment techniques requiring skills other than recall were being discussed. Bloom's taxonomy (1956; Bloom, Mesia and Krathwohl, 1964) had arrived; more attention was to be paid to affective as well as cognitive skills.

These pedagogical advances took a long time to trickle down to the classroom, and in some countries never trickled down at all. Changes in a national system of education are slow to happen; they require money for teacher training and materials, and political will. International schools, on the other hand, were much more independent and had the potential to try out new educational ideas very rapidly. By their nature they also attracted teachers with open minds and attitudes favourable to the promotion of international understanding. Knowledgeable, well-travelled, influential parents, interested in a first class education for their children, completed the contextual fabric of these schools, making them ideal educational laboratories.

It was in such a climate that the International Baccalaureate (IB) diploma programme was born. In 1962 the International School of Geneva hosted a conference for teachers of social studies in international schools. Participants (from countries including Australia, Britain, France, Germany, Switzerland and the United States) recommended that a history course be developed for use in international schools around the world as the first subject of an 'international baccalaureate' – these were the words used in the conference report (ISG, 1962) – to be studied during the last two years of secondary education. It was the beginning of the IB Diploma Programme which will be referred to in this chapter as the IB.

The International Schools Association (ISA) created an offspring in 1964 to structure the project, and this officially became the IB Office (later to be called the IB Organization) from 1968, located in Geneva. In 1970, 10 schools entered students for the first official examinations (IBO, 1970: 20).

A Scot, Alec Peterson, Director of the Department of Educational Studies at Oxford, then shaped the educational philosophy of the IB when he became Director General of the IB Organization from 1967–77. A former head of Dover College and editor for many years of the prestigious journal *Comparative Education*, he was a staunch campaigner against what he regarded as the over-specialization of British education at pre-university level.

A number of factors contributed to the emergence of this programme. Many of the parents who were working for the League of Nations (1920), its successor the United Nations (1945), and in overseas embassies were instrumental in starting international schools in different countries. They often found the local schools inappropriate because their children did not speak the language of the host country, the national qualification was not recognized in their home country, the curricula lacked an international perspective and teaching methods were usually rooted in memorization only. In addition, parents working for the UN and its agencies wanted schools that reflected a similar ideology: the promotion of world peace and international understanding. Teachers in international schools also saw the need to have a programme which corresponded to the international experience of the students and which could educationally exploit their cultural diversity.

In summary, the IB came about through a combination of the following pragmatic and visionary factors to which those involved in curriculum design were committed in varying degrees:

- to promote international understanding and provide an international perspective in the curriculum;
- to facilitate international mobility through a diploma recognized by universities around the world;
- to develop critical thinking skills and the intellectual strength to question conventional beliefs;
- to develop the 'whole person'.

The IB model

For a number of years before he joined the IB project, Peterson was discontented with British education at pre-university level, which he regarded as too narrow. His 1960 report, *Arts and Science Sides in the Sixth Form* (see

Peterson, 1987: 42), closely resembled not only the philosophy but also the structure of the IB Diploma Programme which was to be elaborated, initially without any influence from Peterson, a few years later. The Oxford Department of Educational Studies report emphasized the need for a broader education, which at the same time allowed for a degree of specialization. Peterson believed that scientists needed ethics and that humanities students should know something about the beauty of mathematics. Critical analysis and learning to learn, rather than encylopaedic knowledge and memorization, formed the pedagogical basis of the report. It proposed increasing the number of specialized subjects in the British sixth form from two to four, spread over the humanities and the sciences. A fifth block of time was to be added to cover religious and physical education, the creative arts and a new course of about 60 hours which would enable students to 'make a unity' of their whole learning experience. 'The fifth block should therefore include a course, similar to the best and not the worst of the *classes de philosophie*, on the methodology of the subjects' (Peterson, 1987: 42). Those familiar with the IB will immediately recognize this precursor of the theory of knowledge course.

The structure of the IB Diploma Programme is represented in Figure 3.1.

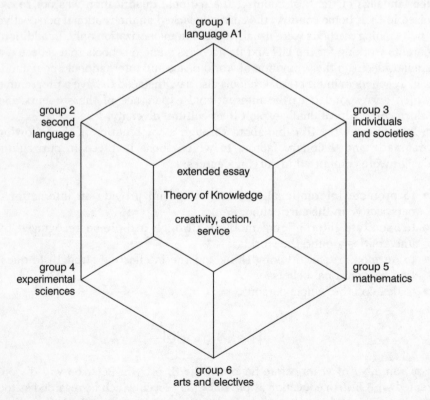

Figure 3.1   Structure of the IB Diploma Programme

Students must choose one subject from each of groups 1 to 5, thus ensuring breadth of experience across languages, the experimental sciences, mathematics and the humanities. The sixth subject may be an arts subject chosen from group 6, or the student may choose another subject from any of the other groups. Further mathematics can be chosen as a second subject in group 5 only if higher level mathematics has already been selected; computer science can only be taken as a second subject in group 5, which means that students must take a mathematics subject first. At least three (and not more than four) subjects must be studied at higher level (HL), which requires a minimum of 240 instructional hours over the last two years of secondary education. The remaining subjects are studied at standard level (SL), which requires a minimum of 150 hours of instruction. The vast majority of IB students take three subjects at HL and three at SL. Standard level courses usually require less depth and breadth of content than those at HL, but this is not always the case – for example, it is not so for further mathematics.

The subjects currently offered in each group are as follows. All subjects are offered at both HL and SL unless indicated otherwise.

Group 1: first language

Literature courses in approximately 80 languages at native speaker level are available.

Group 2: second language

There are currently 14 Language A2 courses for highly competent speakers or for bilingual students.

There are 24 Language B foreign language learning courses on offer, where students would normally have already studied the language for four or five years at school. There are 12 *ab initio* courses (at SL only) for students with no prior knowledge of the language. Latin and classical Greek are included in this group.

Group 3: individuals and societies

This includes business and management, economics, geography, history, Islamic history, information technology in a global society (at SL only), philosophy, psychology, and social and cultural anthropology.

Group 4: experimental sciences

This comprises biology, chemistry, physics, environmental systems (at SL only) and design technology.

Group 5: mathematics and computer science

This consists of further mathematics (SL), mathematics (HL), mathematical methods (SL), mathematical studies (SL) and computer science.

Group 6: the arts

This includes visual art, music and theatre arts (the subjects dance and film are being trialled from 2002).

All students must complete three additional components: theory of knowledge, extended essay and 'creativity action service' (CAS). The maximum score for each of the six subjects at HL or SL is 7, and for the theory of knowledge and the extended essay combined it is 3. Students require a minimum of 24 points out of a maximum of 45 for the award of the IB diploma. No grades are given for CAS, but failure to complete it satisfactorily means that the diploma is not awarded, even if the student has passed the academic subjects. A very small number of students each year fall into this category.

As has been noted so often in the British press and in some reports on education in that country, the IB Diploma Programme offers a breadth and balance that A levels do not. Languages, sciences, maths, humanities and community service are maintained until the end of secondary school. This structure develops the well-rounded citizen. Many educators, parents and universities are dissatisfied with a system that allows students to complete secondary education without a qualification that includes these disciplines. Specializing in any three subjects is unthinkable in continental Europe and in the vast majority of countries around the world where the concept of the 'culture générale' is firmly embedded. Even most of Britain's former colonies have developed their own school leaving qualification where breadth in the traditional areas of learning is compulsory. Breadth is also important from a pragmatic point of view: the idea of a job for life with the same employer has almost disappeared; individuals have to be prepared to recycle themselves for changing circumstances and new tasks. They need preparation for lifelong learning which keeps future options open. Breadth and balance, rather than early specialization, is the key.

UK schools find the IB model also attracts overseas students because it provides a breadth with which they are familiar and it is readily recognized around the world. At the same time it allows for some degree of specialization through its higher and standard levels; the extended essay also allows a student to explore in detail a particular topic within a subject.

The most perceptive students are looking beyond gaining entry to good universities, but are looking at the skills they will need to compete for the top jobs around the world. The IB offers the only means of delivering that kind of breadth at the moment.

Stuart Westley, Master of Haileybury. *Independent*, 8 November 2001.

IB higher level subjects have sometimes been criticized as being easier because they have less content than their A level counterparts. There may be additional content in A level subjects, but academic rigour is more a function of the skills of analysis, interpretation, synthesis, problem solving, creativity, seeing unlikely connections, and clear expression. Content is important, but it is much more a means than an end. Singapore realized this a few years ago when its national education system was not producing 'critical and creative thinkers that would sustain [the country's] future national competitive edge. There was too much content coverage.... Almost overnight, Singapore ordered a 30 per cent downsizing of its curriculum. Singapore has come to realize that it needs to produce more intelligent, less knowledgeable graduates' (Powell, 2002: 32). The evidence later in this chapter is that IB students do not suffer when they attend higher education institutions; on the contrary they are considered to be very well prepared, and they know how to write and express themselves. Most teachers who teach both A levels and IB have said that more work is required to obtain an IB diploma.

> IB students not only have to succeed in a broader range of subjects but the work is harder too. Higher level IB maths is more difficult than A level maths.
> Jackie Kearns, Warden, Impington Village College, Cambridgeshire.
> *Sunday Times*, 18 November 2001.

British proponents of the IB see a stability in its structure, which has not changed since it was first established more than 30 years ago, and which fulfils the needs of an increasing number of students around the world. This is in contrast to the various reforms of A levels that have been mooted and have upset the UK education community. The IB also offers a credible examination process which is criterion-based, highly centralized and places emphasis on the skills that are needed for the world of tomorrow. The academic standard of the IB diploma assessment procedures across subjects has varied very little, if at all, over the last 30 years. The variety of assessment techniques also provides students with different modes of demonstrating their achievements: interdisciplinary group projects in the sciences, short answer questions, essay questions, practical assessments, project work, multiple choice questions, research essays, externally marked essays written as coursework, structured questions, case study questions, data analysis questions, and oral assessments in literature, theory of knowledge and modern languages.

In most IB subjects the teacher's marking of coursework (which is externally moderated) counts for about 30 per cent of the final result, the remainder being final examinations which test the two-year course. This is an attraction for some universities who see this as more demanding than the accumulation of grades by examining segments of the total curriculum at various stages over the last two years of secondary education.

> A key factor [in the growing popularity of the IB] is that, while the IB contains elements of continuous appraisal, it is essentially examined at the end of a 'linear' course. Reformed A levels – split into four ASs in the lower sixth and three A2s in the upper sixth – mean students are examined extensively at the ages of 16, 17 and 18 on free-standing 'modules' of knowledge.
>
> *Financial Times,* 18–19 May 2002

The next section discusses the objectives of the IB Diploma Programme, in which an increasing number of schools see advantages in addition to those related primarily to its curriculum and examination structure, and academic rigour.

Objectives of the IB Diploma Programme

The intent of the IB Diploma Programme is that students will:

1. Engage in a broad, academically rigorous education which still allows for specialization.
2. Learn how to evaluate information and actions critically.
3. Learn how to go on learning.
4. Become intellectually flexible and creative to cope with uncertainty.
5. Develop an appreciation of the human condition in all its local and global manifestations.
6. Discuss and probe global issues and cultural differences to arrive at international understanding.
7. Develop a sense of environmental responsibility.
8. Become informed and responsible local and global citizens.

These objectives are reflected in the syllabuses and examination papers of the IB Diploma Programme and the total curricular experience in schools. Objectives 2, 3 and 4 are pedagogical while numbers 5 to 8 relate to international understanding. Here is not the place to debate the nature of international education. Suffice it to say that the thinking world received the message (delivered in a totally unacceptable way on 11 September 2001), as if it needed any reminding, that our nations are economically, politically, environmentally, technologically and socially interdependent. An international education perspective, defined by UNESCO (1974) in terms almost identical to those of the IBO, is more important now than it ever was. National systems of education are looking to inculcate 'internationalism' into their programmes. The IB Diploma Programme has been practising 'internationalism' since it was founded. This has now become a pertinent advantage of an IB education. The following discussion gives examples that highlight how aspects of the IB programme seek to support international understanding in particular.

Theory of knowledge is a course of 100 hours; it has no exact equivalent in national systems. It is interdisciplinary and challenges students to question the bases of knowledge, to be aware of subjective and ideological biases, to think critically, and to appreciate cultural differences. It is assessed through a major essay externally examined and an oral presentation. Topic questions from the theory of knowledge (IBO, 1999) curriculum guide include:

Do knowledge claims transcend different communities or cultures?

Is it correct to think that what constitutes [good logic] varies from discipline to discipline and from culture to culture?

Is the scientific method a product unique to western culture, or is it universal?

Student Profile: Jalal Al Rasheed

Higher level	grade	Standard level	grade
Chemistry	6	Arabic A1	6
Physics	7	English B	5
Mathematics	5	History of the Islamic World	5

Extended essay: physics/excellent Theory of Knowledge/mediocre 2 points
All CAS (creativity, action, service) requirements have been fully satisfied.
Total diploma point score: 36. Bilingual Diploma awarded.

Jalal intends to pursue a career in engineering at university either in his home country of Jordan or in the United States. He took Physics, Mathematics and Chemistry at Higher Level and wrote his extended essay in Physics. He took his groups 3–6 examinations in English and consequently earned the bilingual diploma since his first language is Arabic. With a combination of an excellent extended essay and satisfactory work in Theory of Knowledge, Jalal gained two points for a total diploma score of 36. He plans to continue volunteer work with disabled children, an activity he came to value through his CAS programme in Jordan.

Students choose to write an extended essay of 4,000 words on a topic that is usually associated with one of the subjects they are studying, but it may be done in another subject. This develops independent research skills and academic rigour in the structure of a research essay. Recent extended essays have been written on the following topics:

- The effects of acid rain on the environment, with a focus on plant life (biology).

- An examination of existing solutions to Latin America's debt crisis in relation to Mexico (economics).
- The contribution of international organizations to the economic development of Geneva (economics).
- Why are the Australian and Singapore stock exchanges more volatile than the major international stock markets? (economics).
- Springtime is silent: the poetry of the Vietnam war (English A1).
- Lillie A. James: opportunity and equal rights through education (history).
- The mathematics of nature: the relationship between fractals, chaos and iteration (maths).
- Euthanasia: the morality of killing and letting die (philosophy).

> I used the knowledge that I acquired [in the IB]... to think creatively alone and in a team, and above all to develop the habit of continuing to learn as a style of life. I learned to learn.
> Jose Obes, General Manager, Boston Bank private pension scheme, Uruguay.
> *IB World*, 12 (1996): 2.

CAS requires all diploma students to spend a minimum of 150 hours over two years pursuing a combination of activities that are related to the arts, physical exercise, and service to others. They develop greater awareness of themselves, concern for others, and the ability to work cooperatively in a group. In a number of schools IB students provide weekly survival (literacy and numeracy) and recreational programmes for street children in both developed and developing countries. Students in an IBO school in Uganda provide information on the prevention of AIDS to the local community. They also, in collaboration with UNICEF, give weekly moral support to families with HIV positive parents, building up memory banks of the family history and values told by the parents and recorded on tape by the students; this will then be available to the children after the parents have died. An international education develops 'attitudes and values which respect human dignity and which transcend barriers of race, class, religion, gender and politics' (IBO, 2001b: 8). In this way many CAS activities contribute very personally to citizenship at a local, national and international level.

> The most memorable part of the IB programme was CAS. Two gratifying experiences were being able to bring joy to many lonely individuals at an old people's home and knowing that during our AIDS awareness campaign we may have corrected dangerous misconceptions.
> Luciano Castagnola, St George's College North, Buenos Aries, Argentina.
> *IB World*, Aug/Sept 1997: 2.

All language courses have as a main objective the promotion of intercultural understanding, and students are required, in language A1, to study world literature: a number of works in translation from cultures unrelated to those represented by the language A1 are studied. The topic options in language A2 include 'global issues' and 'language and culture'. An essay question in the November 2001 English A2 SL examination was: 'Global issues can be a source of conflict between nations. Give examples and say how the conflicts were, or could be, resolved.'

The history course seeks to develop 'the capacity to identify, to analyse critically and to evaluate theories, concepts and arguments about the nature and activities of the individual and society' (IBO, 2001c: 4). It gives suitable emphasis to the process of historical enquiry. One of the three history papers is always devoted to analysing several accounts of the same event written from different cultural perspectives. Other group 3 humanities courses stress the international dimension, such as the global interdependence of national economies and the need to consider different economic solutions in different cultural circumstances. For example, the following question appeared in the Economics papers (May 2001): 'Critically assess the arguments for and against the increased liberalization of international trade. Refer in your answer to both less developed and more developed countries.' The November 2001 Social Anthropology examination paper included the following essay topic: 'Inequalities within and between societies or nations are increasingly evident in today's world. Describe one way in which anthropologists have tried to explain this development...' One of the questions in the May 2001 Psychology examinations was, 'Which cross-cultural communication skills are most important in achieving cultural mediation? How can these skills reduce culture conflict?'

The first aim for the experimental sciences is to 'provide opportunities for scientific study and creativity within a global context which will stimulate and challenge students' (IBO, 2001a: 6). The moral and ethical implications of scientific advances are explored. An aim of all mathematics programmes is to 'appreciate the international dimensions of mathematics and the multiplicity of its cultural and historical perspectives' (IBO, 1998: 5). An example of consideration of the human condition and sustainability is this question from the November 2001 environmental systems paper: 'Suggest what the physical, biological and social limits might be to the growth of the human population on earth.'

During the oral discussion of students' work in visual arts the examiner asks questions such as 'How do you feel the culture of this part of the world has influenced your work?' (IBO, 2000: 16). The role of the arts in enhancing cultural appreciation needs no elaboration here.

The extent to which the IB Diploma Programme attempts to inculcate a code of ethics for good world citizenship has been explored elsewhere (Hill, 2001).

The student experience

Annick Goulet, former IB diploma student at the Collège de Jean-de-Brébeuf, Montréal (1991) summed it up nicely:

> After the IB diploma, I began to evaluate the program in terms of contributions to new life experiences. It was then that I came to consider the IB as a real heritage because it bequeaths to its former students more than well-articulated knowledge and skills in the traditional disciplines. It really inculcates a critical approach, an efficient work method, a way of synthesizing, a discipline and, more than anything else, an openness to the world.

Hayden and Wong (1997) surveyed 29 people at the University of Bath (UK) comprising students with an IB diploma, teachers of the IB Diploma Programme doing post-graduate study, and members of staff of the university including admissions tutors. One of the three questions to the group was whether the IB promoted international understanding. The conclusion was that the school environment and the personal contact with a mix of nationalities that it provided, together with international travel, contributed more to international understanding than the IB Diploma Programme itself. The respondents were not, however, dismissive of the formal IB curriculum and identified the following components as making the greatest potential contribution to international understanding: theory of knowledge, foreign languages, and world literature in the language A1 course.

Jessica Reinisch, Impington Village College, Cambridgeshire:

> I chose to take biology at higher level despite the fact that I strongly disliked all sciences and could not see their relevance for me as an 'arty' person.... After a period of determined struggling with biology and maths I realized how much I was getting out of these lessons.... It made me begin to see the world as an interconnected whole.... Maths and biology helped me look at art quite differently. I discovered new fields such as scientific illustration and geometrical art. I found many parallels between biology and social anthropology which were reinforced by English and German literature. Somehow all these loose ends came together in theory of knowledge.... The IB has made me aware of new ways of looking at the world.
>
> (IB World, 11 (1996): 3)

To monitor the progress of the IB Diploma Programme, all schools receive a survey at five-year intervals from the IBO regional offices. The section for students (in their last year of the Diploma Programme) and teachers includes a question that asks what aspects of the IB subjects and activities promote intercultural awareness. A sample of 72 schools in Africa, Europe and the Middle East comprising 44 international schools, 12 state schools and 16 private national schools provides helpful feedback. The information gathered relates to the period 1998–2000. The total number of teacher and student questionnaires for the 72 schools was approximately 1,700, of which 55 per cent were from teachers and 45 per cent from students. There were approximately 1,030 questionnaire responses from international schools, 300 from state schools and 370 from private national schools.

Elizabeth McGregor, Lauriston Girls' School, Victoria, Australia:

I have learned much through the IB: the purely academic but I have also attained many skills in areas as diverse as research and relating to others. I've developed determination and patience – I will no doubt use these new skills as I look to a career in medicine. I feel that I am well prepared to meet the challenge.

(IB World, 12 (1996): 1)

Respondents often related the IB programme to the school context, so that in the international schools a frequent response was that intercultural awareness occurred principally 'via the cultural mix of students and teachers'. In national state and private schools the corresponding response (from about half the schools) was that intercultural understanding was enhanced through interaction with 'foreign teachers and students, foreign visitors, and intercultural comparisons'.

Very few respondents from international schools mentioned the value of exchange programmes with schools abroad for developing intercultural understanding. A small number of schools in Europe referred to CAS trips to Africa. By contrast, student exchanges abroad figured frequently in the questionnaire responses from national state and private schools, occurring slightly more in the latter. Are they less needed in international schools where other nationalities are present in abundance? Another much less expensive way for national schools to access other cultural points of view is through the Internet; this figured in more than half their questionnaire responses but was hardly mentioned at all by individuals from international schools.

Did teachers and students indicate that the content and delivery of particular subjects had any perceived effect on their appreciation of other cultures? There was no distinguishable difference in responses between the three school types. The most frequently mentioned subjects, in descending order, were: world literature (language A1), modern languages, theory of knowledge, history, art/design, CAS, music, language A2 topic options, theatre arts, world geography, social anthropology and philosophy. All other regular subjects and two school-based syllabuses (proposed by participating

IB schools) – peace and conflict studies and world religions – were mentioned at least once. Similar subjects were identified in Hayden and Wong's survey (1997: 359) as most likely to have a beneficial effect in the promotion of international understanding.

Student Profile: Kate Evans

Higher level	grade	Standard level	grade
English A1	5	Japanese B	6
History – Europe	5	Environmental systems	4
Art/Design	6	Mathematical studies	3

Extended essay: history/good Theory of Knowledge/good: 2 points.
All CAS (creativity, action, service) requirements have been fully satisfied.
Total diploma points score: 31. Diploma awarded.

Kate was born in Australia of Welsh parents and lived in Japan for a few years while her mother was on a business assignment. She wants to study History at a university in Melbourne so took History at the higher level and elected for the European regional paper. Kate opted for Japanese B at standard level which her high school had just begun to offer as a regular group 2 course. She increased her History specialization by writing an extended essay on an Australian history topic, and demonstrated her talent in Art/Design at higher level. Kate chose to take her standard level Environmental Systems and Mathematical Studies examinations at the end of her first year. She was on the girls' diving team and organized a neighbourhood clean-up day as part of her community service.

The IBO questionnaires for this regular five-year review were not established with a rigorous research design in mind. The returns do, however, represent a large sample in which almost all of the 1,700 respondents in both international and national schools refer to the effect of parts of the formal curriculum on the development of intercultural understanding.

Hinrichs (2001) surveyed 53 IB and 50 Advanced Placement (AP) students in two state schools in the same district of Washington State, USA on the nature of international understanding and to what extent their programmes had contributed to this. Care was taken to match the cohorts on a number of external variables including demographic characteristics and prior test scores. Hinrichs synthesized the responses into seven components of international understanding, identified as skills for students to live effectively across cultures, appreciate ethnic differences and diverse beliefs, recognize interdependence among nations, understand global issues, value peace and international interests over nationalism, understand how domestic policies affect the world, and respect democracy and basic human rights. The

IB objectives encompass all of these: for example, the IB 'human condition' includes respect for human rights.

Statistically significant differences were demonstrated. 'IB students included more elements of international understanding as defined by experts in the field, and the answers were longer, more complex, more personal, and demonstrated exceptional insights' (Hinrichs, 2001: 106). More than the AP students, the IB students attributed their conceptions of international understanding to specific IB courses.

An international higher education qualification

Recognition

The IB diploma provides a widely respected international passport to higher education. Early recognition of the IB for university entrance was shepherded by influential international public servants and reformers of national education systems, who were drawn to the IB project in the hope that it would provide a fertile field in which to exchange pedagogical ideas. From the beginning, Mountbatten, as champion of the United World College movement, was successful in gaining university recognition in many countries through his government contacts and world-wide reputation.

Today the IB is accepted for further studies in 101 countries including all of the developed world with the exception of a very small number of countries in the Middle East (the United Arab Emirates, Saudi Arabia and Oman). Higher education institutions in other countries accept IB diploma holders on a case by case basis. A number of the countries where no official recognition exists are politically unstable, and their universities are often closed for long periods owing to student and staff unrest.

There are more than 1,100 schools (43 per cent of them state schools where the IB programme is funded by ministries or departments of education) offering the IB Diploma Programme in 107 countries. (A very small number of countries, mostly in the developing world, host international IB schools but do not officially recognize the IB diploma.) Of these schools, 125 teach in Spanish and 20 in French. A list of IB Diploma schools by country is included as an appendix to this chapter. At the request of students, the IBO forwards electronically thousands of diploma results each year directly to universities. In 2001 these requests, plus information from regional IBO offices, showed that the majority of IB graduates wished to attend universities (in descending order of popularity) in the United States, Canada, the UK, Australia, Latin America, the Nordic countries, and the rest of Western Europe. Smaller numbers of IB diploma holders wished to attend universities in the Middle East, parts of Asia and South Africa.

Recognition is broadly of two types. The most common is where the national education authority or individual universities grant an equivalence between the IB diploma and the national qualification giving entry to higher education. The

IB diploma therefore provides direct access without the necessity to sit further examinations (with the exception of proving facility in a language where required). Countries where this applies include Australia, Belgium, Canada, France, Germany, Italy, the Netherlands, and the UK. This also applies to colleges and universities in the United States, where the IB diploma earns advanced credit of up to one full year depending on results in individual subjects. The other type is where direct equivalence is not granted and students must sit further examinations. Only a small number of countries require this, and the number is diminishing. Students seeking admission to higher education in Spain, Greece and Turkey must sit university entrance examinations after having completed the end-of-secondary school national leaving qualification; the same applies to IB diploma holders. Some Latin American countries also require a national diploma for access to state universities. Most countries or institutions stipulate the study of specific subjects at IB level for certain university courses, and a minimum score for admission to programmes with a high demand, as occurs for students with the national qualification.

The Council of Europe/UNESCO Convention on the Recognition of Qualifications concerning Higher Education in the European Region was signed in Portugal in 1997 and is known as the Lisbon Convention. Signatories also include Australia, Canada and the United States. A number of countries have now ratified the agreement. In 1999 the committee of the Lisbon Convention adopted a *Recommendation on International Access Qualifications* as a subsidiary text to the convention itself. The subcommittee of member states of the Council of Europe/UNESCO which drafted this recommendation used the IB diploma as a model.

In the convention, international access qualifications are defined as secondary school leaving certificates awarded on completion of a programme:

- distinct from the programmes offered within national education systems
- administered by one or more bodies external to national education systems
- having an international orientation and scope per se
- meeting the general requirements for access to higher education
- subject to well-defined and transparent quality assurance mechanisms
- incorporating a core curriculum of sufficient academic rigour.

Each party to the Lisbon Convention is asked to give full consideration to qualifications external to their system and to grant equivalence 'unless a substantial difference can be shown' with the comparable national qualification. Furthermore, countries are urged to show flexibility 'in the spirit of the increasing internationalization and diversification of education'.

Top universities [in the UK] certainly value the added breadth of the IB, and the signal it sends about a student's ability to handle large amounts of material and a range of ideas.

Financial Times, 2002

Performance of IB students in higher education

How successful are IB students in higher education? There is much anecdotal evidence about many individuals, stretching back to the first diploma holders in 1970, and some research on the topic. At conferences and meetings in different parts of the world IB students almost invariably emphasize that they found their first year of university less onerous than they had anticipated because they had already developed independent research skills, had learnt to structure essays and reports, had learnt to organize and prioritize their study activities, had learnt how to study (not just to memorize) – how to assimilate and analyse critically, and had approached issues with an open mind.

Jacqueline Maughan, Impington Village College, Cambridgeshire:

When I was in the final year of the IB I often wondered why I had voluntarily opted for the demands of a six-subject programme instead of A levels. The IB's balance between the arts, sciences and humanities proved a major attraction because it enabled me to pursue my favourite subjects to a high level.... I would not have identified my academic and personal strengths as quickly had I not taken the IB. In terms of my present studies I feel at a tremendous advantage. Adapting to the academic demands of university has been less of a struggle thanks to the emphasis the IB placed on independent research, particularly through the extended essay.

(IB World, 11 (1996): 2–3)

During the period from 1993 to 1999 this writer was regularly in touch with university admissions tutors and lecturers in a number of countries in Europe and elsewhere. They said frequently that IB students were consistently:

- self-confident and independent;
- mature and tolerant towards the opinions of others;
- open to challenges and willing to take risks;
- critical readers and thinkers;
- participating actively in local and global events.

This is not to say that the above qualities are not to be found in other students to varying degrees; clearly they are. The point is that IB students are perceived almost always to demonstrate these attributes.

Moreover, these observations are consonant with findings by Hayden and Wong (1997: 354), where a small sample of admissions tutors 'were all of the opinion that IB students are broadly knowledgeable, are equipped with research skills, are independent and able to work in teams. They are also recognized to be open-minded with respect to other cultural identities and modes of thought'. As Hayden and Wong point out, it is difficult to demonstrate that these characteristics are due to the IB curriculum alone. Nevertheless, these comments echo those that have been made frequently over many years.

Student Profile: Stan Losak

Higher level	grade	Standard level	grade
English A1	5	Polish A1	5
Psychology	5	Chemistry	4
Music	7	Mathematical methods	5

Extended essay: music/excellent Theory of Knowledge/satisfactory: 2 points. All CAS (creativity, action, service) requirements have been fully satisfied. Total diploma point score: 33. Bilingual Diploma awarded.

Stan came to Chicago from Poland four years ago and quickly developed an enthusiasm for jazz. He took English A1 at higher level and Polish A1 at standard level, the latter with a private tutor from the city's Polish community since a course was not offered at the high school. His artistic interests are demonstrated in his choice of Music at higher level, and his decision to write an extended essay in that subject. He registered to take the standard level Chemistry examination in his junior year. Stan was eligible for the award of the bilingual diploma because he has two languages A1. An excellent extended essay and acceptable work in theory of knowledge gave him a diploma total of 33 points. Stan plays the saxophone and volunteers at a shelter for the homeless.

Phil Thomas of the International School of Geneva began a research project for the IBO in 1986 to track IB diploma holders through their university studies. One of the objectives was to solicit from a random sample of students and university lecturers in the United States, Canada and the UK whether the IB was an adequate preparation for tertiary studies (Thomas, 1991: 1). The 26 British universities that responded provided data and comments about 1,036 IB students who sat university examinations from 1971–87. Of these 98 per cent completed good honours degrees. Thomas (1991: 6) sees this as 'an encouraging sign' and goes on to comment that these statistics compare more than favourably with those for GCE A level students during that same period. Thomas' report concludes that the IB is a good preparation for university and that IB grades are reliable predictors of success in higher education. To this writer's knowledge, no subsequent research on the same scale has been undertaken.

Student responses to an IBO survey which each school completes every five years have consistently mentioned, on the positive side, that the IB provides good preparation for higher education, teaches time management, allows students to acquire an overall understanding not restricted to single subjects, teaches students to think not memorize, and prevents students from specializing too early. On the negative side, some students have said that the IB programme is too stressful, the content of some subjects is excessive, deadlines for completion of assignments should be better spaced, and the obligation to do language A1 penalises those without literary appreciation skills.

Flodman, Malmström and Thelin (2002) obtained data on the university destinations of 362 Swedish diploma holders from 44 schools in different countries, the majority of them state schools in Sweden, from 1971–93. Among the 21 questions in the survey instrument given to the students, the following question was asked: 'How valuable do you think your diploma studies have been for university studies, other studies, career, life in general?' Responses were selected from a five-point scale: excellent, good, useful, little value, no value. Of the students 63 per cent attended universities in Sweden, 12 per cent in the UK, 10 per cent in the United States and the remainder in other countries. In relation to this question 84 per cent of the respondents said that the IB Diploma Programme was an 'excellent (54 per cent) or good (30 per cent) preparation' for university. Eighty-one per cent said that it was an 'excellent or good' preparation for a career and for life. Only 3 per cent indicated that the IB Diploma Programme was of little or no value for university study, career and life. A large number of respondents (34 per cent) did not answer the part concerning other studies, and 48 per cent said the IB Diploma Programme was 'excellent or good' as a preparation for this aspect. The survey instrument did not allow for respondents to give reasons for their statements. The study shows a very high level of satisfaction with the IB Diploma Programme.

Duevel (1999) surveyed the registrars and (former and current) IB students of 12 US universities (including Columbia, Cornell, Harvard and Stanford) for her research on whether earning an IB diploma was a predictor of success at university and beyond. The students had come from IB schools both in the United States and overseas. Academic results showed that the successful completion of an IB Diploma Programme was an effective predictor of completion of a first degree at university. IB diploma holders, reflecting as adults on their high school experiences, university performance and career choice indicated that a combination of the following factors of the IB programme contributed to their success:

- challenging integration of topics offering both breadth and depth;
- necessity to be highly productive throughout the two year course;
- requirement to develop strong study skills;
- emphasis on developing strong writing, research, and analytical thinking skills;
- adopting a global view and considering one's role within the wider world (Duevel, 1999: 94).

The real test is whether parents, students and schools continue with the IB and whether more schools are showing interest, since this is an option, unlike a national programme which is usually obligatory. The irrefutable evidence, published in the annual statistical bulletins of the IB Organization and on its public Web site, is that few schools leave the organization and the average world growth rate in the number of schools was around 15 per cent in 2001. Since the IB programme first started there has never been a year when there was not an increase in the number of schools, and the annual percentage increase has not been below 10 per cent. It would appear to be fulfilling the expectations of the vast majority of its students, their parents and teachers in providing quality preparation for higher education. If it were not, and if higher education institutions did not validate the IB diploma, schools would rapidly withdraw and subscribe to another programme.

Contribution to education/social policy

The IB diploma is a programme of international education founded on a set of principles associated with peacefully sharing our planet and giving attention to sustainable development (which might be defined as arriving at a balance between economic growth, protection of the environment and a fair distribution of material wealth). Its primary focus is on a global social policy and not on a national one. This sets it apart from national systems of education. It does not, however, ignore the importance of the nation and its culture(s) as the following comment indicates:

> The honesty of the IB stems from the fact that we require all students to relate first to their own national identity – their own language, literature, history and cultural heritage, no matter where in the world this may be. Beyond that we ask that they identify with the corresponding traditions of others. It is not expected that they adopt alien points of view, merely that they are exposed to them and encouraged to respond intelligently.
>
> (Peel, 1988)

Today, more national systems are endeavouring to integrate an international dimension into their programmes (as has been recommended by UNESCO for many years), and there is much excellent material being produced, for example, by Oxfam (1997) and the British Department for Education and Employment (2000) which later became the Department for Education and Skills. But the overriding orientation of a country's education system is national, and it would be surprising if it were otherwise.

In terms of pedagogy, the IB prizes the development of critical thinking skills, of working collaboratively, of personal development through CAS activities, of research skills, of creativity and initiative, of skills for lifelong learning, of maintaining study across the disciplines and not specializing too early. Howard Gardner (1999: 226) includes the IB in his list of 'families of schools that are already successful' in assisting students to search for the truth, educating for understanding, and encouraging students to become active for the peaceful preservation of our planet.

The educational and social policy of the IB is encapsulated in its mission statement at the beginning of this chapter. Pragmatic and pedagogical objectives are evident in 'international understanding', 'critical thinkers', 'lifelong learners', 'informed participants in local and world affairs'. But the real goal of international education has not been achieved until students attain 'responsible citizenship', become 'compassionate thinkers', and appreciate the 'shared humanity that binds all people together'. This will be measurable only by their actions after they leave school and make their way through life. International education is driven by ideology; it unashamedly seeks to promote certain attitudes. 'A sense of values is needed to inform [the students'] studies and their life purposes as well. Without it, they may be clever, knowledgeable, even wondrously creative, but they will never become citizens of the world nor give it their gifts as should those who have known a true international education' (Mattern, 1991: 216). This is the social policy challenge that international education has set itself.

For any particular country the attraction of the IB is not that it enables students to discuss world problems, to learn other languages, to read other literature, since these have become increasingly possible in many national systems. The uniqueness of the IB is that it is not about other parts of the world, it *is* other parts of the world. As an internationally derived and internationally examined diploma, not representing any one national system, it provides direct international experience and is driven by educational, not political, prerogatives pertaining to global social policy. It is also a unique pedagogical laboratory spanning 107 countries and comprising both independent and state schools. It provides national systems and intergovernmental organizations with a wonderful opportunity to contribute to and benefit from a world curriculum and assessment network. A number of such projects have taken or are taking place across the world.

For example, under the auspices of the European Platform initiative of the European Commission the government of the Netherlands has been teaching the IB diploma English A2 course in 13 state schools since 1998. The government chose English A2 because it represented the level of English proficiency required and because of the content and assessment procedures. Teachers are trained in IBO workshops to teach the course and undertake the internal assessment component, and this provides them with the opportunity to meet with colleagues from other countries.

The IBO has collaborated with its IB schools in Turkey and with the government to create a social studies school-based syllabus, taught in Turkish, which satisfied the requirements of both the ministry of education and the IB diploma. The course is a modification of an existing Turkish subject comprising aspects of national history, geography and philosophy which have, in the new course, been embedded in an international perspective. The course was implemented in 2001.

In cooperation with the Finnish Ministry of Education and the University of Oulu, a pilot project in distance learning for the IB Diploma Programme is taking place between two state IB schools: the Oulun Lyseon lukio in Oulu is giving instruction and support through video links and other information technologies to an isolated partner school, Lyseon Puiston lukio in Rovaniemi, Lapland. This assists the provision of quality education to small schools in remote areas using the latest technology, and the results of the project will be of benefit to both the IBO and the Finnish government.

The IB diploma subjects 'Theory of Knowledge' (TOK), History and Biology will be available in German for the first time in a pilot project from 2002–07 with the German federal government, initially for use in 14 of the government's overseas bilingual schools.

The governments of Japan, Indonesia and Singapore have undertaken research during the last four to five years into aspects of the diploma programme that might be useful in their own reforms; this research continues. The Central American Educational and Cultural Coordination Committee (Coordinacin Educativa y Cultural Centroamericana) of ministers of education initiated in 2001 an academic study of the IB Diploma Programme to analyse the possibility of adopting it, or parts of it, in public schools in central American countries.

Several state departments of education in the United States (California, Florida, Minnesota, Oklahoma, South Carolina, Texas) provide schools with substantial financial grants for one or more of teacher training, books and materials, IB examination fee subsidies, and higher education scholarships; this financial support is usually related to the number of successful IB diploma students each year in the school or district. The education authorities see the IB as providing a reputable, academic benchmark at the end of secondary education and promoting values for a more cooperative world. The vast majority of IB schools in North America are state schools with no tuition fees.

Late in 2001 the Minister for Education in Lithuania asked the IBO to collaborate on the development of a baccalaureate model for senior secondary education in his country. Early in 2002, meetings between the IBO and a Lithuanian working group for the project had begun. It was clear that the international reputation of the IB diploma and its educational philosophy were key attractions.

In these ways the IBO has been able to influence and learn from national systems of education.

In 2000 the IBO began a research project with the UNESCO Institute in Hamburg on inter-generational learning, an increasingly important aspect of social policy as longevity produces ageing populations. The experience in IB schools is being analysed with a view to producing material jointly with

UNESCO for distribution to national systems on how to promote inter-generational learning. The study also seeks to identify the benefits for the students and the retired members of society as they cooperate in learning activities.

Recent innovations

There have been recent innovations in curriculum design, curriculum delivery, and student assessment. In order to provide more choice to students, three transdisciplinary subjects at SL only have been developed for addition to the hexagon; they will be examined for the first time in 2003 during a trial period before they are available on 'open offer' to all schools. 'Text and performance' covers both groups 1 and 6 and combines the study of literature with creative writing and drama. 'Ecosystems and societies' covers groups 3 and 4 and includes topics such as pollution management, human population, carrying capacity and resource use on a global scale; it fuses environmental issues with an ethic for sustainable development. 'World cultures' (groups 3 and 6) examines cultural artefacts and the creative impulse during different periods of time and in different geographical and cultural settings.

The choice of any one of these subjects will satisfy the requirement for two groups, thus providing the opportunity for students to choose more subjects from other groups; in particular it will assist the students wishing to study two arts subjects in their diploma, which was not possible under the previous structure. These new subjects also reinforce the interdependence of learning across disciplines which has hitherto been confined to only a few of the IB diploma components, such as theory of knowledge, environmental systems (aspects of chemistry, biology, geography and geology), design technology (which combines the experimental sciences and the arts), and information technology in a global society (a philosophical approach to technological advances in the information sciences).

Two new subjects, film and dance in group 6, will be examined for the first time in 2003 on a trial basis, and represent a further attempt to strengthen the arts offerings of the IB Diploma Programme.

Collaborative learning is encouraged through an interdisciplinary practical project which must include aspects of at least two experimental sciences, or an experimental science and another subject. For example, four students in one school undertook a 'group 4 project' on the production and delivery of electricity (physics) to homes in their country; they included an economics perspective by exploring the costs of production, delivery and purchase by the consumer. The students visited and interviewed staff at an electricity plant and at the local electricity board to gather primary source information which they analysed and presented as a group.

The use of distance learning techniques to make the IB more accessible to small and/or remote schools is the reason for the pilot project previously referred to in Finland. Current IB regulations prevent offering the programme to students not enrolled full-time in an authorized IB school. The IBO is investigating ways of responding to students wishing to study the diploma who find themselves on an oil rig off the Scottish shore, on board an International Red Cross and Red Crescent boat working along the West African coast, or confined to home because of disabilities. The choice of languages in a school where the student demand is not large enough to fund the employment of a teacher (if one can be found) can be enhanced through distance education; this is also being explored.

Teacher training is an essential part of the IB experience: in 2001 more than 15,000 teachers and administrators attended IB workshops and conferences around the globe. As part of the authorization process, schools must send teachers to IB workshops and participate in professional development on a regular basis. The professional development of teachers using information technology started in a small way in late 2001. The IBO Online Curriculum Centre (OCC), an interactive teacher resource which began in 2000, is being revamped in 2002 to include training modules for specific aspects of the IB programmes. The first trial module was launched in 2001 on presenting, supervising and assessing the Personal Project of the IBO Middle Years Programme (for children aged from 11 to 16).

In 2001 the IBO started a trial project with a small number of IB examiners connected to a restricted site called Examnet. Sending information to examiners around the world, and in return receiving their marks and reports, is labour intensive, costly and subject to delays. Exchanging information and data over the Internet overcomes these problems. In addition to serving an administrative function, Examnet also supports the training of examiners, allows examiners to write examination papers and their mark schemes in a secure collaborative electronic environment, and eventually will enable the IBO to send images of candidates' scripts to examiners for marking on screen.

Limitations of the IB Diploma Programme

Student access to the IB Diploma Programme may be limited by the diploma profile itself, the curriculum or financial concerns. For students who want to follow a narrower selection of pre-higher education courses and drop GCSE subjects that they do not like or in which they do not perform well, the IB is less suitable. In particular, students who have not succeeded at a modern language might see the IB as forbidding. It is interesting to note, however, that a second modern language at pre-university level is a requirement in continental Europe, where students would be bemused to think that there were too many subjects in the IB diploma, as they complete their baccalaureates with 7 to 12 subject examinations in the final year of secondary school.

One drawback for a national system catering for all student abilities is the academic nature of the courses and a lack of vocational subjects. Business and management, and design technology are offered but no other vocational courses. 'A key concern for the British baccalaureate would be to establish different levels of difficulty and include vocational subjects to ensure it is open to as many students as possible, while retaining the intellectual challenge for the brightest' (*The Times*, 24 September 2002: 4). While the IB Diploma Programme has never pretended to be for all students, those of average ability (at least a C average in GCSE subjects) do obtain the diploma if they work consistently and in an organized manner. Students who are less academically able can take more Standard Level courses and not seek to obtain the full diploma, but this militates against the whole IB experience. There is a minimum academic level below which a student will not succeed at the diploma, and there is a necessity to be highly productive throughout the two year course, as Duevel's (1999) study revealed.

In addition to the academic level of the curriculum, two difficulties were cited by a significant number of respondents to the questionnaires (above) sent to many IB schools for IB programme evaluation: work overload and that the obligation to do a language A1 penalized those without literary appreciation skills. (It is worth noting again that in continental Europe the study of the national language and literature is compulsory in school leaving qualifications.) Some students and teachers felt that the internal assessment (course work) preparation in every subject was onerous, and that the sheer content of some of the maths and science subjects was overwhelming.

The potential of the extended essay to promote international understanding through interdisciplinary study has not been achieved; discussions have taken place about allowing students to include cross-curricular global issues as topics, but at the time of writing this is still not possible. A recent reform of secondary education in Switzerland saw a new component: the '*Travail de Maturité*' (modelled on the IB extended essay) of 6,500 words (in addition to 11 or 12 subject examinations), based on a topic in one of the subjects being studied, or a global issue, or some activity or design work that can be evaluated in a rigorous way.

Finally, the IBO needs to develop strategies to make its programme more accessible to those who cannot afford to attend fee-paying private schools or who are not within commuting distance of the government schools offering the IB Diploma Programme without the burden of tuition fees. Student access in the developing world needs special attention. Projects previously cited for the developing world with donor finance are examples of efforts in this direction. The IBO wishes to widen student access so as to provide another educational option, not to replace national programmes.

Conclusion

The IBO is protective of the integrity and quality of its programmes. Schools wishing to teach them go through a rigorous preparation phase, which includes a mandatory visit to the school by IBO officials and compulsory teacher development at IB workshops. The IBO is, however, generous in sharing mutually beneficial ideas with national systems and in exploring ways in which aspects of its programmes might work in local situations. The IBO surveys the educational landscape on a global scale, taking into account trends, ideas and materials identified in reports by organizations such as UNESCO, the Council of Europe, and the Centre for Education, Research and Innovation (at the OECD, Paris) in addition to ideas from national reports. It uses such information in the thoughtful and periodic evolution of curricula and student assessment techniques, consulting widely with the schools offering the Diploma Programme.

But national systems looking to adopt an IB Diploma Programme model need to see how it might be adapted: which parts, methodological orientations, emphases can be applied in a particular national context on a large scale? The English system would benefit from a structure similar to the IB diploma, but adjustments would need to be made in terms of the level of difficulty and assessment procedures – courses of a different nature, for instance vocational courses, might also be added into the structure – if it is to cater for a wider range of student aptitudes.

As a model of education that was ahead of its time, the IB Diploma Programme now finds itself increasingly at the centre. It responds to what schools are seeking: critical thinking skills, preparation for lifelong learning and adaptability, breadth and balance, personal growth through community service, research skills, academic rigour, promotion of initiative and creativity, keeping an open mind, an international perspective, a quality diploma which provides access to the best universities around the world. But the distinctive feature of the IB Diploma Programme is the way it can make a very small but important contribution, through the promotion of international understanding, to alleviating the sense of insecurity that hangs over the world at this time. As an entity independent of all nations it might be argued that it is uniquely placed to do so.

The IBO has been grappling with international education for more than 30 years. It does not have all the answers, but it has considerable practical experience in education for a future world where peaceful coexistence and sustainable development are the overriding concerns. Beyond encouraging its students to reflect on world issues and to ponder the injustices of the economic divide, it provides a global network of like-minded schools where students and teachers from markedly different cultures can and do meet each other, at IBO conferences or through collaborative activities that are initiated between individual schools. Electronic communication enables relationships to be maintained at minimum cost across national borders. They can test their thoughts on each other and learn to appreciate cultural differences. This is the richness of the IB experience.

References

Bloom, B (ed) (1956) *Taxonomy of educational objectives, Vol 1: The cognitive domain*, McKay, New York

Bloom, B, Mesia, B and Krathwohl, D (1964) *Taxonomy of Educational Objectives* (2 vols: *The Affective Domain* and *The Cognitive Domain*), David McKay, New York

Council of Europe/UNESCO (1999) Recommendation on international access qualifications. Vilnius, Lithuania. [Online] http://www.cepes.ro/hed/recogn/groups/recomm.htm (accessed 14 February 2002)

Council of Europe/UNESCO (1997) *Convention on the Recognition of Qualifications Concerning Higher Education in the European Region*, Lisbon, Portugal [Online] http://culture.coe.fr/Infocentre/txt/eng/esucon.165.html (accessed 14 February 2002) For status of signatures and ratifications: http:// conventions.coe.int/Treaty/EN/searchsig.asp?NT=165andCM=1

Department for Education and Employment (DfEE) (2000) *Developing a Global Dimension in the School Curriculum*, DfEE, UK

Duevel, L (1999) *The International Baccalaureate Experience: University perseverance, attainment, and perspectives on the process*, PhD thesis, Purdue University, USA

Financial Times (2002) Exams face up to a tough test, *Financial Times* 18–19 May, UK

Flodman, M, Malmström, H and Thelin, A (2002) Swedish IB diploma holders research study 1971–1993, *IB Research Notes*, **2** (2) (April) [Online] http://www.ibo.org

Gardner, H (1999) *The Disciplined Mind: What all students should understand*, Simon and Schuster, New York

Hayden, M and Wong, C (1997) The international baccalaureate: international education and cultural preservation, *Educational Studies*, **23** (3), pp 349–61

Hill, I (2001) Curriculum development and ethics in international education, *Disarmament Forum*, 3, pp 49–58, UNIDR (United Nations Institute for Disarmament Research), Geneva [Online] http://www.unog.ch/UNIDIR/e-df1–3.htm

Hinrichs, J (2001) *Effects of the International Baccalaureate Program on International Understanding*, thesis in partial fulfilment of a PhD, Berne University, Switzerland

International Baccalaureate Organization public Web site: www.ibo.org

International Baccalaureate Office (IBO) (1970) *Semi-Annual Bulletin*, 5, IBO, Geneva

IBO (1998) *Mathematics Higher Level*, IBO, Geneva

IBO (1999) *Theory of Knowledge*, IBO, Geneva

IBO (2000) *Visual Arts*, IBO, Geneva

IBO (2001a) *Biology*, IBO, Geneva

IBO (2001b) *Creativity Action Service*, IBO, Geneva

IBO (2001c) *History*, IBO, Geneva

International School of Geneva (ISG) (1962) *First Conference of Teachers of Social Studies in International Schools: Report*, 26 August – 1 September 1962

Mattern, G (1991) Random ruminations on the curriculum of the international school, in *World Yearbook of Education 1991: International schools and international education*, ed P Jonietz and D Harrus, pp 209–16, Kogan Page, London

Oxfam (1997) *A Curriculum for Global Citizenship: Oxfam's development education programme*, Oxfam, Oxford

Peel, R (1988) *Report of the Director General to the Council of Foundation*, IBO, Geneva

Peterson, A (1987) *Schools Across Frontiers: The story of the international baccalaureate and the united world colleges*, Open Court, Illinois

Powell, W (2002) Conversations that matter: the use and abuse of communications in our schools, *International Schools Journal*, **21** (2) (April)

Thomas, P (1988) University destinations and performance of IB diploma holders, *Journal of College Admissions*, 121 (Fall), pp 11–14

Thomas, P (1991) *IB Diploma Holders Research Project Progress Report Prepared for the Director General*, IBO, Geneva

Times (2002) A broad but tough test of ability, *The Times,* 24 September: 4

UNESCO (1974) *Recommendation on Education for International Understanding*, UNESCO General Conference, Paris

Appendix: Diploma Programme schools by country
(as at 14 January 2003)

Country		Country		Country	
Antilles (N)	1	Hungary	3	Paraguay	2
Argentina	45	Iceland	1	Peru	12
Australia	36	India	8	Philippines	4
Austria	4	Indonesia	5	Poland	9
Azerbaijan	1	Iran	1	Portugal	5
Bahrain	5	Ireland	1	Qatar	1
Belgium	4	Israel	1	Romania	1
Bermuda	1	Italy	12	Russian Fed	6
Bolivia	1	Japan	7	S. Africa	1
Bosnia/Herzegovina	1	Jordan	3	Saudi Arabia	2
Botswana	1	Kazakstan	1	Senegal	1
Brazil	9	Kenya	5	Singapore	4
Brunei	1	Kuwait	1	Slovakia	1
Cambodia	1	Latvia	1	Slovenia	2
Canada	87	Lebanon	3	South Korea	1
Chile	15	Lesotho	1	Spain	31
China	15	Lithuania	1	Sri Lanka	1
Colombia	10	Luxembourg	1	Swaziland	1
Costa Rica	4	Macedonia FYR	1	Sweden	28
Croatia	1	Malawi	1	Switzerland	14
Cyprus	1	Malaysia	4	Syria	1
Czech Republic	3	Malta	1	Taiwan	1
Denmark	5	Mauritius	1	Tanzania	2
Dominican Republic	1	Mexico	22	Thailand	8
Ecuador	11	Monaco	1	Togo	2
Egypt	3	Mongolia	1	Tunisia	1
El Salvador	1	Morocco	2	Turkey	12
Ethiopia	2	Namibia	1	United Arab Emirates	3
Fiji	1	Netherlands	12	United Kingdom	43
Finland	12	New Zealand	5	Uganda	1
France	8	Nicaragua	2	Ukraine	1
Germany	16	Norway	12	USA	387
Ghana	2	Occ. Palestine	1	Uruguay	4
Greece	12	Oman	1	Venezuela	9
Guam	1	Pakistan	2	Vietnam	3
Guatemala	1	Panama	1	Zambia	2
Honduras	1	Papua–N Guinea	1	Zimbabwe	1

Total: 1060 In 111 countries

4

The French baccalaureates

Françoise Martin-van der Haegen and Michèle Deane

In France, the *Baccalauréat* is considered as a national symbol by all, whatever their political persuasion. Jack Lang (1992), Minister for National Education in a former socialist government, described it as an 'historic monument'. François Bayrou, another former Minister for National Education, who belonged to the more conservative side of parliament, stated (1993): 'Its national character is more than symbolic: it is a benchmark in the relationship between school and nation and it makes the objectives for democratization easier to determine. If the baccalaureate needs to evolve, changes must be carried out carefully.'

This indicates the high status of the *Baccalauréat* in France. In this chapter we will explore the significance of its symbolic nature, particularly in terms of democratization of education. A brief history of the *Baccalauréat* in France will illustrate how it has undergone a significant evolution – which might have led to some complexity – but no real revolution. The various baccalaureates, and more particularly, the '*bac professionnel*' (vocational baccalaureate) will be reviewed and their common points and differences highlighted. Finally, the French *Baccalauréat* and the A level system will be compared, and some conclusions will be drawn regarding the standing of the various French baccalaureates.

The *Baccalauréat*, a national symbol

As explained earlier, because the *Baccalauréat* is a national symbol, ministers for education, whatever their political colours, have hesitated to reform it. For French public opinion, the *Baccalauréat* is the symbol of equality of opportunity and democracy in schools and because of this, examination syllabuses and papers must be decided upon at national level. This is linked to the strong belief that all citizens are equal. The issue of equal opportunities features at the top of national preoccupations at the moment in France. Second, all candidates must be awarded their qualification according to the results of papers they all take on the same days (depending on the categories of baccalaureate they sit). This too is linked to the concept of equality.

These two beliefs are so strong that public opinion will not be convinced that either of these two propositions can be changed. This means that any attempt at changing patterns of assessment, for instance, meets with immediate opposition. It has been suggested that continuous assessment should be introduced. This would allow students to accumulate 'transferable units' to replace either one or several components of the final examination or even the whole examination. However, this has been refused by different pressure groups in the name of equity between students, classes, schools and regions. In 1995 the *Conseil Supérieur de l'Education* (CSE) or High Council for Education (HCE), whose role it is to agree changes to the education system, refused to introduce continuous assessment and decided that most subjects would continue to be examined through written examinations.

There is one major exception to this rule: in 2001 continuous assessment was implemented for the *travaux personnels encadrés* (TPE) or supervised personal projects. Introduced in 2001 in *lycées* for general education, following a survey among students in *lycées*, the TPEs are a new concept. Their purpose is to develop students' sense of initiative. They are cross-curricular research projects based on well-defined topics, and carried out by students in small groups of two or three. At the beginning of each school year, the Ministry selects a number of topics that are valid for the whole of France. Students choose one of the topics on offer and carry out their research using knowledge and methods from a range of school subjects. For instance, the topic 'frontiers' can be researched through texts from French and foreign literature, historical texts and geographical data. At the end of the school year, students present their research project and defend it in front of a panel made up of school teachers from various school subjects, but not by teachers who have taught the students being examined. The assessment of these tasks is carried out by the school and the mark for the TPE is added to the final examination mark. As soon as the TPEs were announced, hostile reactions were vented against what amounts to validation of knowledge by individual schools; the *Agrégés'* Association was particularly vehement. This teacher association regroups teachers with the highest teaching qualification. Traditionally, they have been very sensitive to changes.

It is interesting to note that the introduction of continuous assessment as a part of the vocational baccalaureate has hardly been noticed and has been accepted. This is probably due to the specificity of the vocational baccalaureates, but also to the fact that the various baccalaureates do not have the same status, as will be discussed later.

The Baccalauréat, a reflection of the democratization of education

In France there has always been an examination that the majority of the age cohort was expected to take or pass. During the first half of the century, when not everybody went to secondary school, the *Certificat d'Etudes Primaire* (Certificate of Primary Education) was taken by all at the end of primary school studies. Between 1960 and 1980, the *Brevet* became the examination all pupils had to sit. It was taken at the end of the fourth year of secondary education and validated the 'first cycle of secondary education'. In the 1990s the then Minister for National Education, Jean-Pierre Chevènement, started the slogan '80 per cent of pupils must pass the *Baccalauréat*'. The *Baccalauréat* results for the Académie of Nantes show that Jean-Pierre Chevènement's target was attained by 1999, if not before.

Since the creation of the *Baccalauréat* there has been a dramatic increase in the proportion of the overall age cohort that passed the examination, as Figure 4.1 shows. In 1950 only 5 per cent of pupils of the age cohort passed, in 1960 the percentage had risen to 10 per cent, and it reached 53 per cent in 1993 and 78.2 per cent in 2001. As Jane Marshall noted, 'when Napoleon Bonaparte introduced the *Baccalauréat* in 1809, 31 bacheliers graduated in literature, science, medicine, law and theology. [In June 2000] a record 644,128 candidates sat the exam to qualify for a place in higher education and about 80 per cent [were] expected to pass' (*THES*, 11 August 2000).

This increase in the number of *Baccalauréat* passes is, for French people, proof that the standard of education is rising. It is also proof that the stigma of social discrimination that the *Baccalauréat* used to carry is progressively being eroded. This increase in the number of students passing the *Baccalauréat* is extremely important as 'the 'bac' serves as a passport to higher education' (*THES*, 1995). The higher the *Baccalauréat* pass rate, the more students enter university, which yet again reflects the democratization of education.

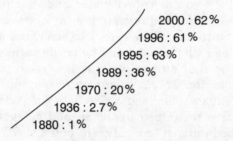

Figure 4.1 Percentage of the age cohort that passed the *Baccalauréat*
Source: French Ministry of Education Web site

How has the French *Baccalauréat* become this national symbol? A quick glance at the history of the French *Baccalauréat* might help start to answer the question.

The history of the *Baccalauréat* in France

The French *Baccalauréat* was created in 1808 by the Organic Decree of 7 March in the section 'University grades and means to achieve them'. The decree stated that candidates had to be at least 16 years old. The exam was a viva voce on Greek and Latin authors, rhetoric, history, geography and philosophy. In 1809, the first cohort of successful candidates comprised 31 students.

From its inception the *Baccalauréat* has been considered as the link between secondary and higher education, and it has validated the end of secondary education and has provided access to higher education. A few important dates have marked its history.

7 March 1808	Creation of the *Baccalauréat*
1821	A science baccalaureate was created
1830	The first written paper was introduced. It consisted of an essay in French or the translation of a classic.
1853	A modern language paper was introduced
1902	All who passed the *Baccalauréat* were given the same rights, irrespective of type of baccalaureate they passed or the 'commendations' they received
1921	Creation of a scientific baccalaureate
1946	Creation of a range of 'industrial techniques' baccalaureates
1953	Creation of a range of 'economic techniques' baccalaureates
1969	Creation of the technical baccalaureate (*Baccalauréat technologique*)
1986	Creation of the vocational baccalaureate (*Baccalauréat professionnel*)

By 1993 there was a mushrooming number of baccalaureates: 16 general, 17 technical and 29 vocational syllabuses and examinations. This was becoming burdensome for the organization of examinations: some 800 papers had to be written for the general baccalaureates alone. Therefore a general streamlining took place, to offer two main pathways which offered fewer options. The first stream was the general baccalaureate which had three options: the *ES Baccalauréat* (economic and social), the *L Baccalauréat* (literary), and the *S Baccalauréat* (scientific). All other baccalaureates were regrouped in the second category, the technical baccalaureate, which offered four different options: *STI* (*sciences et technologies industrielles*, or industrial sciences and technologies), *STL* (*sciences et technologies de laboratoire*, or laboratory sciences and technologies), *SMS* (*sciences médico-sociales*, or socio-medical sciences) and *STT* (*sciences et technologies tertiaires*, or tertiary sciences and technologies).

The history of the baccalaureates has been a succession of evolutions rather than revolutions, illustrating perfectly the statements by Jack Lang and François Bayrou: this slow evolution may have made it appear to French public opinion as immovable as a monument, and has preserved its high status. It is also viewed as an accolade, and is extended to new courses and examinations that need recognition. When the Ministry for National Education wished to state that vocational education was as important as all other forms of education, it created the vocational baccalaureates (*baccalauréats professionnels* or *bac pro*), thus bringing vocational education into the recognized framework of excellence that the republican school represents.

An overview of all baccalaureates

Students in French secondary schools can follow one of three pathways: a general education pathway, a technical pathway or a vocational pathway. Each course of study leads to a different baccalaureate, either the general baccalaureate, the technical baccalaureate or the vocational baccalaureate. Each pathway offers several options to maximize students' choice and opportunities (see Table 4.1).

Table 4.1 Pathways, baccalaureates and options

Pathway	General education	Technical	Vocational
Baccalaureate	General baccalaureate	Technical baccalaureate	Vocational baccalaureate
Options	*L* (literary), *ES* (economic and social), *S* (scientific)	*STT* (*sciences et technologies tertiaires*), *STI* (*sciences et technologies industrielles*), *STL* (*sciences et technologies de laboratoire*), *SMS* (*sciences et techniques médico-sociales*), *STPA* (*sciences et technologies du produit agroalimentaire*), *STAE* (*sciences et technologies de l'agronomie et de l'environnement*), *TMD* (*techniques de la musique et de la danse*), *Hotellerie*	

Figure 4.2 is a map of the three different pathways in pupils' careers in French secondary schools. At the end of the fourth year pupils have a choice as to which fifth year they are going to follow: either a fifth year in the vocational route or a fifth year which will be a 'determination year' at the end of which they will select either the general education route or the technical route. These decisions depend on individual pupils' interests and on the baccalaureate they wish to take.

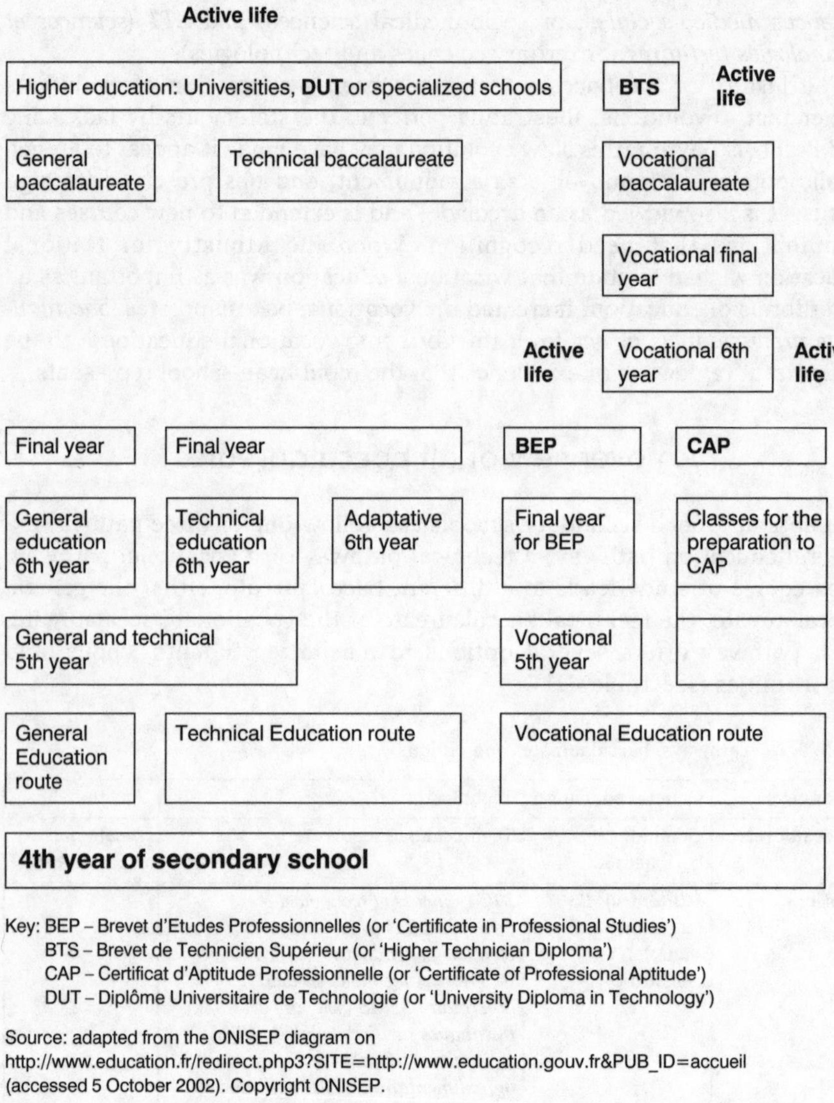

Active life

Higher education: Universities, **DUT** or specialized schools	**BTS**	**Active life**

General baccalaureate	Technical baccalaureate	Vocational baccalaureate

Vocational final year

	Active life	Vocational 6th year	**Active life**

Final year	Final year	**BEP**	**CAP**
General education 6th year	Technical education 6th year	Adaptative 6th year	Final year for BEP	Classes for the preparation to CAP

General and technical 5th year		Vocational 5th year	

General Education route	Technical Education route	Vocational Education route

4th year of secondary school

Key: BEP – Brevet d'Etudes Professionnelles (or 'Certificate in Professional Studies')
    BTS – Brevet de Technicien Supérieur (or 'Higher Technician Diploma')
    CAP – Certificat d'Aptitude Professionnelle (or 'Certificate of Professional Aptitude')
    DUT – Diplôme Universitaire de Technologie (or 'University Diploma in Technology')

Source: adapted from the ONISEP diagram on
http://www.education.fr/redirect.php3?SITE=http://www.education.gouv.fr&PUB_ID=accueil
(accessed 5 October 2002). Copyright ONISEP.

Figure 4.2 Three routes in the second cycle of French secondary education system

The general baccalaureate pathway

Since 1993 this pathway has been streamlined, and it now offers only three different options, a literary option (*Baccalauréat L*), an economic and social option (*Baccalauréat ES*), and finally a scientific option (*Baccalauréat S*). The general baccalaureate is a general qualification that validates general knowledge and culture. Just like A levels, it does not lead directly to a profession. It gives access to higher education: universities, and classes to prepare for the *'Grandes Ecoles'*, the *Institut Universitaire de Technologie* (IUT), or *Institut Universitaire Professionnel* (IUP). We will consider each of the options offered in turn.

Bac L (literary baccalaureate)

This baccalaureate 'focuses on philosophy, literature, languages, history and geography, but also the arts.... It requires pupils to have a real taste for literature and to be able to carry out analysis' (ONISEP, 2002: 25).

Bac ES (economic and social baccalaureate)

'This baccalaureate is for young people who are interested in the socio-economic environment and current affairs. Communication skills and analytic and methodical ability are required. The following are important elements towards success in this specialization: a taste for maths, a curiosity for history and geography and a flair for modern languages' (ONISEP, 2002: 26).

Bac S (scientific baccalaureate)

'This is a baccalaureate for students who find sciences attractive. It calls for ability for abstraction, rigour, reasoning, a sense of observation and a taste for experimentation' (ONISEP, 2002: 27).

The technical baccalaureate pathway

This pathway enables students to gain general knowledge and culture at the same time as professional training. It has to be noted that this professional training does not concentrate on one particular occupation, but is broader and offers training for a line of employment. As indicated in Figure 4.2, there are eight main options in this category of baccalaureates, which are here reviewed in turn.

Bac STT (*sciences et technologies tertiaires*, or tertiary sciences and technologies)

'The STT baccalaureate encompasses all tertiary activities. It is an interesting choice for students who show maturity, a sense of communication, order and method, initiative ... and are also open to the new communication techniques. Written and verbal expression and a real taste for modern foreign languages cannot be neglected' (ONISEP, 2002: 28).

Bac STI (*sciences et technologies industrielles*, or industrial sciences and technologies)

'This baccalaureate offers seven specialities and one speciality in applied arts. Organization and method in one's work, interest for manipulations, the ability to see a project through ... and, of course, curiosity for new technologies and their evolution, are crucial for the future STI baccalaureate holder' (ONISEP, 2002: 28).

Bac STL (*sciences et technologies de laboratoire*, or laboratory sciences and technologies)

'This is a baccalaureate that focuses on laboratory activities. In each speciality (physics, chemistry or biology), students must have a strong taste for manipulations. They must also have real ability in science subjects, and also a good memory rigour in their reasoning' (ONISEP, 2002: 32).

Bac SMS (*sciences médico-sociales*, or socio-medical sciences)

'This baccalaureate which is focused on the socio-medical area offers an education and training for all students who are interested in human relations and health and social work' (ONISEP, 2002: 33).

Bac STAE (*agronomie et environnement*, or agronomy and environment)

This baccalaureate enables students to continue studying in the area of agro-equipment, commercialization and the organization of amenities in rural areas. 'This STAE baccalaureate which is concerned with technologies and agronomy offers two specialities: production systems technology and technologies concerned with rural equipment and organization' (ONISEP, 2002: 34).

Bac STPA (*produit agro-alimentaire*, or agricultural food products)

'The STPA baccalaureate is for students attracted by the transformation and commercialization of agricultural food products' (ONISEP, 2002: 34).

Bac techniques de la musique et de la danse

'This is a baccalaureate for students wishing to make a career as musicians or dancers. If talent is a prerequisite, general knowledge and culture cannot be overlooked' (ONISEP, 2002: 36).

Bac hotellerie

'The purpose of this baccalaureate is to train professionals in the restaurant industry, the reception and hotel industries. Availability, adaptability, initiative, stamina are qualities required to succeed' (ONISEP, 2002: 35).

After passing their technical baccalaureate, students have a choice between entering the world of work immediately or continuing in higher education. If they decide on the last option, four alternatives are open to them:

● They can spend a further two years in a *lycée* in a *Section de technicien supérieur* (STS) or Higher Technician Section where they can prepare for a *brevet de technicien supérieur* (BTS) or Higher Technician Diploma.

The *STS* are classes which are the equivalent of *classe préparatoire aux Grandes Ecoles (CPGE)* for technical education. Entrance into these classes is highly competitive, as small businesses recruit their management from these.

- They can attend an *institut universitaire de technologie (IUT)*, or university institute of technology, in other words a section of the university where they prepare to take a *Diplôme Universitaire de Technologie (DUT)* or university diploma in technology.
- They can go to an *institut universitaire professionnel (IUP)* or university vocational institute, where they take a university vocational diploma. IUPs are not developed in many universities. Despite their names IUPs have no connection whatsoever with the *bac pro*. They prepare students, for example, for careers in banking or in work management (organization of work in companies, quality assurance or management).
- Finally, students with a technical baccalaureate can enter specialized schools, such as commerce schools or management schools.

The opportunity to study for the various types of baccalaureate categories is evenly distributed throughout all the *lycées* in a region, in keeping with the firmly-held French desire for equality.

The technical baccalaureates offer students a vocational route, as does the vocational baccalaureate (*bac pro*). The latter was created in 1985 by the Ministry for Education, to recognize the value of professional and vocational education and to meet specific professional needs. At local level, the education authorities and the representatives of the world of work collaborate to offer options that meet local economical, industrial or commercial needs. For instance, in one *académie*, work on leather is particularly important; the *rectorat* has therefore collaborated with the local chambers of commerce and industry to offer a *bac pro* in 'soft materials' that meets local industrial needs. Other regions that have a mostly agricultural economy offer a range of *bacs pro* that enable students to take up posts that will support the local economy. Generally the *bac pro* has proved very popular, and its numbers soared rapidly between 1987, when it was first awarded to 800 students, and 2001, when over 87,600 candidates passed the examination. This qualification will now be considered in more detail.

The vocational baccalaureate, *le bac professionnel*

Some pupils have already entered the vocational route well before they reach the fourth year of their secondary education. At the end of the second year in the secondary school, pupils who choose to do so, or more often than not, those who have been failing in the general education sections of secondary schools, are directed towards vocational classes. These classes can be in vocational secondary schools called *lycées professionnels*, but the tendency is to keep these classes in ordinary collèges to avoid the problem of pupils become professionalized too early. The debate is still raging, though, to determine the optimum age at which pupils should be encouraged to decide on a vocational path.

At the end of the fourth year, students in a technological school can prepare for a *Certificat d'Aptitude Professionnelle* (*CAP*) (Certificate of Professional Aptitude), a *Brevet d'Etudes Professionnelles* (*BEP*) (Certificate in Professional Studies), or a professional baccalaureate (*le bac pro*). Whichever qualification they choose will take two years' preparation. All three examinations prepare for immediate entry into the world of work. The only difference between them is the qualification level: the *CAP* and *BEP* are level 5 qualifications, the lowest level, whereas the vocational baccalaureate is the next level up, a level 4 qualification.

The *bac pro* offers a range of specialities. As well as a general education programme of study, the vocational route offers students a concrete curriculum which is relevant to the world of trade, commerce or industry and enables students to develop knowledge applied to a specialized area of work. There are 48 different specialities on offer which include, for instance, aeronautics, a range of artistic options (stone carving, graphic communication, fashion), accounting, car maintenance, hygiene and the environment, electrical equipment and installation, maintenance of electronic audio-visual equipment, and services.

The vocational baccalaureate has too many options and facets for any one school to be able to offer them all. The *recteurs* (who are the representatives of the Minister for Education in the regions) share out the various options among the *lycées* in their own administrative areas. They do so in consultation with regional government representatives and representatives from the local chambers of commerce and industry. The partnership with local chambers of commerce and industry is particularly important when the vocational *lycées* select the options they are going to offer, as students studying these options will need corresponding work placements.

Work placements

The aim of the *bac pro* is to educate and train students so that they are equipped to enter the world of work rapidly. Their studies are therefore based on acquiring professional techniques through practical work in class, in workshops or during work placements. Over the last two years' preparation for the *bac pro*, students are expected to spend 18 weeks in work placements related to their specialism, alternating with spells in the classroom.

Since September 2001 the weekly timetable of compulsory lessons has been reduced over the last two years of preparation, so that students can take part in optional activities destined to enrich their learning. The major tool for this enrichment programme is the *projet pluridisciplinaire à caractère professionnel* (PPCP) (cross-curricular professionally-oriented project):

this involves small groups working on cross-curricular projects which involve several subjects, either general education or technical, so as to acquire knowledge (*savoir*) and know-how (*savoir-faire*) linked to work situations. This type of project work fosters team work and enables students to make connections between a range of subjects; it also helps students to develop research and work methods, their sense of initiative and a form of creativity. The *PPCP* correspond to the *travaux personnels encadrés* (TPE), or supervised personal projects, which have been developed for the general baccalaureate in the general education *lycées*.

After passing their vocational baccalaureate, students can enter the world of work or they can chose to continue studying. Some students, usually the higher attainers, can integrate a special class (the adaptative sixth year in Figure 4.2), which enables them to prepare for a technician's baccalaureate in two years and achieve a higher level of qualification (level 3). In addition, the *bac pro*, as with any other baccalaureate, opens the doors to university.

Common points to all baccalaureates

Despite what must appear like a multiplicity of baccalaureates there are many common points to all the various versions. First of all, and because of the French public opinion's desire for equity, all examination syllabuses and papers are centralized: they are decided by the ministry and apply to all.

The composition of examination awarding teams, known as *jury de baccalaureate*, is clearly defined and the same for the whole of France: the chair of the jury is a university lecturer and the other members of the jury are teachers in *lycées*. The organization of the jury and the administration of the actual examination are centralized in the *rectorat* so that members of the jury cannot know the students they are examining, as marks and awards need to be objective. For the same reason, students' names are not visible on written papers.

This respect for equity has a real bearing on the French assessment model. This is why the introduction of coursework and continuous assessment is causing real difficulties, as we mentioned earlier.

One of the precepts of French education is that all students deserve to receive a broad education. Therefore the syllabuses and assessment of all baccalaureates contain a common core of subjects that are studied by all and externally examined for all: French (which is examined at the end of the sixth year), maths, science, history and geography, one modern foreign language, philosophy and physical education. The difference between the various baccalaureates and their categories is in the actual content of the syllabus and examination papers for each. The differences also come from the weightings subjects carry according to each specific baccalaureate and its categories. For instance, in the general baccalaureate, the history and geography paper carries a weighting of 5 in the economic and social baccalaureate: a weighting of 4 for literary and scientific baccalaureates and only a weighting of 1 in the technical baccalaureate.

While the idea of weighting is attractive in so far as it allows all students to continue studying a broad curriculum, if the differential between subjects is too great, this weighting system can also result in some subjects not receiving the attention they deserve. For example, in one of the technical baccalaureates, the weighting for the technology paper is 12 whereas that for the history and geography paper is 1. Students wishing to secure a pass will more than likely concentrate their efforts on the subject where a low mark would have disastrous consequences; in other words, they will pay little heed to history and geography, and thus this subject will become devalued in their eyes. The weightings determine the respective importance of the different subjects in the whole examination, but also in the curriculum for the two years.

In lieu of a conclusion: France–England, comparison, contrasts and reflections

Both A levels and the *Baccalauréat* have a high status in their respective societies: the English 'gold standard' becomes the French 'monument', the benchmark. Both are defined by centralized directives: the Qualifications and Curriculum Authority (QCA) is responsible for examination specifications and ensures a level of consistency in assessment throughout England. Centralization in France goes a step further: the actual syllabus is defined by the Ministry for Education, as are the actual examination papers. However, while in France all the general and technical baccalaureate categories are evenly distributed through the country so that all French children have equal opportunities, in England schools are free to choose the qualifications they offer.

Whereas the A levels could be considered as specialized, the *Baccalauréat* offers a programme of study that provides a broad curriculum (see Chapter 2), reflecting the French belief in a broad, well rounded education. The broad curriculum approach leads to French students having heavy timetables. They work over 30 hours per week in school. Homework and private study are not included in this and are usually very onerous. There have been some attempts at lightening this load: as well as introducing some element of continuous assessment, the establishment of TPEs and PPCPs (which are optional) have reduced some of the time spent receiving instruction.

Both A levels and the *Baccalauréat* are prepared over a two-year period, and both have a half-way examination: the AS levels in England and the *Epreuve Anticipée de Français (EAF)*, or anticipated examination in French, in France. Apart from the TPEs or the PPCPs, there is no continuous assessment in France, and the rest of the papers are taken at the end of the second year.

Both examinations allow students entry to university, with the difference that in the UK, universities sometimes use additional selection tools. This is totally inconceivable in France. When, in 1995, the government suggested a way of decreasing a high failure rate in the first two years of university by introducing more selection, students started demonstrating on the streets in Paris and throughout the country. 'The young inmates of France's overcrowded *lycées* take the formal status of the baccalaureate – any baccalaureate, general, technical, vocational – absolutely literally as the passport to university' (Hughes, *THES*, 3 March 1995). The high rate of failure at university has exercised French academics and the government for many years. According to M André Robert, lecturer at the Paris V University's Sociology of Education Research Unit, 'There is a real problem that must be faced. Some argue for "baccalaureate" reform which would reduce its content, which implies that it would be followed by university entrance examinations. I think we should maintain the level of the "baccalaureate", but introduce more introductory modules at university to bring the students up to the required level' (*THES*, 1997). Does this imply that the *Baccalauréat* does not prepare for university, or that it does not help forecast the level of success that will ensue?

It is a fact that the increased pass rate for the *Baccalauréat* has signalled a democratization of education, and that there is a broader access to university. In 2001 there were 631,429 students registered to sit the *Baccalauréat*: 52.55 per cent for the general baccalaureate, 29.63 per cent for the technical baccalaureate and 17.82 per cent for the vocational baccalaureate. Figure 4.3 shows that apart from the vocational baccalaureate, numbers decreased slightly from the previous year, but this also reflected changes in demography. It illustrates the fact that the general baccalaureate attracts more candidates than the other two baccalaureates put together.

Although all *Baccalauréats* enable students to enter university, Figure 4.4, which shows the proportion of students that enter universities, IUTs, CPGE and STSs according to the baccalaureates they have passed, makes it clear that not all *Baccalauréats* provide equal chances of entry.

Figure 4.4 clearly indicates that students who have passed the general baccalaureate get the lion's share of places at university (approximately 80 per cent), in the IUTs (over 60 per cent) and in the CPGE (nearly 100 per cent). 'Over 300,000 candidates sit the science or arts-based general baccalaureate, which has always been the passport to higher education, leading systematically to university or to a preparatory class for a grande ecole' (*THES*, 1997). Students who have passed the technical baccalaureate do less well, with approximately 15 per cent of university places, 30 per cent of IUT places, fewer than 5 per cent of places in CPGE and the lion's share of places in STS (approximately 65 per cent). Those who pass the *bac pro* and continue in higher education represent approximately 2.5 per cent of university places, less than 2 per cent of IUT places, no CPGE

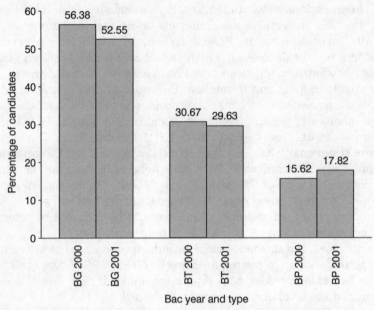

Number of candidates per category of baccalaureates in 2000 and 2001

Figure 4.3   Candidates registered for the different French baccalaureates in 2000 and 2001

places and barely 10 per cent of STS places. The conclusion can only be that the opportunities for accessing higher education via the *bac pro* are far fewer than through the other two baccalaureates, and that the general baccalaureate is still pre-eminent, thus continuing to attract more students.

The recruitment of students for CPGE takes place from January onwards (a long time before the examinations even take place, let alone before results are available), and it creams off the best students. The majority of places in the highly selective STSs go to students with the technical baccalaureate, and nearly a fifth to students with a general baccalaureate. There appears to be no special niche for students who take the vocational baccalaureate. Does this reflect the quality of students taking the *bac pro* or the lack of parity between the various baccalaureates? It is a fact that discrimination still exists; it concerns the different categories of the baccalaurée that are perceived to be more or less prestigious, according to whether they enable students to continue studying in higher education.

The fact that students are totally responsible for their choices of the categories and options would indicate that equality is preserved. Yet, a closer look shows that choices are made according to a range of options suggested by the *lycée*. Not all *lycées* offer the same range of options, and options do not offer same openings in terms of further studies or entry to the world

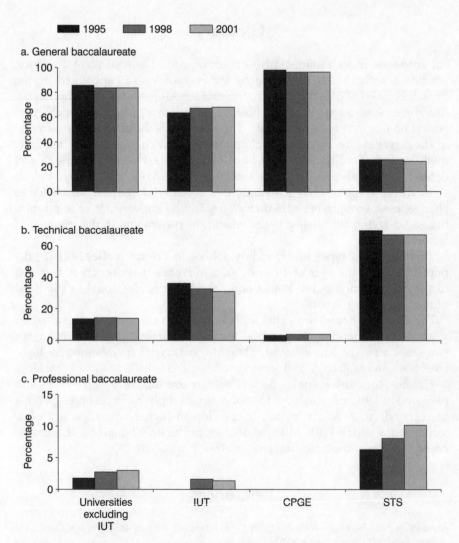

Figure 4.4 Proportion of students in different branches of higher education in France, according to the baccalaureate they took

of work. It is therefore the case that the perception students' families have of the system is paramount in guiding students' choice. If students are not guided properly, a whole mass of young people will be dissatisfied with the baccalaureate they pass: a devalued qualification may cause great dissatisfaction which might be difficult to control socially. A comparison between some of the Paris *lycées* that recruit students for their CPGE from January onwards, a long time before the examination, and vocational *lycées* that offer the *bac pro*, reveals the huge gulf that separates diplomas that bear the same generic name 'baccalaureate'.

Glossary

An **académie** is an administrative education unit, the equivalent of a local education authority. It is headed by the **recteur** who is appointed by the French Counsel of Ministers and represents the Minister for Education in the Académie. The *recteur* is responsible for all primary, secondary and higher education teaching in his *académie*. The **Rectorat** is the office of the *recteur*.

The **agrégés** are secondary school teachers with the highest teaching qualification. Traditionally they have been very sensitive to changes and defend a transmission model of teaching. They have come to symbolize, through the voice of their association, *la société des agrégés*, resistance to change, even though there are many *agrégés* who are very active in promoting and carrying out change in the education system and in the teaching of school subjects.

There are two types of secondary school in France: **collèges** that take pupils between the ages of 11 and 16, and **lycées** that take them from 16 to the *bac*, usually at 18. Pupils enter the **lycée professionel** in the third year of secondary school.

The **Grandes Ecoles** are elitist schools to which students are recruited on selective examinations; preparation for these examinations takes a further two years after the *Baccalauréat*. Their students, who are destined for high-level posts in the French civil service, receive a very high quality of teaching.

The **instituts universitaire de technologie** are linked to universities and prepare students in two years for a university diploma in technology. This corresponds to a determination to develop in higher education a professional route which leads to vocational or professional degrees. It must be noted, however, that such degrees are few in numbers.

References

Académie de Nantes Web site: http://www.ac-nantes.fr/actu/bac/bac.htm (accessed 10 December 2002)

Bayrou, F (1993) *Libération*, 30 Avril 1993, Paris

DPD Web site: http://www.education.gouv.fr/dpd/DPD_WEB/ap_eec42.htm (accessed 10 December 2002)

French Ministry of Education Web site: http://www.education.fr (accessed 10 December 2002)

Lang, J (1992) Journal de 20 heures, *Antenne* 2, 15 June

Office National d'Information sur les Enseignements et les Professions (ONISEP) (2002) *Guide du professeur*, ONISEP, Paris

Times Higher Education Supplement (THES) (1995a) Showdown of evasive v. abrasive, *THES* (3 March) (UK)

THES (1995b) 'Bac' pass row erupts (28 July) (UK)

THES (1997) Beloved 'bac' shows signs of stress (13 June) (UK)

THES (2000) How the baccalaureat has moved forward (11 August) (UK)

5

The Welsh Baccalaureate: two models

Introduction: the context

The curriculum reform debate in Wales has produced two models.

Model A (The Welsh Bac) is the product of work carried out by the Institute of Welsh Affairs (IWA), an independent think tank based in Cardiff. The case for this model first emerged in a social and economic policy review, *Wales 2010: Creating our future* (IWA, 1993). The Welsh Bac is based essentially on the framework and principles of the International Baccalaureate (IB) Diploma, modified to include vocational options and complemented by compulsory core studies. It is designed to be offered at three levels – foundation, intermediate and higher.

Following devolution, responsibility for education in Wales passed to the National Assembly which was established in 1999. The Assembly took up the challenge, and in 2001 put a proposal for 16+ education reform out to tender to a number of examining boards. (In the event only one bid was received: an anticipated proposal from the Welsh Bac group, with the support of the International Baccalaureate Organization (IBO) did not materialize.) The contract was therefore awarded to the Welsh Joint Education Committee (WJEC), the major examining body in Wales, in association with the University of Bath and Fforwm (the body representing Welsh colleges).

The successful model (**Model B: The Welsh Baccalaureate Qualification**) combines a compulsory core key skills curriculum alongside existing AS/A2, GNVQ, NVQ and GCSE qualifications. It will be offered at intermediate and advanced levels. This model is based on the principles underpinning the Graduation Certificate model (see Chapter 6).

The debate surrounding these two models in Wales has centred on a number of issues. These have included concerns about the need to protect the position of Welsh students in the context of the British qualifications market, and the resources viability of the various proposals. The Welsh Baccalaureate Qualification (Model B) will now be piloted in 19 schools and colleges across Wales from 2003.

Model A: The Welsh Bac

John David and Colin Jenkins

Introduction

Three threads have influenced the development of this project, and were brought together by the efforts of three head teachers, the two authors and Eirlys Pritchard Jones, former head of a large comprehensive school in the Rhondda Valley. The first of these threads was a readiness for change, the consequence of the authors having witnessed throughout their teaching careers the floundering efforts to improve the quality of post-16 education. They had witnessed N and F, Q and F and Higginson (DES, 1988), all of which were educationally and philosophically persuasive, but which had all been aborted. Dearing (1996), the latest survey, led through *Qualifying for Success* (DfEE *et al*, 1997) to *Curriculum 2000*, which appears not to be achieving its aims. All of these proposals have demonstrated a clear need for change.

Second, the two authors have had extensive experience of the International Baccalaureate (IB) as teachers, examiners, curriculum developers, and in the case of one of them, a senior administrative and governance role in the International Baccalaureate Organization (IBO). This experience persuaded them not only of the better quality education provided by the baccalaureate but also of its potential accessibility. Critics saw it as a curriculum for the academically able (an A level system in another form). The model, however, lends itself to adaptation to include vocational study and programmes at advanced, intermediate and foundation levels. (These terms, throughout this chapter, are used as defined in the National Qualifications Framework.)

The third factor was the proposal for a Welsh Baccalaureate made in the Institute of Welsh Affairs (IWA) report *Wales 2010* (1993) as part of an economic and social review. The Institute, an influential think tank, has continued with its active support of the proposals, often in the face of strong criticism.

A number of institutions in Wales had already been attracted to the baccalaureate concept in the form of the IB. Atlantic College had been involved since the late 1960s as one of the founder members, and has made significant contributions to the development of the IB. Others in Wales have recognized the merits of a broad and rigorous post-16 curriculum: Swansea College and Llandrillo College have established successful programmes. They were joined in 2000 by Whitchurch High School, Cardiff, where an IB pilot is under way.

The challenge of giving substance to the Welsh Baccalaureate idea was taken up, with the authors attempting to fashion their ideas within the educational and political context current in the mid-1990s. From their IB experience and their analysis of the deficiencies of the post-16 provision in

England and Wales, they perceived that an educational programme should have:

- **breadth** – across domains of knowledge;
- **depth** – providing the rigour required as preparation for further study;
- **balance** – to provide within the curriculum the range of skills now regarded as a prerequisite for further study and for lifelong learning;
- **coherence** – to provide levels of assessment and styles of learning that are stimulating for students and acceptable to the outside world;
- **a core studies element** – embracing connective components common to all participants at all levels;
- **currency** – to ensure its acceptability to higher education and employers;
- **inclusiveness** – making provision at advanced, intermediate and foundation levels, covering both academic and vocational study programmes.

Raising the status of vocational study was seen as a key requirement. For too long 'academic' and 'vocational' education had been provided for separately, on different tracks. Also guiding the curriculum design was the belief that the baccalaureate features indicated above, and already in place in the IB exemplar at the advanced level, could be replicated at the intermediate and foundation levels.

Building such an all-embracing model was, and remains, a challenging task. The authors were made aware of their own limitations and of the severe constraints of national provision in both 'academic' and 'vocational' areas. It was quickly realized that a baccalaureate could not be built from A and AS 'blocks' – they were the wrong size of study unit. A programme that provides breadth as well as depth runs the risk of making excessive time demands on the curriculum. A restructuring of the subject specifications is therefore necessary. The IB provides a successful model for such a strategy, and one that has received widespread approval from higher education. Furthermore, recent experience of schools and colleges with *Curriculum 2000* indicates a degree of disaffection with the individual units.

In 1997 the only existing vocational 'bricks' were NVQs and GNVQs. The latter, as initially conceived, were cumbersome, and their take-up was limited. Inevitably, our first models conformed to the limitations they set. The Dearing Report (1996), disappointing in many ways and limited by its brief, introduced a welcome flexibility by proposing six and three unit vocational programmes: this enabled the enhancement of the baccalaureate qualities of student study programmes containing vocational components.

Practically, the model had to satisfy students in a range of circumstances. Some would wish to, and be able to comply with, all the study requirements concurrently; others might take a 'staged' approach in building up to the full award as part of a process of lifelong learning. In this context it was felt that having a clear target would be motivational.

To summarize, we saw our task as being the design of a curriculum giving breadth, depth, balance, coherence, rigour, inclusivity and currency. Coherence meant the inclusion of vocational study within an overall package rather than its being given a separate 'track'. A coherent plan also required the design of provision at advanced, intermediate and foundation levels. The development of the curriculum needed to be viewed as a whole, with student needs as central, rather than as an exercise in adjusting student requirements to fit existing qualifications and patterns.

> I am delighted that the Institute of Welsh Affairs has chosen the format of the International Baccalaureate for their new Welsh Bac. In my view this is far superior to A levels both in required spread and in the mutual support of subjects. The consultation exercise about the acceptability of the Welsh Bac to Higher Education institutions is impressive – by the number as well as by the variety of institutions consulted and also the attention given to specific subjects. I wish the new examination every success.
>
> Professor Sir Hermann Bondi KCB, FRS Formerly Master, Churchill College, Cambridge; Chief Scientist, Ministry of Defence; Director, Natural Environment Research Council

> As currently conceived, the Welsh Bac is an educationally coherent, forward-looking qualification which should not only prepare students for admission to universities such as UCL but which should also provide an enriching and enabling education to school students across the full range of ability.
>
> Nigel Percival, Deputy Director, Educational Liaison, University College, London

The model

The construction of the model was heavily influenced by the format of the IB Diploma. Its 'units' were constructed to complement each other and to provide a coherent framework. The GCE A level system and other existing post-16 systems had never aspired to such coherence, or indeed to any 'completeness' in the range of skills acquired by a student. The IB model in both its curriculum and assessment strategies had addressed this need with conspicuous success. Where the IB did not provide a lead was in the vocational field, and in the provision of levels of study necessary to benefit the majority of the cohort. In this respect the IB diploma was similar to A levels.

For decades government thinking on post-16 education has focused on advanced level provision. The *Qualifying for Success* consultation (DfEE *et al*, 1997) was a recent example of this. Another was the research report *An Overarching Certificate at Advanced Level* (1999) produced by the Further Education Development Agency (FEDA) and the Institute of Education, London, which was restricted by the research remit from the Qualifications,

Curriculum and Assessment Authority for Wales (ACCAC), the Northern Ireland Council for the Curriculum, Examinations and Assessment (CCEA) and the Qualifications and Curriculum Authority (QCA). This remit did not permit them to consider modularity, or qualifications of different design or size to A levels or GNVQs. In our judgement it is unnecessary to impose such a constraint, and we claim that a baccalaureate structure and the skills it gives students could and should apply at advanced, intermediate and foundation levels. We believe that the benefits of a baccalaureate programme are not the exclusive right of the 'academic' student.

Basic principles

These are the main principles of the Welsh Bac:

1. A programme that provides an academic and/or vocational focus according to the needs of individual students, and that incorporates a substantial common curriculum for all students.
2. International elements suited to a world in which national barriers to trade, communication and co-operation are diminishing: a global perspective is essential for the 21st century.
3. National elements related to the position of the modern Wales in the world – its economics, sociology, governance, culture and language.
4. Learning a second language.
5. A study of the humanities and the social sciences.
6. A study of mathematics.
7. Study of one or more science subjects.
8. Study of an aesthetic or artistic subject.
9. A broad contextual programme on ways of understanding and the theory of knowledge.
10. A course on information technology.
11. A requirement for a community partnership involvement.

These features provide the founding principles for a coherent education programme for each student, combining academic and vocational provision in varying proportions according to the needs and choices of the individual. These basic principles, while in one sense setting out the programme's requirements, are even more significant when seen in terms of the right of each student to a broad, balanced, skills-based education.

The Welsh Bac programme

The Welsh Bac curriculum therefore:

- provides breadth and balance;
- achieves academic/vocational integration;
- is designed at three levels – advanced, intermediate and foundation;

- ensures continuity of a Welsh Studies element within an international context;
- requires an element of community partnership.

All this is included within the curriculum framework (see Figures 5.1 and 5.2).

Study time

We envisage the following over a two-year course:

- 240 hours study per higher level subject;
- 120 hours study per standard level subject;
- 150 hours study for core studies.

Thus a typical programme of three higher level, three standard level subjects and core studies would require 1,230 hours over two years. This is comparable with, and certainly no more than, the study time requirements of *Curriculum 2000*.

Core studies

The core – a mandatory requirement for all those aspiring to the full diploma – should be a powerful mechanism for providing coherence as well as exploring the place of each individual in the modern world. A connective study such as the IB's theory of knowledge programme teaches critical thinking and considers the ways in which judgements can be fairly made and opinions formed. A 'global issues' programme counterbalances and sets in context the Welsh dimension. The IT programme is essential to provide current information and communications technology skills, and the community partnership requirement promotes community understanding and responsible citizenship supported by community action. Some might argue that this is an impossibly idealistic menu. The reality is that it is already being achieved by the IB programme. The 'academic' subjects focus on appropriate knowledge and skills in their disciplines, while the core focuses on connections, judgement, civic awareness and the opportunity for action.

Assessment

Assessment strategies across the programme are aimed at evaluating a range of skills. These skills are acquired as an integral part of the broad, coherent programme of study, and not as a 'bolt-on' extra. The skills required are:

- knowledge of the subject matter of the courses taken, together with the appropriate subject skills;
- literacy and the ability to communicate in writing;
- oral skills;

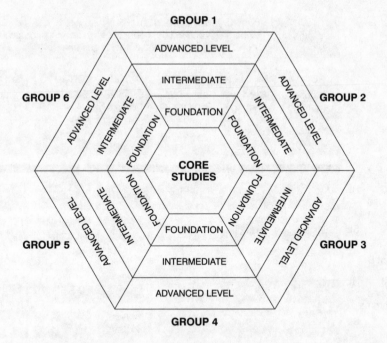

GROUP 1

GROUP 6

GROUP 2

GROUP 5

GROUP 3

GROUP 4

CORE STUDIES
Community partnerships and action, connective studies, individual study projects, any additional statutory requirements

GROUP 1	GROUP 2	GROUP 3	GROUP 4	GROUP 5	GROUP 6
Culture, Language & Literature	Second Language	Humanities GNVQ/NVQ units	Science, Maths & Technology GNVQ/NVQ units	Art, Aesthetics GNVQ/NVQ units	Student Choice

How are individual choices made?

All students take Core Studies.

- Students may choose a course from each Group. Note that Wales Studies can satisfy Group 1 and/or Group 3 (Humanities) or Group 5 (Arts/-Aesthetics) requirements, freeing up a further choice group for specialisation if desired.
- The Maths/Science combined course at Standard Level satisfies the mathematics and science requirements.
- Having made six choices, a student then decides on three to be taken at Higher Level and three at Standard Level. This allows the specialisation necessary for admission to higher education.
- Students may take GNVQ courses at Advanced, Intermediate or Foundation level. Support studies in other Groups (Languages, Maths, etc) would be available at the corresponding levels.
- Students would take national vocational qualifications at level 1, 2 or 3. These vocationally specific programmes complement the academic element of the Baccalaureate and provide realistic work experience. For example, a student wishing to study international hotel management would include an NVQ in Hospitality Management and Modern Languages in the programme of study chosen.

Fulfilment of all requirements gains the Award of a WelshBac Diploma, annotated at the appropriate level.

- Each subject is scored on a 1 to 7 (top) scale; a 4 constitutes a Pass.
- A diploma will be awarded according to a set of rules where weaker performance in one subject may be compensated by a stronger performance in another.
- Students not aiming for, or not completing, the full diploma programme will receive a Certificate in recognition of successful achievement in each subject.
- A diploma may be achieved by concurrent study or by accumulation.

Levels of Study

In principle the possibility exists for a programme to be constructed from units at various levels. Much depends on institutional constraints as to how much of this can be offered. As the illustrated programmes indicate, academic and vocational units may be combined.

The flexibility of the programme at the three Levels (Advanced, Intermediate and Foundation) provides a ready basis for adaptation to a 14–19 educational construct rather than to just post-16 as in its present format.

Figure 5.1   Overview of the Welsh Bac

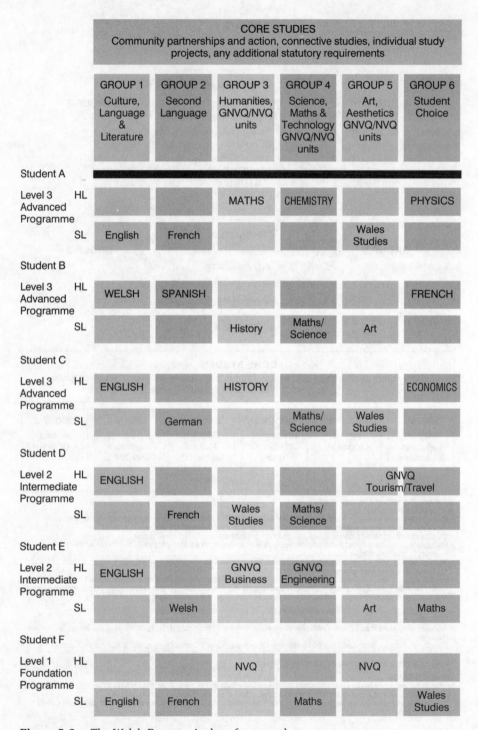

Figure 5.2   The Welsh Bac: curriculum framework

- ability to marshall an argument and to support it with reliable data;
- data analysis;
- numeracy;
- information technology;
- linguistic competence;
- teamwork.

A student successfully completing the full programme would possess a skills base that would be personally satisfying as well as being attractive to higher education and employers. The programme therefore provides a challenging and motivating education designed to raise standards of provision and the achievement of each student, at whatever level, for the benefit of the individual and society.

As referred to earlier, the IB has had a strong influence on the construction of the Welsh Bac model, which often prompts the question, 'Why not use the IB?' There are two factors to consider in responding. First, the preparation of a comprehensive model which will cater for the majority of the cohort requires the integration of vocational courses, and differentiation in the planning of courses at the foundation, intermediate and advanced levels. Currently the IB does not include such features. Second, there is the practical consideration of cost. The worldwide operation of the IB and the heavy administrative costs associated with this mean that the cost of examination is very high, and beyond the capacity of most state-maintained schools. However, we would estimate that the examination costs of our model, in the hands of a local examination board, would be similar to those for an A level-based programme.

The challenge

Throughout our work on the Welsh Bac we have been guided not only by the educational principles it embodies but also by social, economic and political concerns. The key phrases promoting educational philosophy in recent years have included 'overarching qualification', 'parity of esteem', 'raising the status of vocational education', 'skills' (basic, key and generic), 'inclusiveness' and 'community partnership and citizenship'. Our design meets these criteria: our aim has been to ensure that all students, regardless of their ultimate career aims, have experience of all areas of learning and are multi-skilled.

In recent years UK government concerns, irrespective of party, have centred on improved pass rates, particularly at A level. Focus on this one aspect has meant the absence of any serious debate about the question of pass rates in the key subjects of mathematics, languages and the sciences. In mathematics there has been a dramatic fall in number of students, graduates and qualified teachers in the subject. The Nuffield Languages Inquiry

Table 5.1 Development of the project: a summary of the key stages in the process

1993	Publication by the Institute of Welsh Affairs (IWA) of *Wales 2010: Creating our Future* (IWA, 1993)
1994	Initial approach to Welsh Joint Education Committee (WJEC)
February 1996	Initial Welsh Baccalaureate proposals launched by IWA to encourage wide consultation. Enthusiastic response from schools, colleges, higher education, business and industry. Publication of the Dearing Report (1996)
March 1996	Labour Party education policy document *Aiming Higher* (1996) published. This articulated the challenge as follows: It cannot be sensible for some of our brightest young people to achieve excellent A Levels at 18 and still not be, in any full sense, well educated. Breadth is a sounder preparation than narrow specialization for progression into higher education, employment and active citizenship.
June 1996	Conference organized by IWA to discuss the proposals with representatives of all political parties, education and business
February 1997	Publication of handbook *The Welsh Bac: Educating Wales in the Next Century* (Jenkins *et al*, 1997) by the IWA, followed by meetings, conferences and the distribution of a questionnaire. Results of questionnaire sent to all schools and colleges in Wales, and consultation with higher education and business, reported in *The Welsh Baccalaureate: Matching International Standards* (David and Jenkins, 1997). Summary of results: total response: 61 per cent; interested in the development: 86 per cent; prepared to take part in a pilot scheme: 38 institutions.
May 1997	*Qualifying for Success: A consultation paper on the future of post-16 qualifications* (DfEE *et al*, 1997) issued. Scope limited by policy statement: 'This Government is committed to GCE A Levels.' The Welsh Office issued the London document with no modification. Views were not sought on the Welsh Bac proposals. The Curriculum and Assessment Authority for Wales (ACCAC), in response to the Welsh Office document *Qualifying for Success* (1998), devotes a large part of its letter of advice to a dismissal of the Welsh Bac.
October 1997	Meeting with Minister for Education at the Welsh Office, Peter Hain MP. He urges a UK-wide consultation with higher education to establish the currency of the proposed qualification.
September 1998	Publication by the IWA of *The Welsh Bac: From Wales to the world* (1998)
September 1999	Devolved Welsh Assembly established, with education one of its major responsibilities
1999–2000	£30,000 grant received from Council of Welsh TECs to finance consultation research project with higher education in England, Scotland and Northern Ireland to be undertaken by questionnaire, in-depth interview and conference. Consultation report published, *Beyond the Border: The acceptability of the WelshBac to higher education institutions outside Wales* (Black and David, 2000). Questionnaire sent to 145 institutions: 72 replies, with 94 per cent approval rating for the proposal. Interview responses endorsed the principles and practice of the Welsh Bac.

September 2000	Conference and launch of the IWA consultation report *Beyond the Border* (Black and David, 2000). Labour-Liberal Democrat partnership agreement commits the Assembly government to pilot a Welsh Baccalaureate, based upon the IB 'so as to protect their (ie the students') position in the developing qualification market'.
December 2000	Assembly Cabinet advised by its Education Department to change its commitment in respect of the use of the IB and thus to change the partnership agreement
January 2001	Welsh Assembly invites tenders for development and administration of a Welsh Baccalaureate pilot scheme. Tender specification documents accompanied by a 'technical analysis' from ACCAC which includes the statement: 'The Assembly may wish to explore whether there is an alternative and more viable model for the Welsh Baccalaureate, drawing on the concepts that underpin designs for Overarching and Graduation Certificates.'
May 2001	One tender only received – from the WJEC – based on A/AS levels, vocational courses and the Key Skills qualification. It is successful.
September 2001	WJEC Information and Guidance booklet published for their proposed Welsh Baccalaureate Qualification (WBQ)
March 2002	WBQ proposals submitted to ACCAC and gain approval, constituting final confirmation of rejection of the Welsh Bac proposal

(2000) highlighted the limited take up of languages post-16. The Dainton Report (1968) investigated why there were so few candidates for university places in science and technology. Lord Dainton's remedy was a broader curriculum for all pupils post-16. (As his obituary in *The Times* (December 1997) reminded us, 'These recommendations fell on stony ground, however, and have yet to bear fruit.')

Now, at long last, concerns are being expressed about the dire economic consequences of these deficiencies – but the curriculum design to remedy them has still to be implemented. *Curriculum 2000* and the Government Green Paper *14–19: Extending opportunities, raising standards* (DES, 2002) both fail to address the issue, though we believe that a solution from the latter is possible.

The Welsh Bac model as outlined in this chapter sets out the type of curriculum required to meet the readily identifiable needs of our society. The challenge is a considerable one, but to ignore it or fudge the response serves society ill, and underprepares and underestimates our young people. The Welsh Bac (or its possible English adaptation) at the three levels of provision, with its general academic and vocational components, common core, range of disciplines and qualifications strategy, provides a comprehensive programme. It is one that would win respect within the UK and beyond. We owe it to those who have supported and encouraged us, whether in education, business and industry or politics, to continue to advocate and clarify the merits of the Welsh Bac. We feel that its principles and concepts could make a significant contribution to the continuing 14–19 debate.

Model B: The Welsh Baccalaureate Qualification

Robert Adams

Background

The constitution of the National Assembly for Wales in 1999 devolved a great deal of responsibility for education onto the Assembly. This enabled the Welsh Assembly government to strike out on a largely independent course, with a distinctively Welsh approach to the oversight and development of the national education system. In curriculum terms, one of the major examples of this autonomy was the announcement of the creation of a Welsh Baccalaureate qualification (WBQ) and the publication of an invitation to tender for the running of a pilot project for its detailed design and development. The Welsh Joint Education Committee (WJEC), the examinations board for Wales, tendered for this work and was successful in securing the contract. This chapter describes the design process of the qualification and the curriculum programmes that will lead to its award.

Introduction

Early in March 2001 an invitation was issued by the Office of the National Assembly of Wales (NAW) to Awarding Bodies in the UK to tender for the development and piloting of a Welsh Baccalaureate qualification, as outlined in the National Assembly's paving document *The Learning Country* (NAW, 2001). This qualification was intended to promote access, social inclusion, and retention among post-16 students in Wales, would raise achievement of Welsh students, and so would contribute to the rejuvenation of the Welsh economy; it would have a distinctive Welsh flavour, and would lead to a broadening of the curriculum for students at both Levels 2 and 3 of the National Qualifications Framework (NQF). It would also bring parity to vocational and academic qualifications. At the same time it was recognized that students taking part in the development should have their interests and futures protected. (The invitation documents made clear that a decision on a Level 1 qualification would be taken during the course of the project, informed by the development of the Level 2 and Level 3 versions.) Also, students would be able to pursue their courses, experiences and activities in English or Welsh.

The WJEC responded quickly and set up a small group, comprising the chief executive, the senior assistant secretary (curriculum) and the head of the Research Unit. A likely project director, the former director of education for Carmarthenshire, was invited to join in the preliminary discussions. Also at this early stage, the need for a person experienced in the world of further education and work-related education was identified and added to the team.

The need for an agency to conduct the internal and formative evaluation of the project was soon identified, and Professor Jeff Thompson of the University of Bath Department of Education was invited to take on this role. He agreed, and brought to the WJEC's deliberations a wealth of experience, particularly with the International Baccalaureate Organization, which has its Curriculum and Assessment Centre in Cardiff. By March 2001, this team had met with the WJEC Examinations Management Team, who formally recommended that the WJEC prepare and submit a tender nominating the project team to carry out the preparatory work and, if successful, to manage the project.

Outline of the tender

Interpreting the need both to protect the students' interests in the developing qualifications market, and to develop a viable qualification in that climate, the Project Team concluded early on that the terms of the NAW's invitation would best be met by a pragmatic curriculum design that was based partly on existing qualifications at Levels 2 and 3. Moreover, the required broadening of students' programmes could be brought about by the incorporation of the existing Key Skills qualifications, which could also be mobilized to drive the curriculum innovation that the team viewed as essential to satisfy the social and economic, as well as the educational, aims of the development. Above all, this innovation aimed at harnessing all of a student's activities, including enriching experiences and a 'learning by doing' approach (both inside and outside school or college) to his or her development of essential skills.

Subsequent events have shown that this vision of the future of the curriculum is shared by policy makers in Wales. The consultation paper on the 14–19 provision, *Learning Country: Learning pathways 14–19* (Welsh DET, 2002) places the Welsh Baccalaureate at the centre of change. I quote: 'These [essential] skills are best developed through experience and practical application in community groups, voluntary activities, sports or cultural activity or in the work place, as well as in day-to-day learning environments' (*ibid*: 3), and, 'We want to extend their learning beyond the school or college gates to include other opportunities and experiences which enable them to develop and apply a wide range of essential skills' (*ibid*: 8).

This analysis led to the establishment of the overarching 'core plus options' model that is the fundamental characteristic of the proposed qualification. The core would be compulsory, and would comprise a series of experiences and activities that would contribute to students' developments in all six key skills: the three main skills – communication, application of number, and IT – and the three wider ones – working with others, improving own learning and performance, and problem solving. It was emphasized that this would not preclude students' using their option studies to furnish evidence for attainment in any of the key skills. It was intended that all the opportunities for meeting the requirements of key skills assessments could, with careful design and guidance, arise naturally from students' curriculum activities, and, equally, should arise from their own inclinations and interests. The key to the success of the curriculum would indeed lie in capturing the students' interests and enthusiasms.

The options would comprise students' choices from the whole existing range of qualifications, appropriate to their attainments, needs and aspirations, and not restricted to the offerings of the WJEC, but embracing those of all awarding bodies in the UK. Also, in order to promote flexibility no restrictions would be placed on combinations of subjects that might be pursued as part of students' options. In this way, students would be encouraged to take up vocational qualifications, and the status of vocational qualifications might therefore be enhanced.

Certain desirable educational experiences for 16-plus students were embedded in the core. These included work-related education, including a placement for each student with an employer for at least a week, plus some form of entrepreneurial experience such as the Young Enterprise scheme. (For students following vocational qualifications, this would arise naturally as part of their programmes.) Also some elements of personal and social education, including preparation for citizenship, would contribute to the core. This would also include a period of community participation. The distinctively Welsh element would be added by means of a series of activities and experiences designed to engage students' interests in life in contemporary Wales, as a member of a local community, but in the context of Wales as a whole, Europe and the wider world.

The Project Team recognized at an early stage that guidance and mentoring of students would be essential in fostering retention, completion and achievement, and in particular in leading students toward the preparation of evidence for their attainments in the key skills. As a result, tutorial support for each student was included in the evolving model as a means of bringing coherence to each student's curriculum programme. Again, subsequent policy developments in Wales have reinforced these principles: the *Learning Country: Learning pathways 14–19* (Welsh DET, 2002) document already referred to comments that 'all young people would need close professional support and guidance in setting their short and longer-term goals and in agreeing their individual learning pathways' (*ibid*: 23).

Underlying the whole design of the core was the principle that it would lead naturally to, and its success be recognized by, attainment in the Key Skills qualifications.

These were the parameters that the Project Team used to develop the curriculum model that was to form the basis of the Welsh Baccalaureate qualification at both Levels 2 and 3 of the NQF. By the end of June 2001 the bid had been submitted to the NAW, and after a series of discussions and negotiations, the contract to develop and pilot the qualification was awarded to the WJEC. The team was expanded to include two development officers and a project manager, together with administrative support. Working groups were set up by the Project Team to include experienced practitioners, to put flesh on the curriculum model. As well as a general Curriculum Models Working Group, four other groups were established corresponding to the main elements of the core. These were: Key Skills; Wales, Europe and the World; Work-Related Education; and Personal and Social Education (PSE). An Information and Communication Technology (ICT) Group was also set up to advise on information technology aspects of students' programmes and the place of ICT in general within the project. It was envisaged from the outset, for example, that pilot institutions would be linked to each other and to the project centre by an extranet. At the same time, the NAW set up a Contract Monitoring and Steering Group to which the Project Team has reported regularly and will continue to report throughout the life of the project.

The curriculum model

The model, common to both Level 2 and Level 3, is shown diagrammatically in Figure 5.3. This portrays the components of the qualification described above with notional weekly time allocations, and emphasizes the critical role of tutoring in achieving coherence in students' programmes and experiences.

The core is shown as comprising Key Skills and 'mandatory components'. (The 'additional qualifications' might, for example, include a Duke of Edinburgh's Award, a sports award, or a language qualification.) The mandatory components are intended to contribute to students' key skills development, and to provide rich sources of evidence for their assessments in all six of them. A summary of the structure of these components is shown in Table 5.2.

The rationale for the model is that, despite initial teething troubles over their introduction in schools and colleges across Britain, the way forward does indeed lie with the development of key skills in our young people. Not only will this automatically broaden their studies and their perspectives, but it will offer to all young people a curriculum that is relevant to their future needs as participants in the social and economic life of Wales.

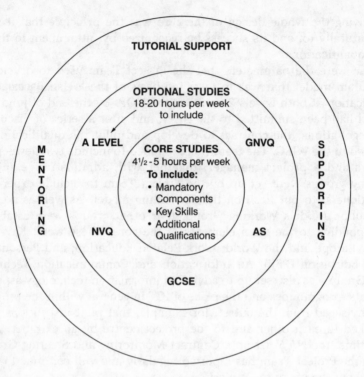

Figure 5.3   The Welsh Baccalaureate curriculum model

In this way, access, retention and completion by those young people will be promoted.

The fundamental tenet of the team, as expressed in the Welsh Baccalaureate model, is that it is possible to devise a means of fostering attainment in the key skills through a 'whole curriculum' approach. Moreover, in fostering this attainment through students' whole programmes, mediated by careful tutoring, the diversity of activities and experiences in conjunction with any student's chosen options would ensure breadth and balance. There is almost universal agreement that the traditional post-16 diet of three A level subjects represents premature specialization and a narrowing of perspective for most students. Attempts have been made in recent years to add breadth to post-16 studies by introducing first Advanced Supplementary GCEs and later Advanced Subsidiary (AS) GCEs. The addition of subjects from domains of similar subjects, such as for the International Baccalaureate (IB) Diploma programme, is not the only approach to breadth and balance. These can also be achieved in other ways, notably by enabling students to undertake and participate in a variety of types of educational experience, such as those proposed by the WBQ programme.

Table 5.2   Components of the WBQ core

Component	Summary
Personal and social education (PSE)	Five elements: • positive relationships; • good health, including sexual health; • rights and responsibilities of active citizens; • education for sustainable development; • community participation.
Wales, Europe and the world	Eight 'key issues' drawn from four elements: • political issues; • social challenges and responses; • impact of economic and technological change; • heritage and cultural perspectives. A language module
Work-related education	Two elements: • working with an employer; • enterprise activity.
Key Skills	All of the above, as well as options, to contribute to the development and accumulation of evidence for key skills

Once again, the model subsequently became adopted as part of the vision of the future for Wales, the *Learning Country: Learning pathways 14–19* (Welsh DET, 2002) document commenting that 'The proposed continuum of learning would include the six Key Skills, plus Wales, Europe and the World, work focused experience and community and voluntary opportunities' (*ibid*: 12), and explicitly states that, 'The content of the proposed continuum of learning is closely related to the requirements of the Welsh Baccalaureate' (*ibid*: 13). For the exploration of this insight, the Project Team are indebted to the Evaluation Team from the University of Bath Department of Education, whose presentation 'Towards a typology of baccalaureate qualifications' to a meeting of the Curriculum Models Working Group forms the basis of Chapter 2 of this book.

Critical to this curriculum process is the management of the relationship between an individual student's core and options: the 'interaction' as it is known to the team. In general terms, every student will have different option programmes, and each will contribute to attainment and 'evidence accumulation' in the Key Skills assessments in different ways. The curriculum innovation sought by the project is achieved through tutoring and guidance to enable students to take responsibility for this interaction.

Assessment

The options, comprising existing qualifications, will carry their own assessment arrangements, which students will undertake in the normal way. Also, in pursuit of the Key Skills, national assessment arrangements will be in place for tests and portfolio assessment, and these too will be undertaken by students. In addition, students will be required to show evidence of having experienced elements of the core. For the unit 'Wales, Europe and the world' each student will be expected to produce an 'individual investigation' based on some aspect of his or her life in Wales. The team is eager to explore with pilot centres the possibility of developing more adventurous forms of presentation of the outcomes of these investigations, rather than the customary essay. Evidence of experience in PSE and work-related education will be through students' keeping diaries, or other suitable means of recording, supported by witness statements (for example, from employers) where appropriate. The only part of the core programme, aside from the Key Skills programmes, that is differentiated is the individual investigation. This will be assessed against different criteria at Level 2 and Level 3. All other parts of the core are available to students of all abilities.

The main thrust of the curriculum development, as referred to previously, will be to establish whole-curriculum approaches across the core and options to Key Skills portfolio building. In the midst of these developments the Green Paper *14–19: Extending opportunities, raising standards* (2002) was published by the DfES in England, proposing a Matriculation Diploma. This bears a close resemblance to the proposals for the WBQ, though it differs in the precise requirements in existing qualifications and Key Skills attainment for its award.

The focus on the 14–19 phase as a sensible educational entity, current in Wales as well as in England, puts the WBQ, as a strictly post-16 development, in an interesting position. Developments post-16 in the pilot schools will undoubtedly trickle down into the pre-16 curriculum in any case, but if attention formally shifts on to the 14–19 curriculum, then the project will face major adaptation in mid-stream. It is difficult to predict the form this trickle-down will take, but the NAW's paving document *The Learning Country* (2001) in Section 52 suggests that legislative action might need to be taken in Wales to allow more flexibility in the 14–16 curriculum, to allow pupils to follow mixtures of vocational and academic qualifications, and to permit the more effective pursuit of key skills.

Awards

The actual requirements for the award of the Welsh Baccalaureate Diploma at Level 2 (Intermediate Diploma) or Level 3 (Advanced Diploma) are shown in Table 5.3. It will be seen that a Core Certificate will be awarded to show completion of the requirements of the award beyond the option requirements.

Table 5.3 Welsh Baccalaureate Qualification: requirements for award

Level 2: Welsh Baccalaureate Intermediate Diploma	
Core requirements – Welsh Baccalaureate Intermediate Core Certificate	Five key skills certified at Level 2 or above, with evidence of the sixth having been pursued; completion of a satisfactory individual investigation; evidence of curriculum coverage, including work placement
	Five GCSE subjects at grade C or above, or their equivalent
Level 3: Welsh Baccalaureate Advanced Diploma	
Core Requirements – Welsh Baccalaureate Advanced Core Certificate	All six key skills certified at Level 2 or above, three of which must be at Level 3, of which at least one must be drawn from Communication, Application of Number or IT; completion of a satisfactory individual investigation; evidence of curriculum coverage, including work placement
Option requirements	Two GCE Advanced subjects at grade E or above, or their equivalents

At the time of writing, the team has responded to an invitation by the NAW to make proposals for a Level 1 WBQ, and has recommended that such a development should take place, provisionally to be known as the Welsh Baccalaureate Foundation Diploma.

The qualification at both levels has been designed with a two-year (usually years 12 and 13) programme in mind, and the two sample student profiles below are presented in this way. It is acknowledged, however, that some students may wish to complete the Level 2 Intermediate Diploma in one year, and then progress on to the Level 3 Advanced programme. Such students would probably have met most of the options requirements for the award of the Intermediate Diploma, say two or three GCSE grades A* to C, and could expect to complete their core programme in a single year.

Typical students' programmes

In the boxes on pages 112 and 113 are two specimen examples of students' programmes, Student A at Level 2, and Student B at Level 3, designed to illustrate applications of the model for individual students.

Student Profile Level 2: Student A

Background: A below average student (NQF level 1 working towards level 2). By age 16 she had become disenchanted with schooling so she reluctantly sat her GCSEs, emerging with two grade 'C' and six grades D, E or F. Returned to school largely because she had no clear idea about possible career prospects.

Programme: A large part of her initial time in the sixth form was taken up with tutoring/mentoring. It was decided to make the core the focus of this student's programme – and, because of her initial uncertainty about the future, to treat it as a series of two year-long component 'blocks'. So for Student A, in Year 12 the core (5 hours' contact time) consisted of Preparation for the World of Work, closely linked to PSE, together with appropriate community participation.

During Year 12, Student A developed an interest in a possible career in leisure and tourism. She obtained a work placement with the ground staff at a local leisure and recreation park. She took Key Skills set programmes in Communication, Application of Number and IT, all at Level 1. Gradually, she developed signposted programmes within the options. Throughout the year there was an emphasis upon tutorial support, largely to maintain her motivation and to tease out possible career pathways.

Her main option programme comprised a Vocational GCSE in Leisure and Tourism, GCSE PE, and a resit of GCSE Double Award Science and Mathematics.

In Year 13 Student A continued with her core studies, ie PSE, Preparation for the World of Work, aspects of community participation, and now, specific and relevant aspects of Wales and the World. Following success in Key Skills Level 1, she further developed her competence in Communication, Application of Number at Level 2, and in IT at Level 3. In addition, she showed increasing competence in working with others in work experience activities. She achieved Level 3 in Working with Others, and Level 2 in Improving Own Learning and Performance and Problem Solving. The various work placements during the two years provided the focus for all the Key Skills.

Tutoring continued to maintain Student A's motivation by showing her that 'someone is interested'. Success generally in Year 12 led to a wider choice of options in Year 13. She was able to follow a GCE AS course in Geography, and complete her Vocational GCSE in Leisure and Tourism. She also took an NVQ Level 2 in Groundpersonship. Key Skills were developed and practised in the options.

Outcome: Student achievement Level 2: **Welsh Baccalaureate Intermediate Diploma** comprising GCE AS Geography, Vocational GCSE in Leisure and Tourism, NVQ Level 2 in Groundpersonship, GCSE Double Award Science, PE, Key Skills Level 2 in Communication, Application of Number and Problem Solving, and Level 3 in IT, Working with Others and Improving Own Learning. Welsh Baccalaureate Intermediate Core Certificate.

Student Profile Level 2: Student B

Background: Student B is an above-average student (NQF level 3) who wishes to follow a career in engineering. As a result, he decided to leave school at 16 and go to the local further education college. At school he obtained 9 GCSEs, all at grade C or above.

Programme: Central to his overall programme were the tutorial discussions and measures needed to prepare for an applied science programme. Appropriate core components highlighted in Year 12, in a 4.5–5 hour teaching block, included PSE, Preparation for the World of Work, and aspects of community participation. Wales and the World programmes ran through Years 12 and 13, together with Key Skills programmes at Level 3 in Communication, Application of Number and IT. These programmes were closely linked with work experience in local engineering firms. These were paralleled by the options in Year 12, which included Vocational GCSEs in Science and in Engineering. He also resat GCSE Design and Technology (taken as part of core time/studies).

In Year 13, the Vocational GCE courses were developed as follows: Engineering into a 3-unit ACVE; also a 3-unit ACVE in ICT was added. Student B also decided to take GCE AS in Mathematics and Design and Technology. The use of Key Skills signposting allowed Student B to see their relevance in general education and training.

The Year 13 core programme (4.5–5 hours) allowed Student B to complete in depth his Wales and the World portfolio, as a part of which he undertook individual research into aspects of engineering in Europe and their links with Welsh industry. He also continued his PSE studies and discussions within the Preparation for the World of Work component. Key Skills were developed within the options and also as part of the core. His Key Skills programme emphasized Application of Number, Problem Solving and Working with Others. They were all taken successfully at Level 3. He also took a Computer Literacy and Information Technology (CLAIT) programme.

Throughout Years 12 and 13, Student B received considerable help and guidance through the tutorial system. Partly as a result of this, he was advised to consider widening his programme into extracurricular activities. As a result he participated in the Duke of Edinburgh Award Scheme, and helped in a charity shop at the weekends.

Outcome: Student achievement Level 3: **Welsh Baccalaureate Advanced Diploma** comprising: 3-unit ACVEs in ICT and Engineering, two GCE AS levels in Mathematics and in Design and Technology, Vocational GCSE in Science and Engineering, GCSE in CDT. Individual Key Skills in Communication, Application of Number, IT, Problem Solving, Working with Others and Improving Own Learning, all at Level 3. Duke of Edinburgh Silver Award. CLAIT award. Welsh Baccalaureate Advanced Core Certificate.

Pilot centres

In parallel with the work of the curriculum development group, the Project Team was busy cultivating prospective pilot schools and colleges to join in the development and to undertake to enter students for WB programmes, beginning in September 2003. By April 2002, a total of 19 institutions – 11 FE and tertiary colleges, and 8 schools spread across Wales – had committed themselves to take part in the development and to enter students for the pilot cohorts in 2003, 2004, 2005 and 2006. The centres were publicly identified for the first time at the launch of the Welsh Baccalaureate by the NAW Minister for Education and the Chief Executive of the WJEC at Builth Wells High School in April 2002. The contract with the NAW requires further pilot centres to be recruited: another six to enter students for the first time in September 2004 and then five more to enter students in September 2005.

Current developments

Upon completion of the draft specification for submission to ACCAC in March 2002, the working groups who had designed the specifications for the elements of the core, and commented on the proposed model, were disbanded. It had been necessary to distribute the development work in this way, but an inevitable consequence was that the elements of the core began to take on a life of their own: they came to be regarded by their custodians, the respective working groups, almost as subjects. The focus on the core as a means of facilitating attainment in the Key Skills thus shifted.

The next phase of the project, the development of materials for curriculum development and INSET, will seek to redress this change of emphasis. Pilot centres are being consulted over the implications for school and college organization of the required curriculum innovation, and they will participate in the design and commissioning of the material. At the same time a review of good practice in the delivery of key skills in schools and colleges is being undertaken. This will give the team a basis on which to identify the needs that the materials will be addressing, and to formulate the messages it will need to deliver to schools and colleges.

From the administrative point of view, the project will now have to work with 19 institutions: the team will effectively be enlarged by the addition of a representative from each of them. Work is starting on the setting up of an extranet, probably to be hosted by a commercial organization, to facilitate communication within the project, and to become itself part of the curriculum innovation as a medium of distance learning and information provision. The WJEC is also host to the Welsh National Grid for Learning Project, and fruitful collaboration between that project and the WBQ project has begun. Also, the active marketing and promotion of the qualification to students, teachers and lecturers, governors and parents will now begin in earnest.

It is intended to put in place a system of consultative moderation, by which each school or college will have available the guidance of an experienced consultative moderator to advise on aspects of the core and Key Skills provision. This will be in addition to the formal moderation of Key Skills assessments which will be conducted by the awarding body whose provision the centre adopts.

During the entire pilot process, the team and the evaluation team from the University of Bath will be monitoring and refining the curriculum and INSET materials, with a view to improving them in order to provide support for institutions across the whole of Wales to offer the Welsh Baccalaureate to their students.

Since the inception of the pilot, the Welsh Baccalaureate Qualification has assumed a central place in the vision of the future of education in Wales, initially post-16, but ultimately to take its place in the evolving 14–19 provision, as was demonstrated earlier. The project is now at the critical stage where ownership of the development spreads outwards from the central team into the pilot institutions, in order that they should realize the project's ideals in practice. If the development so far has been successful, then the process of making the Baccalaureate work in schools and colleges should fulfil the intention of the *Learning Country: Learning pathways 14–19* document: 'To secure the package for all, we need to ensure there can be flexibility and choice at local level to allow innovation and creativity to flourish and provide exciting options that will motivate young people to remain in learning until at least the age of 19 and beyond' (Welsh DET, 2002: 33).

References

Black, C and David, J (2000) *Beyond the Border: The acceptability of the WelshBac to higher education institutions outside Wales*, IWA, Cardiff

Cambridge, J C, Hayden, M C and Thompson, J J (2001) *Towards a Typology for Baccalaureate-Style Curricula in Post-16 Education Systems: an unpublished report for the Curriculum Models Working Group of the Welsh Baccalaureate Qualification Project*, Department of Education, University of Bath

Dainton, (Lord) Dr F S (1968) *Enquiry into the Flow of Candidates in Science and Technology into Higher Education*, HMSO, London

David, J and Jenkins, C (1997) *The Welsh Baccalaureate – Matching International Standards: A report on consultation with Welsh education institutions, business and industry*, IWA, Cardiff

Dearing, Sir R (1996) *Review of Qualifications for 16–19 Year Olds*, SCAA, London

Department for Education and Employment (DfEE), Department of Education Northern Ireland, Welsh Office (1997) *Qualifying for Success: A consultation paper on the future of post-16 qualifications*, DfEE, London

Department of Education and Science (DES) (1988) *Advancing A levels: Report of a committee appointed by the Secretary of State for Education and Science and the Secretary of State for Wales*, HMSO, London

Department for Education and Skills (DfES) (2002) *14–19: Extending opportunities, raising standards*, DfES, London

FEDA/Institute of Education (1999) *An Overarching Certificate at Advanced Level: Report to QCA, ACCAC, CCEA*, FEDA/Institute of Education, London

Institute of Welsh Affairs (IWA) (1993) *Wales 2010: Creating our future*, IWA, London

IWA (1998) *The Welsh Bac: From Wales to the world*, IWA, Cardiff

Jenkins, C, David, J, Osmond, J and Pierce, J (1997) *The WelshBac: Educating Wales in the next century*, IWA, London

Labour Party (1996) *Aiming Higher: Labour's plans for reform of the 14–19+ curriculum*, Labour Party, London

National Assembly for Wales (2001) *The Learning Country: A paving document*, National Assembly for Wales, Cardiff

Nuffield Languages Inquiry (2000) *Languages: The next generation*, Nuffield Foundation, London

Welsh Department for Education and Training (DET) (2002) *Learning Country: Learning pathways 14–19*, Consultation document, Welsh Assembly DET, Cardiff

Web site references: http://www.wbq.org.uk; http://www.welshbac.com

6

The Graduation Certificate

Geoff Lucas

Introduction

Prior to July 1999, the term 'graduation certificate' would have meant little to those involved in education and training in the UK. If it signified anything at all, it was most likely to have conjured up images of higher education degree certificates rather than awards pre-18. To those familiar with the United States it might have suggested graduation ceremonies linked to the High School Diploma. In the public mind this association would have been reinforced by the film (and latterly theatre version of) *The Graduate*. The publication of *Bridging the Gap* by the government's Social Exclusion Unit (SEU, 1999) in July 1999 brought together these existing associations and connotations and recast them anew. At the same time, by juxtaposing the words 'graduation' and 'certificate' it rooted this new concept firmly in the context of the 'overarching certificate', a form of group award which was linked to, but fundamentally different from, more traditional forms of baccalaureate.

This chapter traces the origins and development of the 'graduation certificate' developed by QCA (the Qualifications and Curriculum Authority). It analyses its contribution to thinking about overarching certificates in general, and its relationship with bac-style awards in particular. It is different from most other chapters in this book on two counts. First its subject is a theoretical model which has never been implemented nationally, although some local versions exist (notably Surrey and Liverpool) (QCA, 2001). (Details of the Surrey model are included in Chapter 7.) Second, it deals with something that was extremely ephemeral, at least so far as the broader 'graduation' concept was concerned. Its legacy, however, in terms of the content of more recent proposals for an overarching award (DfES, 2002) is likely to be more enduring.

The main thesis of the chapter is that graduation certificates (and their subsequent reincarnations) are, in fact, closer in concept and design to 'records of achievement' than to the other bac-style awards covered in this book. This does not, however, preclude the development of a hybrid that shares the best features of both of these distinctive traditions. The challenge for policy makers in England over the next five years is where on the continuum from the simplest form of 'record of achievement' to a full blown 'baccalaureate' they wish to place any future national overarching award. It is with this issue that the chapter concludes.

The Graduation Certificate in context

'Graduation': the policy context

From the beginning the graduation certificate was something of an anomaly in terms of curriculum and qualifications policy. Its launch in a chapter in a report by the government's Social Exclusion Unit (1999) locates it in a broader social and educational policy context. The primary focus of *Bridging the Gap* as a whole, and Chapter 8 on 'Education, training and work' in particular, is how to tackle the fundamental and interrelated problems of social exclusion, non-participation in education, training or work post-16, and low achievement (particularly as evidenced through formal qualifications).

The report starts with an analysis of what goes wrong and why so many of this country's young people – at any one time 161,000 or 9 per cent of the age group – are outside education, training and work for long periods after the school-leaving age of 16, and 'why it matters that they are' (SEU, 1999, Chapter 1: 8). It contrasts 'the clear structure for those who do best at school' (full time education post-16, resulting in high status qualifications and access to a good job or higher education) with the lack of such 'a clear goal' or 'rite of passage' for the 9 per cent who are left out. It notes that these young people are 'disproportionately from poor backgrounds in deprived areas... suffer multiple disadvantage, and... are much more likely to be unemployed, dependent on benefits, to live in unstable family structures, and to be depressed about their lives'. It calls for a radical approach to overcome such obstacles to success for this group of young people, within an overall approach designed to significantly improve the life chances of all young people.

Although Chapter 8 of the report is essentially about educational policy, the report as a whole (and its combined recommendations) had implications for several different government departments. It is no coincidence that the SEU's report was launched at a time when 'joined-up thinking' was being given substance by the creation of a new post within the cabinet to oversee and promote 'joined-up working', as envisaged in the White Paper, *Modernising Government* (CM 4310). The location of the SEU within the Cabinet Office itself and the close interest of the Prime Minister, Tony Blair, gave the report a propitious start in life. The confidence of the report's authors that there was the political will and authority to override traditional departmental and territorial boundaries is nowhere more evident than in Chapter 12, entitled 'Making it happen'. Here a detailed structure for further work was set out with both a joint Ministerial Group (albeit led by the Secretary of State for Education and Employment) and a cross-departmental implementation group (led by the DfEE) to oversee such work. An accompanying table and action plan went so far as to set out the remit and action expected from each of the four groups to be set up to take forward the four main strands of work arising from the *Bridging the Gap*. One of these was graduation.

Graduation: the social and educational contexts

Bridging the Gap set out four main elements as part of a new national strategy to raise levels of participation and achievement in education, training and work post-16. The first of these was to be 'graduation' (a broad holding phrase intended to represent 'a clear outcome to aim for by 19'). The other three were to be:

- a variety of pathways to 'graduation' which would suit the needs of all young people (whether in general education, vocational training or work);
- financial support, building on the pilots of educational maintenance allowances to engage the most disadvantaged groups, with a Youth Card to assist with transport and other costs (since launched as the Connexions Card);
- a new multi-skill support service for all young people, but particularly targeted at those most at risk of underachievement and disaffection (since launched as the Connexions Service).

Although this chapter focuses on graduation, it is important to recognize the linked and mutually reinforcing nature of these four main strands. From the beginning it was always stressed that the 'graduation' idea would be ineffective without the support of the other three. The converse, however, is not necessarily true. Indeed, the fact that work on both EMAs and the Youth Card has gone ahead in advance and independently of the graduation proposals bears this out. The other three strands, particularly the financial and broader support mechanisms, did not depend upon the existence of something such as graduation. Nevertheless the latter was intended to provide a powerful focus for what might otherwise have appeared to be rather disparate elements.

Graduation itself was initially conceived of as both a product (in the form of a certificate) and a process (with an American-style high school graduation ceremony playing an important part in recognizing and celebrating the achievement of the graduation certificate). In the original documentation associated with the proposals (notably the SEU report but also in the remit letter from Baroness Blackstone, Minister of State at the DfEE, to Sir William Stubbs, Chairman of the Qualifications and Curriculum Authority (QCA)), the concept of 'graduation' is defined both broadly (as a 'visible, universal and attractive goal' for all young people to aim for) and narrowly (as a certificate obtainable by age 19, through different learning routes, involving the achievement of formal qualifications to at least Level 2 standard, ie 5 GCSEs, grades A*–C, or their vocational equivalent). Nowhere in the initial proposals is there any explicit link with earlier work by the QCA on an 'overarching certificate at advanced level', although it is clear that the two concepts have a number of things in common, to which reference is made later in this chapter.

Graduation: early concept and models

Table 6.1 reproduces a possible design for a graduation certificate as provided in the SEU report. The text accompanying this stresses that this is 'purely by way of example' and the ministerial remit to QCA specifically asked the Authority 'to consider how the other elements identified in the report [other than formal qualifications at level 2] might be included and achievement measured'.

It was the design of the graduation certificate that was the main focus of the first year of QCA's work on graduation. An advisory group was set up

Table 6.1 One possible design for the graduation certificate (July, 1999)

Qualifications (and units of qualifications)	Achievement to at least Level 2 in formal qualifications such as GCSEs, GNVQ, NVQ or equivalent qualifications
Key Skills	Attainment at Level 2 and above in the key skills of communication, application of number, information technology
Curriculum enrichment and community participation	Demonstrable achievement in activity in areas drawn from a menu of options, such as citizenship/volunteering, sports, the arts, general studies, experience and skills gained through work
Personal development and achievement	A record of personal development and achievement, harnessing some of the features of the National Record of Achievement (Progress File), created and sustained with the ongoing support of a mentor

Note: the Ministerial letter to QCA's Chairman (13 July 1999) states that graduation should require achievement of 5 GCSEs A*–C (or the vocational equivalent). It does not specify any specific subjects. *Source:* SEU (1999), Chapter 8: 68.

to steer the work, with representation from the main government departments involved, the business sector and education (including the voluntary sector). The first meeting of the Graduation Expert Advisory Panel (as it was called) considered six key issues that were central to understanding and clarifying what 'graduation' meant. These are worth including here in some detail, since they remain the key questions that any future graduation certificate (or variant of it) will need to address. The initial answers to these questions are also provided.

The purposes of graduation (what it was for)

The primary purposes were considered to be to:

- increase participation in learning amongst 16–18-year-olds;
- raise levels of attainment for all (with Level 2, and 5 GCSEs A*–C in particular, as the normal expectation);
- broaden the range of achievements to be formally recognized and valued (to include, for example, work-related learning, citizenship/volunteering, sports and the arts).

The target groups (who it was for)

The main target groups were considered to be:

- 16–18-year-olds currently outside education, training and work;
- other 16–18-year-olds (for whom graduation would also be meaningful).

Two other groups of learners were also thought likely to seek or be eligible for graduation even though they were not the main targets for the initiative:

- pupils aged 16 or under who met the requirements early;
- older learners who might take longer to achieve graduation, for whom some form of equivalent recognition was desirable.

The nature of the achievement to be recognized

This refers to what is required, in terms of both breadth/volume and depth/level of achievement. The essence of graduation, which reflects the purposes set out above, was identified as:

- formal qualifications at or above Level 2 standard;
- a set volume of achievement of formal qualifications (5 GCSEs A*–C or the vocational equivalent);
- greater breadth of achievement (for example, through enrichment activities and community participation).

The nature of the recognition (whether it was acknowledged through a certificate and/or some other means)

The assumption was that 'graduation' would be recognized by the award of a certificate. However, other ways of recognizing graduation (eg through the National Record of Achievement/Progress File) were also noted, and these became significant in later discussions.

The value of graduation (both to young people and to those who recruit them)

The success of the graduation proposals would be dependent on the actual and perceived value of the certificate. The graduation concept needed to be more than a piece of paper or a collection of qualifications, and had to attract young people across the target population. The SEU report acknowledged that while some aspects of graduation would be intrinsically motivating, others would require extrinsic rewards to engage learners (such as financial incentives), particularly for those who did not currently participate voluntarily post-16.

The term 'graduation'

The title of the graduation certificate would influence its appeal, and it was recognized early on that 'graduation' carried many existing (and misleading) connotations for potential users. It is hardly surprising, therefore, that the term 'graduation certificate' was eventually to be superseded by the more general term 'overarching award'.

Throughout the first year of the QCA's work on graduation, attention returned frequently to these key issues. In many respects, the answers to the first four questions would determine the design of the graduation certificate (or more accurately certificates, if different levels of achievement were to be recognized). Pressure for different levels of certification came, in fact, from two different directions. First, it came from those who worked with young people who were unlikely to achieve Level 2 qualifications by age 19, including (but not only) those with learning difficulties and/or disabilities (some of whom would never meet the Level 2 target at any age). In 1999/2000, when work began on graduation, these learners represented almost a quarter of the age cohort. If such a sizeable group were not to be part of the graduation concept, it is difficult to see how the proposals could be truly 'inclusive'.

Second, pressure came from those who saw a need for a higher level certificate (at advanced level), to provide progression for learners who achieved the Level 2 certificate early (at 16 or 17), and more generally to raise the overall status and appeal of graduation in the eyes of young people, employers and higher education. Both of these concerns played a significant part in the development of models of the certificate which were to be the subject of consultation.

Graduation: certificate models and consultation

In the summer of 2000, the QCA conducted two consultation exercises on graduation: one quantitative, the other qualitative. Questionnaires were sent to some 1,600 individuals and 2,500 organizations, covering a range of issues to do with the concept of graduation, not just the certificate. The key messages from the questionnaire responses can be summarized as follows.

Support for the concept

- Most people supported a certificate for everyone at around the age of 18/19.
- The key purpose of such a certificate was seen as recognizing wider achievements, particularly the reporting of achievements in interpersonal skills and personal attributes.
- A certificate based on Level 2 qualifications was accepted as the appropriate level by most people (but see below).
- There was a need to develop methods to recognize achievement en route to the Level 2 certificate.
- A version of the certificate based on Level 3 qualifications was seen as a means of providing a challenge for more able learners.
- There was strong support for flexibility in how and where graduation was achieved, including the workplace.
- People accepted that 18+ was an appropriate target age for awarding the certificate, but did not want to see rigid age restrictions on when the award could be made.
- The availability of the certificate to adults received general support.

Content of the certificate

- The content of the certificate should include (in order of level of support):
  - key skills (communication, application of number, IT, working with others and improving own learning and performance);
  - national qualifications;
  - wider achievements.

Conditions for success

- National recognition of achievements (qualifications plus wider activities) and the use of the certificate by employers were seen as the most powerful motivators.

- There was a strong feeling that the certificate needed to be actively launched, publicized and supported by government if it were to succeed.
- Integration with the rest of the Connexions strategy would be necessary, and links with other agencies working with young people were seen as crucial.
- The certificate could form the basis of a four-year process of learning, starting from age 14 with an individual learning plan. This could help bring greater coherence to 14–19 education as a whole.
- The provisional name 'Graduation Certificate' did not appear to strike a chord with most people.
- There was support for some kind of public ceremony in which certificates were awarded.

Face-to-face interviews and discussions with some 350 young people and over 300 employers, higher education tutors and other providers of education and training largely supported the questionnaire response, but focused in greater detail on the content of the graduation certificate.

Models of the graduation certificate

Four 'models' were presented to participants, and they were invited to comment in particular on the main components of each rather than on the models as a whole. All four models contained the three main components that commanded most support in the questionnaire survey (key skills, national qualifications and wider achievements). One of the models floated the idea of an Entry Level/Level 1 certificate as well as an advanced (Level 3) Graduation Diploma. Another focused on learning processes (not just content), with the explicit aim of developing the learners' skills for independence, social responsibility and employment, as well as their general education. A third model embodied the notion of 'learning domains' through which certain negotiated activities would take place, leading to the acquisition of skills and formal qualifications. The models and components were each evaluated in terms of their accessibility (to learners), credibility (to young people and end users) and simplicity (to understand). Essentially, however, the key components remained largely the same as those proposed in the original SEU model (Table 6.1).

Participants were also asked to consider how a graduation certificate made up of such components might be adapted to meet the needs of adult learners, and how they might relate to other forms of overarching certificate at advanced level that had previously been proposed. The origins of the latter were the Dearing review of qualifications for 16–19-year-olds (Dearing, 1996) and subsequent development work by the QCA on such a certificate following the government's *Qualifying for Success* consultation in 1999 (DfEE, 1997). The links between the graduation certificate and these other forms of overarching certificate are the focus of the next section.

The graduation certificate as a form of overarching certificate

Since the early 1990s a number of forms of overarching certificate have been proposed at national level, although the term itself is relatively new. Its first appearance in official documentation would appear to be in the newly elected Labour Government's 16–19 consultation document *Qualifying for Success* (DfEE, 1997). The term was then adopted by the QCA, and used in subsequent ministerial correspondence as a generic term for any form of certificate made up of several component parts, each of which had some form of quality assurance and currency in its own right, but which, together formed a 'group award' with an overall rationale and coherence.

The School Certificate and Higher School Certificates which were replaced by O and A levels in 1951 were early forms of overarching certificate. The 1991 White Paper *Education and Training for the 21st Century* (DES/ED/WO, 1991) resurrected the idea under the guise of Ordinary and Advanced Diplomas (the former covering a number of key National Curriculum subjects, the latter a set level of achievement at advanced level broadly equivalent to HE matriculation requirements).

Although neither of these proposals went any further at that time, the idea of an Advanced Diploma was picked up in the Dearing Review in 1995/96 (Dearing, 1996) and given a new lease of life. This time, however, the focus was primarily on achievement at advanced level. The possibility of an intermediate and even foundation level version was acknowledged by Dearing, but was never fully developed at that time. But the idea of a differentiated form of certification, by 'volume' of achievement rather than level, was a key part of the Dearing proposals.

At advanced level, two forms of overarching certificate were proposed, with their different status clearly indicated by their names. These were to be, first, a National Certificate (linked firmly to the achievement of the government's national targets for education and training at that time, with a minimum expectation of 2 A levels, a full GNVQ or NVQ at Level 3 plus the three key skills of communication, application of number and information technology at level 3); and second, a National Diploma, like the Certificate but with additional requirements for the equivalent of an additional A level and coverage of four out of five broadly defined 'domains' across the programme as a whole. These domains (or 'areas of study' as Dearing called them) were mathematics; the sciences, technology and engineering; the arts and humanities; modern languages; and the way the community works (including business, economics, law, government and politics, psychology and sociology).

It was the requirement for coverage of specified areas of study that locates the Advanced Diploma firmly in the tradition of baccalaureate-style awards. The Diploma was conceived primarily as a vehicle to encourage and recognize the achievement of both depth and breadth of learning, with scope for additional breadth coming from subsidiary studies through the introduction of the new Advanced Subsidiary (AS) qualification, alongside the main A levels or GNVQ subject area. A more occupationally specific version of the Diploma, with an NVQ Level 3 as its core, was entertained by Dearing but never fully developed in the report, although the revamped modern apprenticeships owe something to the Diploma concept. (It is perhaps worth noting, in passing, that modern apprenticeships are themselves a form of group award or overarching certificate as defined earlier in this chapter).

The inspiration for Dearing's Advanced Diploma came more from previous (failed) attempts in England to broaden the advanced level curriculum (notably the Q & F and N & F proposals of the 1970s, and from Scottish Highers) than it did from European baccalaureate models or the IB. Ironically, the latter was clearly influential in shaping one of Dearing's other recommendations: the promotion of critical thinking, both within a revamped General Studies A level and as a free-standing AS qualification. The IB's theory of knowledge component was the basis for both of these Dearing proposals, but unlike in the IB, they were not an integral part of the Advanced Diploma itself. Had the latter required a component such as critical thinking/theory of knowledge, it may well have had greater appeal and attraction to some students and end-users by virtue of the value this would have added.

This brief retrospect into the Dearing proposals for a Certificate and Diploma has a direct relevance to the main subject of this chapter, the graduation certificate. Although, as has been argued above, the Diploma concept is clearly recognizable as being in the bac tradition, the Certificate in contrast had no such aspirations. Other than a very modest profession to broaden post-16 programmes through the addition of Key Skills (and then only the first three, not the wider Key Skills such as working with others, problem solving or improving one's own learning and performance), it is hard to see what added value the Certificate had to offer. This has always been, and remains, one of the key challenge facing any form of overarching certificate that is not in the baccalaureate tradition, where added value clearly derives from subject breadth (and often considerably more).

The 'added value' of the graduation certificate

The graduation certificate as first proposed by the SEU and subsequently developed by the QCA aimed to address this potential shortcoming through the inclusion of certain 'wider achievements', beyond formal qualifications and key skills. QCA's advice to ministers in December 1999 contained a revised version of the SEU exemplar certificate in which achievement was divided into two parts: Part A – National Qualifications and Part B – Wider Achievements (Table 6.2).

Table 6.2 An early QCA model of the graduation certificate (December 1999)

Part A: National qualifications	Part B: Wider achievements
Level 2 key/basic skills: • communication/literacy; • application of number/numeracy; • information technology. Level 2 qualifications: NVQ, GNVQ, GCSE, approved combinations (equivalent to 5 GCSEs). (National quality assurance)	Profile of achievements in the following areas: • additional skills (including the wide key skills); • experience of work; • community involvement; • personal interests and awards (eg in sport, music, the arts, driving theory etc). (Local/institutional authentication)
Routes to graduation: • school/college; • workplace; • individually negotiated learning (eg involving a mixture of the above and other settings such as the community, young offenders institutions etc).	Support for graduation: • individual guidance and mentoring (eg from the Connexions Service personal adviser); • personal development, possibly linked to Progress File and the Key Skill of improving own learning and performance.

As has been indicated earlier, the consultation in the summer of 2000 clearly supported such an emphasis on 'wider achievements', and this strand remained constant in subsequent versions of the graduation certificate, leading up to the QCA's advice in July 2000, at the end of the initial project phase. The July 2000 advice simplified the 'wider achievements' component still further into two more open-ended requirements: first, an individual achievement: meeting a personal challenge (for example, in creative, cultural, sporting, entrepreneurial and caring contexts); and second, a group achievement: working with others (for example, in the workplace and community).

It was hoped that such a formulation would promote the essential personal and interpersonal skills that graduation was trying to develop. It would also give maximum flexibility to young people and providers to choose the specific activities that would develop these skills, as well as the particular contexts in which they could be acquired and demonstrated. The advice also recommended that significant achievements (or 'milestones') *en route* to graduation should be recognized and celebrated alongside full graduation, using the Progress File (the replacement for the National Record of Achievement being piloted at that time).

This, at least, was an attempt at drawing a clear dividing line between the Graduation Certificate (which needed national quality assurance and currency) and Records of Achievement (which did not have and never really gained national currency). Indeed, the issue of quality assurance becomes critical when trying to establish whether the Graduation Certificate could ever be more than just a form of Record of Achievement.

How successful graduation might have been with regard to the value it added, over and above its component parts, can be judged by comparing its contents with those of three other types of overarching certificate that had

been, or were being, developed at or around the same time as the early grad-
uation certificate. Table 6.3 summarizes the contents of the Dearing National
Certificate, the College Diploma being developed with the FE sector by the
Further Education Development Agency (FEDA), and a Level 3 Overarching
Certificate commissioned (but never published) by QCA from FEDA and the
University of London Institute of Education (ULIE) in 1998. Moving from
left to right across the grid, it is evident that the Dearing National Certificate
had little 'additionality' to offer; in contrast, the FEDA/ULIE overarching
certificate appeared to offer most, in particular through its proposed 'connective' (or linking) study, an extended piece of project work designed to encourage students to integrate and synthesize the various discrete aspects of their
overall programme in new and imaginative ways.

Since none of the models in Table 6.3 have ever actually been implemented, it is unwise to speculate which might have proved to be most
appropriate, attractive, motivating and manageable in practice. It is safe to
say, however, that those models that are multi-dimensional, that aim to
address both the content and processes of learning, and that include an
additional 'integrating element' (akin to the theory of knowledge in the IB),
would seem to have most to offer from a number of perspectives. Above all,
they are clearly far more than just a record or certificate of achievement.
This is one of the two key issues which the Graduation Certificate (or, more
accurately, its successor) must address if it is to make any lasting contribution to the development of the 14+ curriculum over the next few years.

The other challenge is the quality assurance and currency of those additional elements that are not qualifications and which do not, therefore,
have their own quality assurance built in. This became a central strand of
the next stage of the QCA's work on graduation. Both the tone and content

Table 6.3 Main components of different forms of overarching certificate

	National Certificate (Dearing)	Graduation Certificate (SEU)	College Diploma (FE)	Overarching Certificate (FEDA/ULIE)
Depth/specialization	2 A levels (or equivalent)	Qualifications (and units)	Main career pathway	Specialist study
Additional breadth	Key Skills	Key Skills	Key Skills	Key Skills
Process aspect		Curriculum enrichment and community participation	Complementary skills/studies	Broadening studies
Other?		Personal development and achievement	Individual adult learning Work readiness/ experience	Management of learning Connective (linking) study

of the QCA's July 2000 advice made sure that there was no immediate prospect of ministers committing themselves to implementing the proposals at that stage. Indeed, without further work on quality assurance, graduation was never likely to be adopted as a viable policy initiative.

Quality assurance issues

The development of a framework for the quality assurance of the wider achievements (or 'activities' as the QCA came to call them) that were a component of the certificate was central to phase 2 of the QCA's work from autumn 2001 onwards. From the very beginning this had always proved problematic. While some of these activities (such as music awards, the Key Skills qualification and the Duke of Edinburgh award scheme) already have their own systems of quality assurance, many of the more informal activities engaged in by young people do not. Even the choice of the word 'activities' as opposed to 'achievements' could be seen as indicative of the type of quality assurance that might apply. When, for example, does an activity become an achievement? How is a 'demonstrable achievement' defined? Any one (or more) of the following might apply:

- meeting an agreed/external standard or benchmark or set of expected outcomes;
- commitment, as evidenced in the length of time spent participating in an activity;
- distance travelled (the improvement or gains made since starting);
- overcoming a particular challenge;
- self-organization (establishing some kind of autonomy or planning to meet a target and meeting it).

This range of interpretations is well illustrated in an extract from a paper on graduation submitted to the QCA by Henry Macintosh in the spring of 2000. Using 'hockey' as the example of an activity or achievement, he formulated the following statements, all of which could be used by an individual as evidence:

> I play hockey.
> I play left wing at hockey.
> I have played hockey since I was the age of five.
> I currently play hockey for Bath First XI.
> I have played hockey for Bath First XI for the past five years and have only ever been dropped as a result of illness.
> I am currently a member of the English National Hockey squad.
> I have played for England in international matches on 11 occasions.

These statements – which incidentally could be spoken, word processed or written – all indirectly suggest differences in the quality of the hockey played, although there is no direct reference in any of the statements to quality. They are all also capable of being evidenced and checked in a wide variety of ways, for example by witness testimony, newspaper cuttings, photography, film or match programmes. None of them, however, say anything comparative, nor do they say anything directly about how good the player is or needs to be.

They key question is: are we prepared to travel along and explore this kind of route for graduation, and even more important, are we prepared to sell hard and nationally a graduation certificate based upon these lines? We will need to decide upon what basis the certificate is awarded. Do we need to provide evidence about everything, whatever everything may mean, or are we prepared simply to award the certificate on the basis of selected evidence in relation to selected aspects of the model? These are crucial issues. If, however, we are not prepared to be flexible, then graduation will turn out to be yet another vehicle for short changing the already short-changed.

The real dilemma for policy makers is highlighted in Henry Macintosh's last sentence. Where is the optimum balance between quality assurance and flexibility to be struck in a national (as opposed to a local) award?

The history of the National Record of Achievement (NRA) is instructive in this respect. From the 1940s through to the 1980s, initiatives to provide pupils with broader statements of achievement when they left school were largely locally-based and founded on 'a concern to recognize attainments of those students who have traditionally not received examination certificates' (Broadfoot, 1986). It was not until 1984 (DES, July 1984) that the government committed itself to a national record of achievement prepared within a framework of national policy and principles.

The records of achievement sponsored by the government during the 1980s were not qualifications. There were both strengths and weaknesses in this position. One of the key strengths was that summary records could be presented as owned by students, thus providing scope for widening the concept of achievement beyond that considered amenable to formal assessment. In terms of weaknesses, summary records lacked wider credibility. Not only were all students entitled to them, but they only contained positive statements. Faced with such undifferentiated and undiscriminating documents, employers and trainers were reluctant to use them for selection purposes.

The body responsible for the NRA at that time was the National Council for Vocational Qualifications. NCVQ did not accredit bodies to quality assure the NRA; instead, it outlined the roles and responsibilities of individuals, teachers/trainers/supervisors and managers, and the principles of recording achievement (NCVQ, 1992). This approach was partly informed by a national survey of quality assurance for the NRA (Brockington and Fettes, 1993), the findings from which showed that, first, internal quality assurance was seen as important by all sectors, but a whole new bureaucracy for external quality assurance of the NRA was not wanted; and second, links needed to be made explicit between the NRA and existing quality assurance systems, such as Investors in People and inspection frameworks to minimize duplication of effort and resources.

It is perhaps not surprising that, faced with such issues almost a decade later, the QCA recommended a similar approach in December 2001 in its final (unpublished) report to the DfES on the implementation of a graduation certificate. The report acknowledged the tension between 'an award that is inclusive and one that has credibility with employers, HE and hence young people themselves'. It goes on to say, 'There is also a tension between the need to verify standards and the need to minimize workload and bureaucracy. In the case of the wider activities the quality assurance framework described below... provides a solution that is sufficiently robust without imposing a burden of a new kind of assessment or recording' (para 17).

The framework outlined in Annex 3 of the report attempts to balance these two imperatives: quality assurance and the avoidance of bureaucracy and duplication. The solution to this tension, it is suggested, lies in distinguishing between standards applicable to providers of wider activities (such as voluntary and statutory youth providers, school and colleges) and standards applicable to individual programmes (award schemes and programmes selected by individual young people).

The framework also establishes objectives for the wider activities themselves, the principles that should underpin them, and the processes by which young people are supported. The need for support is envisaged in relation to young people's choice of appropriate activities, to setting targets, to reflecting on what they have learnt, and to ensuring that they have met the requirements and can provide evidence of their participation and development. Responsibility is, therefore, shared.

Finally, since the inclusion of the wider activities in the award is designed to encourage young people to develop a range of personal and interpersonal skills (both for work and for life in general), a matrix of such skills is also provided. The report proposes that further work should be undertaken to pilot both the framework itself and various model 'transcripts' of achievements. The transcript is described as 'a document that provides the summary record of a young person's achievements in each of the components of the award. It lies between a formative process such as Progress File and a certificate presented at a ceremony' (para 6.1). Once again, explicit links between the graduation certificate and the Records of Achievement/Progress File are made in official documentation.

The other link, which is highlighted throughout the December 2001 report, in between the graduation certificate (as originally conceived) and what is called an 'overarching award'. It is clear that the December 2001 report was written in full knowledge that the Green Paper of February 2002 would place the development of an overarching award at the heart of any future 14–19 framework.

Graduation: resurrection and rebranding

Following the QCA's initial advice in July 2000, the graduation certificate was effectively placed on the policy back burner. Although not extinguished, it was not seen as a priority by ministers at that time, in spite of a fleeting moment in which the graduation concept might have found its way into the Labour Party election manifesto in the spring of 2001. But this would have been a high risk strategy given the scale of the further work which still needed to be done.

The cabinet reshuffle following Labour's election victory in June 2001 saw Estelle Morris promoted to Secretary of State. Suddenly the graduation certificate was back in the policy limelight. Although the term 'overarching award' had now taken over from 'graduation certificate', one of Estelle Morris's first speeches in her new role showed that earlier work on the latter had not been in vain. Speaking at the QCA Annual Conference in London on 26 June 2001, the Secretary of State referred explicitly to a possible place in the future for some kind of overarching award, which acknowledged and celebrated achievements beyond qualifications. Personally, she said, she would like to see community service being recognized as part of such an award, and in response to a question, she added that enrichment and extracurricular activities might well have a place. While formal qualifications would continue to be the most important element, she was keen to explore an overarching award that recognized these wider achievements. Significantly, she also referred to the possibility of certification at different levels. Under new management (and having shed its name), the graduation certificate looked set to rise from the ashes.

Concrete evidence for this was to be found in the 14–19 Green Paper, launched in February 2002 (DfES, 2002). What is perhaps most surprising about the model of an overarching award put out for consultation in February 2002 (Figure 6.1) is how close it was in design in many respects to both the original SEU model (Table 6.1) and QCA's December 1999 version (Table 6.2).

The diploma was to consist of three main components:

- a 'main qualification strand' (still linked firmly to the 'threshold' notion of Level 2 and Level 3 qualifications achieved);
- a 'common strand' (also of a threshold nature, in this case Level 2 attainment in literacy, numeracy and ICT);
- a 'wider activities strand' (designed to promote and recognize the development of activities which would encourage young people 'to live richer, fuller lives and play a part in the community') (DfES, 2002, para 4.13).

Unlike the original (and subsequent) graduation proposals, however, the inclusion of this third strand was far more tentative. The Green Paper states, 'We would welcome views on whether wider activities should be required to achieve the award, and, if so, how they should be recognized' (para 4.14).

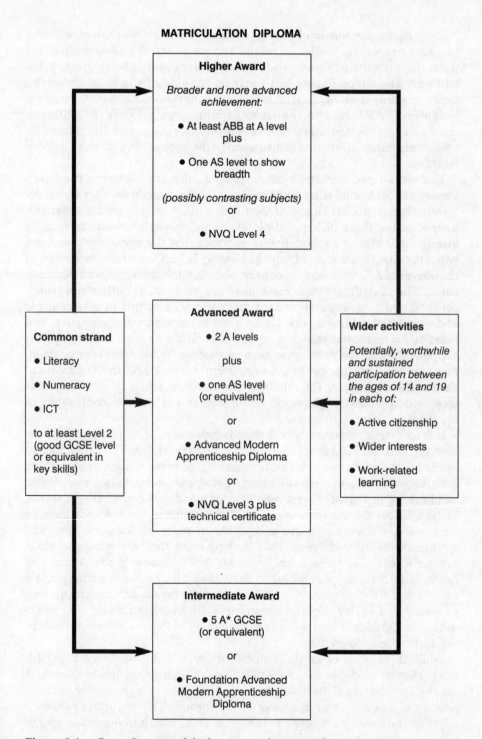

MATRICULATION DIPLOMA

Higher Award

Broader and more advanced achievement:

- At least ABB at A level plus

- One AS level to show breadth

(possibly contrasting subjects)
or

- NVQ Level 4

Common strand

- Literacy

- Numeracy

- ICT

to at least Level 2 (good GCSE level or equivalent in key skills)

Advanced Award

- 2 A levels

plus

- one AS level (or equivalent)

or

- Advanced Modern Apprenticeship Diploma

or

- NVQ Level 3 plus technical certificate

Wider activities

Potentially, worthwhile and sustained participation between the ages of 14 and 19 in each of:

- Active citizenship

- Wider interests

- Work-related learning

Intermediate Award

- 5 A* GCSE (or equivalent)

or

- Foundation Advanced Modern Apprenticeship Diploma

Figure 6.1   Green Paper model of an overarching award

Once again, the tension between needing to ensure that the assessment of young people's activities is 'robust and meaningful' while avoiding 'the potential bureaucracy and burden on teachers and others' (para 4.14) surfaces. The Green Paper clearly errs on the side of a light touch assessment regime, and explicitly refers to schemes such as Millennium Volunteers, ASDAN, and the Duke of Edinburgh's Award as automatically meeting the requirements for active citizenship and the pursuit of wider interests, although not necessarily the recognition of work-related learning.

The second and perhaps most surprising difference between the Green Paper proposals and what went before was the suggestion that a simpler alternative – 'a Certificate of Achievement' – might suffice after all, instead of the three different diplomas. This alternative reads both as an afterthought and as a sop to potential critics that the whole diploma idea, with its three levels (one of which, Higher, is really only an extension of the Advanced Level) was in danger of being too complex and sophisticated. The 'Certificate of Achievement', in contrast, is little more than a consolidated and undifferentiated record (or transcript) of all academic and vocational achievements. No mention is made of wider activities, and there is no threshold that has to be crossed for its award. Indeed, it is supremely inclusive in its attempt at providing 'a common leaving document for all young people in the same form' (para 4.16). In the context of earlier discussions in this chapter about records of achievement, it is clear where the Certificate of Achievement fits on the continuum of certification from ROA to Bac.

It is less clear, however, where the Matriculation Diploma fits. While the Intermediate and Advanced levels mirror very faithfully earlier design briefs for the graduation certificate, the Higher version hints at something both broader and more challenging. Paragraph 4.10 says, 'the Higher would recognize greater achievement (very good and contrasting A levels, or NVQ Level 4)'. As with the graduation certificate, broad vocational or occupational alternatives are acceptable in place of academic (general) qualifications. The diagram that accompanies the text goes one stage further in defining 'greater achievement' as at least a grade A and two grade Bs at A level, 'plus an AS to show breadth'. Such a formulation is a far cry from the heavily prescriptive, domain-based Advanced Diploma proposed by Dearing. Yet the concept of a differentiated award – a threshold, type Certificate and a more challenging Diploma – closely resembles the earlier Dearing models.

While there is no rationale or justification given in the Green Paper for the particular model of the Higher Diploma, a final paragraph in Chapter 4 on the International Baccalaureate is a stark reminder of the relative paucity of ambition and challenge of the former. This is further acknowledged in the passing reference to the value of critical thinking and theory of knowledge in which, we are told, the government 'will develop a new

A level to ensure that it can be studied and recognized within our proposed Matriculation Diploma'. Whether or not this is a belated attempt to address the unaddressed issue of the value added of such an award, already referred to in this chapter, is unclear.

The Matriculation Diploma proposals in the Green Paper could be seen as the coming together of two different traditions: the record of achievement (at two levels, Intermediate and Advanced) and a more sophisticated 'Higher' level award which offers a pale and diluted version of an overarching certificate designed to promote and reward breadth. Whether such a hybrid (a multi-level, differentiated award with a dual concept of achievement) could ever work remains to be seen. It is certainly hard to see how such a design could improve the coherence and intelligibility of an already over-complex system. On the other hand, the alternative 'Certificate of Achievement', for all its simplicity, hardly takes us beyond a primitive and rudimentary record of achievement (and even that is apparently limited to the achievement of qualifications).

Looking ahead

Technically, in policy terms at least, the graduation certificate passed away towards the end of 2001. Its legacy, however, has outlived its name. At the time of writing it is unclear which Green Paper model of an overarching award will be taken forward. However, it is now over a decade since overarching certificates of one kind or another first found their way into mainstream educational policy post-16. The concept has since been pushed down to the 14+ age range, making the likelihood of different levels of certification even more likely.

What was different about the graduation certificate (in contrast to other forms of overarching certificate) was that it began life as an intermediate level (Level 2) certificate. Pressure for a stepping stone to Level 2 has been a persistent feature of all subsequent development work. In contrast, other initiatives (notably the Dearing review) focused almost exclusively on the more prestigious (and, by definition, less inclusive) advanced level of certification. Although there were calls for a foundation and intermediate level version, the advanced level was always seen by Dearing as the key to getting the concept established. Other levels could then follow. The graduation certificate, in comparison, was launched in a policy context of social inclusiveness which was, ironically, consistently undermined by ministerial reluctance to entertain a pre-Level 2 version. Yet a Level 2 certificate without an advanced level award to progress to was seen as exclusive from a different perspective. Those learners for whom Level 2 presented no real challenge were unlikely to be motivated by an intermediate level award. This in itself would send powerful signals to the learners who were the real target for the initiative, as well as to potential users.

In conclusion, then, it would appear that there are still formidable obstacles to be overcome if an overarching award based on current models is ever to be successful. The main challenges for the future would appear to be:

- The creation of three levels of certification (foundation, intermediate and advanced) to match the three main levels in the National Qualifications Framework most appropriate to 14–19 education training and work. The refusal in the Green Paper proposals to entertain a foundation level diploma, with the award of a local 'record of progress' instead, is hardly satisfactory. While it is arguable whether there should also be an entry level certificate, there is a continuing need to address the issue of how progress towards foundation level can meaningfully be recognized and rewarded.
- The balance between commonality of content and components from 14–19 (such as in the wider activities that all young people should pursue, albeit with an element of choice) and differentiation (by level of achievement rather than age).
- The need to show how an overarching award (at each level) is more than the sum of its parts. The inclusion of an element that integrates or connects the other components and programme elements is one possible way forward. The lessons from the IB and other bac style awards, which provide a curriculum (not just an assessment) framework for learners, are worth drawing on here. One powerful incentive, given recent and continuing concerns about the overall burden of the assessment leading to formal qualifications, would be to find a way of making the overall volume of assessment of the certificate less than the cumulative load of the assessment of its individual parts.
- The need to protect and promote the wider achievements (or activities) component without adding to the overall assessment burden. That a degree of quality assurance of these aspects is necessary is indisputable. Whether this can be achieved in a non-bureaucratic and manageable way still needs to be tested in practice.
- The need for the certificate or diploma to have currency and credibility with employers, higher education and young people themselves. The failure of the National Record of Achievement in this respect underlines the importance of the two preceding points: the necessity for minimal quality assurance of the non-qualifications aspects, and the desirability of a clear and explicit value-added aspect. If these two can be got right, and the content of the certificate is seen as appropriate and relevant to life, work and further study, then currency and credibility will follow.

Conclusion

Although there are formidable challenges to overcome if any form of over-arching award is eventually to be implemented, this is one area of national policy where ministers (rightly) seem prepared to be patient. Changes to the advanced level curriculum have always been a slow and difficult process. It took some 50 years for A levels to change, 35 years for the Advanced Supplementary (AS) to be introduced and a further 15 years for it to be replaced by the new Advanced Subsidiary. Set against these timescales, overarching awards are still at a very early stage of development.

As group awards, overarching certificates inevitably depend upon select-ing the right individual component parts first, and then tackling the issue of what added value the certificate itself brings. This may involve the creation of some new component parts, some of which might themselves be qualifi-cations, as hinted at in the Green Paper proposal for an IB style Theory of Knowledge A level. The lead times in changing qualifications are notoriously long. Introducing a new qualification takes even longer. Most curriculum and qualifications reforms in the last decade have been criticized for being rushed, with inadequate time for teachers and institutions to prepare. Timescales for the national introduction of an overarching award look set to be more realistic, and the Green Paper proposals for 'pathfinders' (local collaborative groupings of schools, colleges and others to pilot the 14–19 proposals and the diploma in particular) are to be welcomed. A policy deci-sion to proceed by 2003, with further development work, proper piloting, trialling and evaluation built into the development cycle, would mean that 2005/2006 might be the earliest feasible date for its introduction. The contribution of the graduation certificate to this process may have been brief and ephemeral, but its legacy in terms of the content and design of any future overarching award looks set to endure.

References

Broadfoot, P (ed) (1986) *Profiles and Records of Achievement: A review of issues and practice*, Cassell Educational, London

Brockington, D and Fettes, T (1993) *Quality Assurance for the NRA*, NCVQ/DfEE, London

Dearing, Sir Ron (1996) *Review of Qualifications for 16–19 Year Olds*, SCAA, London

Department for Education and Employment (DfEE) (1997) *Qualifying for Success: A consultation paper on the future of post-16 qualifications*, DfEE, London

Department of Education and Science/Employment Department/Welsh Office (DES/ED/WO) (1991) *Education and Training for the 21st Century*, HMSO, London

Department for Education and Skills (DfES) (2002) *14–19: Extending opportuni-ties, raising standards*, HMSO, London

National Council for Vocational Qualifications (1992) *Action Planning and the National Record of Achievement*, NCVQ, London

Qualifications and Curriculum Authority (QCA) (2001) *Managing* Curriculum 2000 *for 16–19 students*, QCA, London

Social Exclusion Unit (1999) *Bridging the Gap: New opportunities for 16–18 year olds not in education, employment or training*, HMSO, London

7

| Four perspectives on reform |

This chapter brings together four differing perspectives on the post-compulsory curriculum, each of which is designed to provide the reader with an insight into contemporary attitudes to reform held by the various users and end-users of the system.

The first two contributors, Jonathan Stewart and Phil Butler, were invited to reflect upon recent initiatives in the maintained and college sectors respectively, to introduce an overarching award that would formally recognize achievement beyond the scope of existing qualifications, as well as encourage greater breadth in individual programmes of study.

This emphasis on breadth and curriculum enrichment provides the focus of the third contribution from Graham Able, which represents the views of a significant group of stakeholders in the A level system – those from the independent sector – and explores the advantages of adopting a baccalaureate-style qualification.

Finally, the views of employers are presented by Sue Peacock, who argues the case for the introduction of a broader, overarching qualification not only to establish parity of esteem between general and vocational awards, but also to ensure that the skills needed for the workforce of the future are effectively delivered through a more inclusive curricular framework.

George Abbot School and the Surrey Graduation Certificate

Jonathan Stewart

The school

The *Curriculum 2000* reforms initially appeared to provide schools and colleges in England and Wales with the opportunity to implement a qualifications framework that could offer students a genuinely broader curriculum than had previously been available, while still upholding the so-called 'gold standard'.

George Abbot School is a large 11–19 mixed comprehensive school in Guildford with a sixth form of approximately 400 students, most of whom study for A level qualifications. In the light of the government's reforms outlined in *Qualifying for Success* (DfEE, 1997), George Abbot School, like so many other institutions, started considering the kind of curriculum package it could offer its students. In true post-Dearing spirit, the notion of a broader curriculum and the opportunity it gave students to be accredited for both academic and extra-curricular achievement, was fully supported. The vision of citizenship within the National Curriculum, outlined by David Blunkett, the then Secretary of State, had always met with considerable support at George Abbot School. The enrichment programme already offered by the school to post-16 students allowed for flexibility: it was not therefore difficult to make it compulsory within a revised sixth-form curriculum. It was, however, disappointing to find that the student progress file, effectively a remodelled Record of Achievement, was to be postponed for a few years. Sadly, this was to prove true of other initiatives embodied in *Curriculum 2000*, and in the school's view, the government abandoned the chance to introduce genuinely radical reform in favour of a more cautious and piecemeal approach.

None the less, the implementation of *Curriculum 2000* seemed an ideal context in which to introduce a local, overarching certificate alongside a broader curriculum. In effect, what was being offered was a type of baccalaureate programme that offered students real flexibility in their choice of options at A level. To ensure that students would follow a genuinely broad curriculum, General Studies or Critical Thinking was made compulsory for all students to AS level unless they opted for the Community Sports Leadership Award (CSLA). The approach, however, was something of a gamble. By introducing a broader curriculum the school had to convince both Year 11 students and their parents that doing more than they might have to at other sixth form centres or colleges was in their interests. *Curriculum 2000* was eventually placed at the heart of the school's recruitment strategy, which was used not only as a means of briefing students and their parents about the key changes ahead, but also to enable them to subscribe to the vision of a broader and more inclusive sixth form curriculum.

One of the main aims of this version of *Curriculum 2000* was to set a broad, challenging and relevant goal for students in post-16 education, and reward them for a full range of achievement rather than for qualifications alone. Such an intention is endorsed by the recent QCA report entitled *On the Implementation of a Graduation Certificate* (2001), particularly in relation to the notion of the added value inherent in such a qualification. While the school was of the opinion that the implementation of this kind of initiative would enhance students' prospects of admission to higher and further education or employment, subject staff were also keen to improve the overall standard of achievement at the post-compulsory level. This was particularly true for those students who tended to drop down to a two A level programme by the middle of their sixth form career.

The model

The model offered to students for entry in September was as follows:

- An academic core at Advanced level consisting of their AS/A2 subjects including General Studies/Critical Thinking or CSLA.
- A core skills programme within General Studies/Critical Thinking, which would be assessed by the core skills tutor and placed in the student's portfolio. In order to graduate, students would need to achieve Level 3 criteria in at least two of the main core skills.
- Application of number, communication and IT.
- A citizenship element consisting of 45 hours' worth of school or community service plus 30 hours of individual achievement.

The academic core would, it was acknowledged, take care of itself, but core skills would be taught via General Studies or Critical Thinking. (The exception was IT, which would be taught discretely within the General Studies rotation.) An in-house core skills model rather than the external key skills programme was adopted for three simple reasons. First, the key skills on offer at the time appeared to be over-prescriptive, and the assessment regime too cumbersome in the context of their value for the end-users, higher education institutions (HEI) and employers. (Interestingly, the CBI's report *Towards a Skills Revolution* (1989) had argued that the softer skills such as 'working with others' and 'problem solving' were, in fact, more useful to employers.) Second, since key skills were not compulsory, there seemed to be no obligation to make students take on the additional burden of what appeared to be a time-consuming and overly complex programme. Finally, as there was no financial incentive, the overall case for key skills seemed a weak one.

No distinction was made between vocational A levels and their academic counterparts, as they are timetabled and grouped in the same way. This lack of distinction was felt to be essential if a graduation certificate is to be valued by all and not seen as either an elitist or second-rate award. A more important factor was that students understood that they were embarking on an 'advanced level' programme of study.

Students applying for a place at George Abbot School were thus offered the chance to 'graduate' from the sixth form, and were placed on a programme that would subsequently allow them to achieve this if they so wished. In the year of the introduction of the revised curriculum, the sixth form had its highest number of students following an advanced level programme in the history of the school. In addition, students were offered an LEA-endorsed 'Surrey Sixth Form Graduation Certificate'. The sixth form team and the graduation consortium continued to work on the concept of the student portfolio, which the school then piloted with Year 13 students.

As part of the school's curriculum development plan, a wide-ranging review of *Curriculum 2000* was initiated with the following objectives in mind:

- to review the progress of the new specifications;
- to record areas of concern and so identify strategies that would address them;
- to examine the extent and quality of subject induction programmes in Year 12;
- to review pastoral elements of sixth form induction;
- to identify the strengths and weaknesses within the sixth form overall.

Evidence was taken from subject departments, and a third of the student population in Year 12 were asked to complete a questionnaire which focused on:

- the quality of lessons (specific identification of subject 1–4 scale);
- homework (variety/deadlines);
- preferred teaching styles;
- the quality of the applications/recruitment procedure;
- positive aspects of the sixth form;
- areas for improvement within the sixth form.

A focus group of students was established, whose membership reflected a range of options and academic ability. They were asked to comment on their understanding of *Curriculum 2000*, to give their views on graduation, and to discuss the time allocated to homework and part-time study.

The response to this curriculum review produced some interesting results. First, regarding workload, students and staff felt there had been a visible increase. Although extracurricular work continued, commitment to it may have been compromised. Students commented that four AS subjects were as demanding as A levels, and that there was not enough time to grasp the content in some cases. Significantly, there was a feeling among both staff and students that in some instances studying had become a process of 'ticking items off' on the specifications rather than exploring them in detail.

Second, in terms of the level of demand asked for by the AS examinations, students complained that examination overload had become a profoundly negative factor in their sixth form experience. Subject staff commented that some examination questions had been more generic than students were expecting, and that coursework assignments were being set while preparation for examinations was already underway.

Third, when asked about the quality of teaching and learning, students expressed confidence in the quality of education they were receiving, but voiced concern that education in its broader sense has been lost. It was as if learning were perceived solely in terms of assessment, rather than as a stimulating experience *per se*.

Fourth, students generally welcomed the idea of greater breadth and appreciated the fact that they had greater 'choice' because of an expanded curriculum. Significantly, the philosophy behind General Studies was applauded by most of the students, but they felt it still lacked credibility because of the rather ambivalent attitude adopted towards the subject by many HEIs.

Finally, some important questions were raised by the review process, such as whether AS exams might not be taken in July, and whether the assessment regime at this level could not be made more flexible. Tutors and subject staff added that the increased maturity in Year 13 students compared with those in Year 12 might not lead to an increase in entries for modular examinations in January of Year 13. Students obviously felt frustrated, as one commented, 'to be guinea pigs again'. And as another remarked: 'We shouldn't be seen to be fumbling around in the dark. This is our future!'

However students appeared to accept, if not embrace, the graduation concept. They recognized that they were doing more than their A level forebears, but accepted the fact that in order to compete in the global arena of the 21st century jobs market – and indeed, higher education – the model currently offered by George Abbot School is a fitting one.

Beyond this school-focused initiative, post-16 consortia meetings organized by the Surrey LEA allowed heads of sixth forms to discuss the graduation idea with colleagues. Two other schools subsequently became involved, Collingwood in Camberley and Warlingham School in the east of the county. This, in turn, gave rise to the Surrey Sixth Form Graduation Certificate, which has subsequently been endorsed by the LEA, the Learning and Skills Council as well as the Regional Compact Accord HEIs in Surrey, Hampshire, Berkshire, Sussex and the southwest London area. As a result of this liaison, the graduation certificate model has been modified further to meet the needs of this wider group. Resources and templates to support the certificate have since been developed, and a further nine schools in Surrey now plan to follow the graduation model.

In conclusion, the school feels confident about the curriculum model it is providing, and this view is endorsed by the fact that many Surrey schools are now seeking to join the graduation certificate consortium. (A similar model is also underway in Liverpool.) Students are now offered a genuinely broad curriculum through the compulsory core of General Studies/Critical Thinking. At the same time the desire for flexibility of choice in the academic content of their curriculum has also been met. Moroever, students have participated in the planning for the graduation ceremony in September 2002 at the University of Surrey, and around 75 per cent of the cohort should graduate in the summer of 2003 (a figure that should be exceeded with the current student body in Year 12).

What started out as a bold experiment now looks set to have increasing currency given the proposals outlined in the Government's Green Paper *14–19: Extending opportunities, raising standards* (DfES, 2002). The main difference appears to lie in the concept of the matriculation diploma and a separate certificate of achievement proposed in the paper. By creating such a division, the government may well be in danger of reinventing the academic and vocational divide which the graduation certificate has sought to eliminate.

The QCA report on the implementation of a graduation certificate model states, 'Graduation or an overarching award would add status to enrichment or wider activities and enhance young people's prospects' (QCA, 2001). The debate surrounding the implementation of an English baccalaureate is timely and relevant, as *Curriculum 2000* continues to pose problems. There is still much work to be done, but it is to be hoped that the graduation model will have a key influence on the 14–19 consultation process ahead.

The College Diploma: a case study

Phil Butler

Introduction

The development of the College Diploma resulted from work carried out from November 1998 onwards, by a representative body of people working in the post-16 sector for further education and learning. The term 'College Diploma' is a working title used by the group, which later suggested that the award be retitled 'the Learning and Skills Diploma'. The Diploma is seen as a signature award for the post-16 sector: all learners, both 14–19 and adult learners, can work towards achieving it. Learners can accumulate credits towards the Diploma in a range of learning environments including schools, sixth form colleges, colleges of further education, work-based learning providers and some higher education institutions. The award can also be achieved through distance learning.

The College Diploma is not perceived as a new qualification to add to the 16,000 plus qualifications already available to learners after the age of 16. It is seen rather as an overarching signature award, which will encourage learners in the 14–19 age group to follow a broader range of learning opportunities, together with the aim of promoting lifelong learning after the age of 19.

The main purpose of the College Diploma is to enable learners to have their success and achievements recognized and celebrated at any level and at any time (although the expected age of achieving the award is 19 years old and upward). Moreover, a learner could achieve the Diploma at 'certificate' level by successfully completing achievements in the five proposed fields for recording and celebrating success.

The College Diploma in context

The College Diploma was developed during the period 1998 to 2001 and conceived at a time when the post-16 sector in further education was looking for its own brand of signature award. Schools had the newly-proposed 'Graduation Certificate', while universities had degrees. Further education had a mass of confusing qualifications which, it was felt, needed an overarching framework in order to give recognition to a broader range of learner success, and to identify simple and clear pathways for further learning for all groups in our society, especially under-represented groups.

The development of a signature award for the sector was proposed by a number of further education and sixth form college principals. A management group was then formed which invited curriculum practitioners from the sector to join a development team to work on the new qualification. This development team, including representatives from 12 further education colleges from across the country, met for the first time in November 1998. Its brief was to devise a signature award for the post-16 sector, one that offered a broader and inclusive curriculum and would lead to a continuous raising of standards in the sector. It would also be delivered through a flexible, credit-based, coherent and unitized curriculum.

The team looked at the strengths of the English system, with its depth of knowledge and rigorous forms of assessment linked to national standards. It also took account of a number of key issues in the post-16 sector, which schools, colleges and work-based learning providers in the UK were facing at that time. These included:

- a mass of 16,000+ qualifications offered to learners, parents and employers, which had conflicting rules of combination, and lacked clear, simple goals and career pathways for the learners;
- the academic–vocational divide in qualifications, which devalued the vocational pathway compared with the traditional academic route;
- the need for inclusion, providing access to learning from wider groups in society and the encouragement of lifelong learning.

In addition, the development team considered curriculum models of best practice from around Europe. It also examined the community college system in the United States, and individual members visited San Diego City College in California and Harold Washington College in Chicago to look at the Associate Degree model. The Associate Degree is offered by community colleges, and provides a nationally recognized overarching award within the United States: it is flexible, coherent, credit-based and unitized. It also allows people to work towards the final award at their own pace, offers a broader-based curriculum, and has a student transcript at its centre for recording and celebrating learner success on an incremental basis.

Some of the key elements of the Associate Degree were eventually incorporated into the development of the College Diploma, in particular the student transcript, which not only recognizes achievement but was perceived as a means of increasing the motivation of learners.

Above all, the curriculum group saw the College Diploma as an inclusive award, something to which all learners could aspire, and which they could work towards. To achieve this goal, existing attitudes towards – and measures of – learner success were to be viewed differently. Succinctly, learner success would be recorded, reported and celebrated at the credit level, as and when the learner achieves. In this sense, learners working towards the Diploma were regarded as being just as important as learners actually achieving the full award. None the less, the group acknowledged that gaining full qualifications would still be seen as the goal for most learners in the foreseeable future. It also recognized the need to provide excellent guidance before, during and at the conclusion of a learner's programme.

The structure of the Diploma

The developmental process was led by the City College Birmingham, supported by 11 other colleges located in England (Barnsley, Birmingham (South), Bournemouth and Poole, Cambridge, Cornwall, Halton, London (Greenwich, Lewisham, South Thames and Tower Hamlets) and Nottingham (New)). This group was, in turn, supported by two community college systems located in the United States (Chicago and San Diego). Representatives from the awarding bodies Oxford, Cambridge and RSA (OCR), Edexcel, City and Guilds, NCFE and the National Open College Network provided guidance, while further support and advice was received from representatives of the Further Education Development Agency (FEDA) and the Learning and Skills Council (LSC).

The group met on a regular basis over a period of two years, and consulted widely with representatives from other interested groups, such as employers and higher education. Initial contact was also made with representatives from organizations working on developing models for credit accumulation and transfer in England, Wales, and Northern Ireland.

To obtain further feedback on the ideas, format and framework of the proposed Diploma, a number of presentations were made around the country. The concept of a College Diploma was thus presented to a group of over 50 teaching staff from a number of colleges, to obtain the views of what became designated as a group of 'critical friends' – a body of teaching and learner support staff who commented on the structure and the feasibility of the proposed award on a practical level with students. Comments on the Diploma were also obtained from representatives from higher education and employers, through discussions held with the members of the curriculum team. Generally, the comments received were very supportive in favour of piloting of the award.

Following this period of consultation, the College Diploma was finally presented to a national conference held in London during the summer of 1999, and at the Association of Colleges (AoC) conference in Harrogate. It was also presented to a group of chancellors from various community college systems based in the United Sates during a conference held in Dublin the following year.

The five fields

The proposed framework incorporates five separate fields of learning to record learner success and achievements in:

- Field A, Individual learning (nine credits at any level).
- Field B, Key Skills (three credits at Level 3).
- Field C, Experiences of the world of work (one credit at Level 1 / two at Level 3).
- Field D, Main career pathway (twenty four credits at Levels 3 or 4).
- Field E, Complementary studies (three credits at Level 2 or above).

Each field contains an agreed number of credits, which a learner must achieve to gain the full award. The number of credits indicate the importance of each of the five fields in relation to the Diploma as a whole. To receive the full award, learners must achieve success at the credit level indicated in the five fields. While credits at any level can be recorded in each of the fields, only those that reach an agreed level can be included towards the award of the full College Diploma.

To gain the full award, the learner must achieve a total of 48 credits. Through the credit accumulation transfer process, each qualification or part of a qualification is given a credit rating. These are then recorded in the Learner Transcript as and when they are achieved, in the belief that incremental achievement encourages learners to progress from their initial success.

Field A, Individual learning (nine credits)

Field A covers individual learning, and is considered to be the most important field in the College Diploma. This field is regarded as important because any achievements by a learner at any level can be acknowledged: for instance, 14-year-old school children taking a taster course in a vocational area at a local college or work-based provider would have this achievement recognized through the Diploma. Enrichment programmes can also be recognized here, if the learner wishes to have recognition for such achievements.

In addition, the curriculum group thought that this field was likely to be the area of learning where most adults coming back into learning after a break would start their programme of study. To be inclusive and allow all learners to gain some recognition for their achievements, students within this field may include credits gained at any level from Entry through to Level 4 (HE). Therefore, everyone would be working towards the full Diploma, and thus in one important sense 'everything counts'.

Field B, Key Skills (nine credits)

Field B covers Key Skills, which are seen as important credentials in the world of work today. Key Skills achieved at Level 3 will count towards the full College Diploma. Key Skills at Levels Entry, 1 and 2 are still seen as important and can be counted in other fields, such as Field A, or they can count towards Part 1 of the Diploma if desired.

To gain the full College Diploma, Field B must contain three credits at Level 3 in information learning technology, application of number and communications.

Equivalent qualifications or parts of qualifications can be used to count in this field where appropriate, for example, an AS module for Mathematics.

Field C, Work (three credits)

The wide-ranging scope of Field C recognizes and records on the transcript both the learners' experiences of the world of work and/or their readiness for the world of work. The credits allocated to Field C can be claimed from vocational or professional qualifications. Credits can also be claimed through recognition of actual work experience or the demonstration of readiness for work (for example, recent training). This field does not exclude learners who might have obtained skills but have yet to experience the world of work.

Credits demonstrating transferable employment skills (for example, the wider key skills such as problem solving) are also accepted. Similarly, credits that demonstrate awareness of the world of work could also be included, while learners can equally claim accreditation for prior learning.

Field D, Main career pathway (twenty four credits)

To provide the underpinning depth and breadth of study, Field D is seen as the main career/vocational pathway of the College Diploma. It provides the solid spine of achievements for the award in a wide range of qualifications at Level 3.

More importantly, vocational and academic qualifications are given parity of esteem through the system of credit rating. Credits can be claimed in terms of both full and part-achieved qualifications, as promoted under *Curriculum 2000*. To demonstrate a clear career pathway, a coherent combination of differing units and modules would be expected by both employers and higher education.

The achievement of full qualifications is still seen as important under the present national system. Thus Field D would reflect any changing individual aspirations in the area of work, higher education and in the case of adults, opportunities to return to learn.

Entry-Level 2 credits can be recorded in this field and counted towards Part 1 of the College Diploma. Credits achieved at Level 4 (for example, those for foundation degrees) can also be included.

Field E, Complementary studies (three credits)

Field E is concerned with recognizing achievements that are complementary to the main career pathway, but are not recognized in other fields in the Diploma. This allows the learner to include other skills, interests and strengths, and to emphasize the individual thinking behind the choice of certain career pathways.

Complementary studies also allows for the recognition of skills from a wider area of learning, for example languages, science or citizenship. It additionally provides recognition of transferable generic skills (for example text processing, problem solving and critical thinking). Higher level Mathematics could also be included.

Field E can additionally function as an alternative field that can record complementary achievement when other fields of the College Diploma are seen to be full.

Examples of complementary studies include:

Main career	Complementary skills/studies
Media production	Shorthand/A Level Government and Politics
Hairdressing	Cosmetology/Accounting/Marketing/Customer Service
Medicine and related	Counselling/Grief counselling/Accounting

Part 1 of the College Diploma

Some learners may decide not to work towards the full award of the Diploma since they may not feel that they have the confidence to gain credits at the higher levels. To give these learners recognition for their achievements, and encouragement to continue with their programme of learning, they can be awarded Part 1 of the award, as illustrated below:

- Field A, Individual learning: six credits at any level.
- Field B, Key Skills: three credits at Level 1 in the each Key Skill.
- Field C, Experiences of the world of work: one credit at Level 1.
- Field D, Main career pathway: one credit at Level 1.
- Field E, Complementary studies: one credit at Level 1.

The current status of the College/Learning and Skills Diploma

A great deal of development work and consultation has gone into the production of the College Diploma. However, with all the changes that occurred in the year 2000–01 (including the formation of the Learning and Skills Council), resources and energy were diverted away from this new award. The entire initiative was devised in order to present a motivating and prestigious goal for learners, a vehicle for promoting a modern curriculum for students in the 14–19 sector, as well as adult learners. Although well received by the organizations within the post-compulsory sector, the Diploma never achieved the recognition and support from the Department for Education and Skills (DfES) – or indeed from the government – that it really deserved. Attention has instead focused on the proposed 'Graduation Certificate' for the 16–19 age group.

None the less, the original curriculum group is still interested in taking the College Diploma forward as an example of a model of successful curriculum innovation which promotes inclusion, lifelong learning, and widens participation. However, the need for external support and additional resources for such a project remains a vital factor.

Close links with the community college system in the United States have been maintained, especially with the development of an International Associate Degree Program, which has been offered successfully by a group of partner colleges in the UK. It is interesting to note that the government's vision for future curriculum reform embodied in the consultation document *14–19: Extending opportunities, raising standards* (DfES, 2002) includes the proposal for an overarching Matriculation Diploma award for the sector, a proposal that bears striking similarities to the College Diploma.

In the light of these recent developments, the College Diploma group feels even more strongly that the Diploma should be given serious consideration.

It is inclusive, will raise standards, encourage lifelong learning and the desire of our citizens to return to learning. The slogan on the side of the bus from the City Colleges of Chicago reads: 'Education is not a preparation for life: education is life', and we believe this to be so.

Table 7.1 The College Diploma structure

Field A	Field B	Field C	Field D	Field E
Individual adult learning	Key Skills ICLT Number Communication	Work readiness/ experience	Main career pathway	Complementary studies/skills
9 credits	9 credits	3 credits	24 credits	3 credits
Any level (entry level–3/4)	KS Level 3/4 (3 credits per KS area)	2 at Level 3 + 1 Level 2 (or L3)	Level 3 (may include L4)	Level 2 or above
Individual claim All credits registered on transcript Recognizes local, personal and national specialism/ perspective	eg European Driver's Licence (ECDL) and KS Level 3 Level 4 and A level/AS.AVCE Advanced modules and Equivalent vocational credits	eg NVQ units or OCN units in Careership or Professional qualification or APEL of current/ previous experience	Full qualification eg 2 A levels or combination of units eg AVCE, NVQ or Access to HE (1:1) or Equivalent credits in L3 vocational qualifications (**FULL** qualifications are important)	Unit(s) of language (modern/ community) or Unit(s) of citizenship or Comp skills eg business/ accounting or Generic skills eg text processing or Intermediate level units that are different from Field D

An independent view of the baccalaureate

Graham Able

The curriculum framework proposed in this section owes much to the ideas discussed with several different groups and with many individuals over the last four years. These discussions have, in turn, reaffirmed my own commitment to the English tradition of a liberal education, and while the need for some prescription is recognized, this is accompanied by a strong desire to retain depth while creating more breadth and delaying specialization. Above all, a return to differentiation is sought, which will set individual learners appropriate and attainable targets.

Although the independent sector is largely confined to institutions offering only the more academic routes towards 18+ qualifications and higher education, a number of the ideas here have been influenced by the views of those with a wider range of teaching experience.

One can regard the International Baccalaureate and the traditional English A level system as the two limits of a pendulum swing. What follows is an attempt to stop the pendulum in the middle and achieve the best of both approaches. In addition to this, there is convincing evidence that the most important skills for a successful and productive adult life are learnt in the co-curricular activities – I am using the American term since it emphasizes their importance, rather than the British 'extra-curricular' – fostered by schools and not easily susceptible to formal teaching in the classroom. Given that these skills are of great importance, some recognition of the co-curricular would seem to be appropriate, although any formalized assessment in this area would be difficult and probably self-defeating.

The key to this 'ideal' model is the freeing up of the final three years of secondary schooling for advanced level work, which would inevitably have a terminal impact on GCSE as we know it. It also implies a raising or lowering of the leaving age for compulsory education by at least one year, despite the fact that there is an increasing national expectation that all will continue 'in learning' to age 18. In addition, some might argue that a threshold level of attainment might be a better criterion for leaving full-time education than the arrival of a particular birthday.

Although the National Curriculum was, on balance, an improvement on the *laissez-faire* approach to the curriculum in many schools up to that point, it was originally too prescriptive to Key Stage 4, and possibly remains so to Key Stage 3. One can, however, accept the relevance and sense of nationally examined and accredited qualifications in mathematics, English, science and perhaps a modern foreign language, taken at a stage where pupils may sign off from some of these and start to pursue major differentiation in their studies. The preferred model would see this happening at the end of Year 10 (or at whatever age was deemed appropriate for a given student to reach this stage). All other subjects, some of which would be discontinued at this point, could be assessed and accredited by individual schools, and this process checked by sampling or inspection.

From Year 11 differentiation and specialization could then occur. Those taking a more academic route could cope with at least seven AS levels over the following two years. This would give genuine broadening to the advanced curriculum: there is an argument for some prescription, but this should leave much more scope for choice than the restrictive regime of the International Baccalaureate. One could support compulsory mathematics and English and probably a foreign language as well, although not necessarily a modern one.

Alternatively, a domain approach could be used to ensure sufficient breadth at this level.

For those wishing to take more vocationally orientated routes at this stage, genuinely different qualifications, tailored to the needs of students, would be preferable to the apparent current trend of sacrificing this approach on the false altar of supposedly demonstrable equivalence. For example, the BTEC/City and Guilds approach has produced much more positive results for students following such courses than the GNVQ/Vocational A level route designed to replace it. Students' needs at this stage are different, and we should have enough flexibility in any new system to encourage the maximum number of young people to enjoy their education beyond Level 2 and gain meaningful qualifications from it. The failure rates in the 2001 GNVQ/Vocational A levels results were a national disgrace: we must learn from this and develop vocational routes that are effective, enthuse students and produce worthwhile qualifications. In this respect, the possible role of apprenticeships should be considered carefully as a part of the post-Level 2 vocational curriculum.

Year 13 could be spent by those taking an academic route as now, on three or exceptionally four A levels. In order that these should be totally fit for purpose, there is a strong argument for the inclusion of some more difficult advanced-extension award-type questions in all subjects. More finely differentiated grades (possibly A1 and A2) could be awarded, and this would help in the selection process for the most popular and demanding university courses. It would also obviate the need for additional examinations for which not all schools prepare equally. There would remain a completely free choice of subject in this final year. It is essential that any new differentiated top grades are based on more challenging questions and on defined criteria. A statistical A* grade based on current material would be more a test of mechanical accuracy than a badge of intellectual distinction.

Given the concerns about plagiarism – which have been greatly magnified by universal access to the Internet – coursework should also be restricted to that which can be accomplished under test conditions in classroom, laboratory or studio. Much of what is done currently is time-consuming and of dubious academic merit. On the other hand, there is much to be said for an extended essay/research project, which could be taken on any of the subjects studied to AS level as part of the overall requirement. This would provide good training for higher education and beyond.

Turning to the importance of the co-curricular, one could envisage a minimum participation level, measured in hours, in each of three areas: service, cultural and athletic. At least one of these activities should involve working in a group. There is also an argument for including a minimal level of work experience for all students. Together, these activities help students develop interpersonal skills, self-awareness and self-discipline, all of which are essential for their future success. Group activities are particularly important, as the ability to work in partnership with others is an essential life skill for adult life. In each case, the number of hours required should be sufficient to show sustained participation, but not so extensive as to restrict flexibility.

When it comes to minimum standards to achieve a broader qualification along the lines of a baccalaureate-type diploma, these could include a minimum of two passes at A level (or its equivalent) and at least three others at AS level. However, the question of prescription is a difficult one. Certainly any diploma should demand a minimum of Level 2 qualifications in mathematics, English, a foreign language and science, but many would wish to see a requirement for at least the first two to AS level. Perhaps the best compromise would involve the use of generously defined domains for some enforced breadth beyond Level 2. For instance, there could be a requirement for an AS or equivalent from each of the following three domains (the lists are illustrative and not meant to be exhaustive):

- **Quantitative/numerical:** this would include mathematics, the sciences, economics and business studies.
- **Communications/linguistics:** English, modern or classical foreign languages would all be offered.
- **Philosophical:** this could be the theory of knowledge (from the International Baccalaureate), critical thinking, religious studies or philosophy.

Domains (a concept supported by Dearing) would have the added advantage of being more readily adapted to vocational qualifications. At all levels there is a strong case for subsidiarity, so that a higher qualification would automatically subsume a lower one. Thus on a points-count system, once a student has achieved an A level in Mathematics, the points for any Level 2 or AS examination in this subject would no longer count. Similarly, a student progressing confidently to an AS level in French could safely bypass any assessment for the Level 2 qualification. This would reduce further the need for external assessment, and allow lower levels to be bypassed where appropriate.

If competence in ICT is still regarded as an issue – and increasingly, this will not be the case with generations brought up to treat computers in the way that some of us used slide rules in the past – then some sort of competence-based certificate in ICT would seem much more appropriate than a formal academic examination. Such a qualification could be issued by schools and colleges or it could be delivered via online, on-demand testing. Graded tests – as in music – could be a useful mechanism to encourage progression.

Table 7.2 sets out the curriculum pattern this model would anticipate from Year 7 through to Year 13 on an academic route. Similar patterns would apply to those opting for a more vocational approach.

Table 7.2 Possible curricular pattern

Year 7 Year 8	KS3 National Curriculum (condensed)
Year 9 Year 10	KS4 Core of mathematics, English, science and modern foreign language + options
Year 11 Year 12	AS levels (or vocational equivalents) in 7 subjects with some domain-based prescription for breadth. Critical thinking or theory of knowledge as a core element.
Year 13	A levels (or vocational equivalents) in 3 or 4 subjects. Some more challenging questions to give added discrimination in top grades.

Table 7.3 shows the requirements for the award of a baccalaureate-style diploma under this model. Such diplomas could be differentiated both by an overall points score and by the individual results contained therein. Thus there would be no good reason for awarding merits or distinctions on the diploma itself.

Table 7.3 Minimum requirements for diploma

At KS4	National qualification at Level 2 in mathematics, English, science and a modern foreign language
At AS level	At least 5 passes to include domains of (a) mathematics/science (or equivalent) and (b) communication plus theory of knowledge/initial thinking
At A level	Any 2 passes (or equivalent)
Other evidence of ICT competence	
Co-curricular	50 hours service activity 50 hours work experience 50 hours cultural activity 50 hours sporting activity

The strengths of this model are that it allows more students to spend longer on more advanced work. It broadens the scope of their studies beyond that of the traditional English sixth form, and yet it retains, or even increases, the depth of A level study for those following an academic route. For the more vocationally orientated students, it should embody sufficient flexibility to include more young people in a meaningful educational process for longer and with more enthusiasm. It also gives overdue recognition to the importance of co-curricular activities in the wider educational process.

The model also demands the restructuring of many schools and colleges that currently stop or start at the 16+ divide, but I hope that improving the substance of our education is more important than defending imperfect and inflexible structures.

An employer's perspective

Sue Peacock

Employers do not generally subscribe to the hard-line view that education should be solely or even primarily to provide for the needs of employment. However, education – or more accurately, learning – should be a preparation for life, and employment is a very significant component of life. It is therefore of no service to our young people – nor to the economy – if education, particularly towards the school-leaving age and beyond, does not contribute in some fairly substantial way towards the future employability and employment prospects of young people.

The continued presentation of the vocational and academic routes as being mutually exclusive is deeply unhelpful, especially when the routes continue to be presented in a hierarchical manner, with the academic firmly at the top and the vocational firmly at the bottom. Academic and vocational learning and qualifications are complementary and not mutually exclusive, and most people require both academic and vocational learning to achieve occupational competence.

Occupational competence at any level is made up of four components:

- a body of subject or discipline knowledge;
- knowledge and understanding of the workplace;
- ability to apply knowledge in the workplace;
- skills required to do the job.

The relative importance of the components, together with the balance between them, varies depending on the type and level of the occupation, but all are required. The first of these components is normally best delivered through a standard programme of education, and might be accredited by the achievement of the General Certificate of Secondary Education (GCSE) or General Certificate of Education (GCE) A levels in vocational or academic subjects, National Diplomas, Higher National Certificates or Diplomas (HNCs or HNDs) or degrees. The other components are best delivered largely in the workplace, with appropriate periods of training in other environments, and may be accredited by the achievement of a National Vocational Qualification (NVQ), or other existing vocational or professional qualifications, or units of such qualifications.

In order to achieve occupational competence, the majority of people require both institutionally-based and work-based learning, leading to a mixture of academic and vocational qualifications. Employers are, therefore, generally in favour of the thrust of the proposed reforms to the 14–19 curriculum as trailed in the Education White Paper, *Schools: Achieving success* (DfES, 2001) and subsequently the more detailed proposals in the consultation paper *14–19: Extending opportunities, raising standards* (DfES, 2002), with their stated aim of trying to break down the academic/vocational divide. In particular, the majority welcome the greater flexibility proposed in the paper, and the statement that the aim is for many more young people to gain some experience of vocational education. The proposals to remove the structural and legal barriers that prevent flexibility in learning at Key Stage 4 are very much welcomed, as is the parallel pilot initiative to enable students at that stage to undertake part of their learning in a work-related environment, leading to occupationally relevant qualifications. Employers particularly welcome the fact that these programmes, for the first time, are not being designated and promoted only for low ability and disaffected pupils, but for the full ability range.

It would be an enormous step forward if the majority of young people undertook some vocational learning as part of their programme between 14 and 16, and it is therefore vital to get across the message that taking vocational options opens up opportunities and does not close off subsequent options. The support for an integrated approach to the curriculum from 14–19, aimed at breaking down the artificial barrier at 16, is thus a positive development, providing it does not create another artificial barrier at 19, which in turn could have a particularly detrimental effect on modern apprenticeships, which frequently last well beyond the age of 19.

So what do employers feel about the introduction of an overarching award within this new curriculum? First, they are in general more concerned that the process, content and structure of the curriculum is right than they are with the specific shape of any qualifications. If the process is not right and does not offer the breadth and flexibility required, then the qualification becomes irrelevant. There is also the view that existing qualifications (with some minor modifications) would serve the purpose: the important issue is that young people can access the qualifications and modes of learning most appropriate to them and their aspirations.

Therefore any overarching or baccalaureate-style qualification must be valued by learners, education (particularly higher education), employers and the public at large as being greater and more worthwhile than the sum of its parts. Such a qualification will cost money to administer and award, and will not be paid for unless it is deemed to provide added value. Moreover, it should be inclusive in the sense that it must embrace all modes of learning – including work-based learning – and should provide opportunities for young people of all abilities.

It is, however, unlikely to be valued by candidates, education, employers or the general public if it is a single certificate with no obvious differentiation. A model that has different levels so that it is considered worthwhile by all learners, yet gives a realistic target for less able learners so that it is truly inclusive, is more likely to be valued by stakeholders and end-users alike. A single, undifferentiated qualification to which almost anyone can aspire will not be valued by those of above-average ability and is unlikely to be taken up widely.

Clearly, the encouragement of greater breadth in 14–19 learning should be one of the aims of any proposed reforms. Most employers would favour a model that embraces vocational as well as academic qualifications, rather than the model of the International Baccalaureate (see Chapter 3) which involves a mix of subjects largely from different academic domains. Furthermore, a model that is built on existing qualifications and part-qualifications would also be preferred, and thus the proposals for the development of the Welsh Baccalaureate (described in Chapter 5) may well offer an appropriate framework, although the presentation of this model suggests that the 'core' is of greater importance than the primary qualifications.

Key Skills are of considerable importance to employers and should be a fundamental component of any overarching qualification. However, there should be much greater flexibility in the delivery and assessment of Key Skills. For example, young people studying A level Mathematics or a National Diploma in Engineering should not be required additionally to achieve the application of number (AoN) Key Skill. That is, there should be a much greater list of 'proxies' and qualifications that are deemed to be acceptable alternatives to one or more Key Skills in order to avoid duplication and boredom.

In 1996 Dearing presented a report on the future of 16–19 qualifications. One of the recommendations of that report was for overarching certificates at Intermediate and Advanced levels, each containing a primary qualification or qualifications at Levels 2 and 3 respectively, with Key Skills and additional components. The primary qualifications were, in the language of the time, GCSEs, Intermediate General National Vocational Qualifications (GNVQs) and Level 2 NVQs at the Intermediate level, A levels and Advanced GNVQs and Level 3 NVQs at the Advanced level. With the facility to mix and match units and other part qualifications with whole qualifications, this is probably the model that most closely matches the requirements of employers. However, it would be worth investigating the reasons these proposals were not taken forward. There may be some lessons for the current situation here.

So what would a baccalaureate-style qualification look like? A preferred framework would incorporate three levels of awards, Advanced (Level 3), Intermediate (Level 2) and Foundation (Level 1). There are however some problems and concerns about the use of the term 'Foundation', since this is used in so many different contexts, including Foundation Degrees at Level 4 and Foundation Modern Apprenticeships at Level 2, that it is beginning to cause confusion.

The qualification should have three main components:

● primary qualifications;

- complementary Key Skills;
- additional components.

Advanced level

Primary qualifications

- three A levels plus one or more (Advanced Supplementary) AS levels;
- two A levels plus two or more AS levels;
- NVQ level 3 plus 'technical certificate' or other relevant qualification (Advanced Modern Apprenticeship (AMA) Diploma);
- other combinations of whole or part qualifications of approximately equal weight, value and level to the above.

Note that:

- A levels include both vocational and academic options.
- The NVQ option equates broadly to the AMA Diploma, the details of which are yet to be finalized.
- 'Technical certificate' includes qualifications such as Edexcel/BTEC National or Higher National Certificate of Diploma; vocational or academic A levels; AS levels, or other relevant vocationally-based qualifications.

Key Skills

All candidates should hold Key Skills in application of number and communication to at least Level 2, or a qualification recognized as a proxy or acceptable alternative. IT should also be encouraged.

Candidates should in addition be encouraged to undertake at least one Key Skill at Level 3 in an area complementary to their primary study subjects. For example, those studying mathematics, science or engineering should undertake communication rather than application of number, and those studying English or history should undertake application of number rather than communication.

Additional subjects

Candidates should present at least two additional options for the achievement of the qualification. Options should include the so-called wider Key Skills of improving own learning and performance, working with others and problem solving, and broader courses including citizenship, work-related studies and other cultural, sporting and community activities. The latter may be undertaken outside the main place of study.

Intermediate level

Primary qualifications

- five or more GCSEs grades A*– C (vocational or academic subjects or a mixture of the two);
- NVQ level 2 plus 'technical certificate' (Foundation Modern Apprenticeship (FMA) Diploma);
- other combinations of whole or part qualifications of approximately equal weight, value and level to those above.

Note that:

- The NVQ option equates broadly to the FMA Diploma, the details of which are not yet finalized.
- 'Technical certificate' includes academic or vocational GCSEs, BTEC first certificate or other relevant vocationally based qualifications.

Key Skills

All candidates should have at least Level 1 Key Skills in communication and application of number, or a recognized proxy or alternative qualification, and should be encouraged to progress to Level 2 in at least one Key Skill in a subject complementary to their main programme of study. IT should also be encouraged.

Additional subjects

As for the Advanced level, candidates should present at least two other additional options, which could include the wider Key Skills, citizenship, work-related and other cultural, sporting or community activities.

Foundation level

Primary qualifications

- five or more GCSEs grades D–G (vocational or academic subjects or a mixture);
- four or more GCSEs, with at least 2 at grades A–C (or a mixture as above);
- NVQ Level 1, plus other relevant additional whole or part qualifications;
- Other combinations of approximately equal weight to the above.

Key Skills

Candidates should be encouraged to attempt Level 1 Key Skills in communication and application of number, or a recognized proxy or alternative.

Those who have difficulty should be encouraged to undertake basic skills in literacy and numeracy as an alternative.

Additional subjects

As at other levels, candidates should present at least two additional options for receipt of the qualification, including wider Key Skills, citizenship, work-related activities and cultural, sporting or community activities.

The above model in the light of the government's recent Green Paper

The above suggestions differ from those put forward in the government's February 2002 consultation paper. This proposes a Matriculation Diploma with three levels – Intermediate, Advanced and Higher. The Higher level is for those with three high grade A levels plus an AS level or a Level 4 NVQ. There is no proposal for a Foundation level within the Diploma, and it is suggested that those who reach age 19 without achieving the necessary components for one of the three levels of the diploma should be given a 'Record of Progress'. A Foundation level within the Diploma would, however, be considerably less divisive.

The desirability of splitting the Level 3 Diploma into Higher and Advanced is to be questioned. However, if this part of the proposal is taken forward, it is essential that the Higher level includes higher level Advanced Modern Apprenticeships (AMAs). As far as the recent proposals are concerned, only an NVQ Level 4 of the work-based qualifications qualifies for Higher status. In engineering and other related sectors, many young people undertake an HNC alongside a Level 3 NVQ, and it is important that models of this sort should qualify for Higher status, if that route is eventually chosen. It would also be helpful presentationally if the NVQ 4 option was presented as an 'Advanced Modern Apprenticeship' with NVQ 4 and the Technical Certificate, for example an HNC. Without this, AMAs would immediately be perceived to be of lower quality than some A level combinations, and the argument about parity of esteem would be lost before it had begun.

The major concern as far as work-based learning is concerned is that the government's paper suggests that the Diploma should be awarded only at age 19. This would exclude a very high proportion of modern apprentices and some others following other programmes. Many AMAs take three or four years to complete their apprenticeship, and would not have completed by the age of 19. They would be eligible only for the 'Record of Progress' which is unlikely to be valued by anyone, or a level of diploma that they were qualified to claim at age 16. Recent statistics show that 45 per cent of AMAs and 30 per cent of FMAs are 19 or older when they commence their apprenticeships. Few of these would qualify for the relevant Matriculation Diploma by age 19, unless they were already qualified on entry through achievement of other qualifications, and even then, with AMAs, their qualification would be likely to remain at a lower level than their potential level of achievement on completion of their AMA.

A great deal more thought needs to be given to whether this Diploma is strictly about marking achievement at 19, or whether it is open to people of any age if they achieve the necessary requirements. There has never been a precedent for a qualification to be strictly age-related, and this would seem to run counter to the government's own drive for social and educational inclusion. Such a proposal would erect an artificial barrier at age 19 – exactly what most employers do not wish to see.

The inclusion of work-related learning as one of the 'wider activities' is to be welcomed although this option is, of course, irrelevant when the primary programme and qualification are work-related. It is, however, essential that any work-related learning is well structured and planned and leads to recognizable outcomes, such as full or part qualifications. If this is not the case, we shall not have progressed from the current model of 'work experience', parts of which are extremely poor and more likely to put young people off than to attract them to the occupation in question.

The devil of all this is very clearly in the detail, and it is to be welcomed that the proposals are presented as a medium to long term plan which will not be rushed through until the detail has been sorted out.

References

Confederation of British Industry (CBI) (1989) *Towards A Skills Revolution*, CBI, London

Dearing, R (1996) *Review of Qualifications for 16–19 Year Olds*, SCAA, London

Department for Education and Employment (DfEE) (1997) *Qualifying for Success: A consultative paper on the future of post-16 qualifications*, DfEE, London

Department for Education and Skills (DfES) (2001) *Schools Achieving Success*, DfES, London

DfES (2002) *14–19: Extending opportunities, raising standards*, DfES, London

QCA (2001) *On the Implementation of a Graduation Certificate*, QCA, London

8

A baccalaureate system for the English context

Ann Hodgson and Ken Spours

Baccalaureates and the reform of the English curriculum and qualifications system

In comparison with other European systems, England is unusual in not having a national grouped award that is recognized both as a school-leaving certificate and matriculation for higher education. The most well known approach to marking achievement at the end of secondary education in European systems is the award of a national or international baccalaureate-style qualification, which demonstrates achievement in a range of subjects and contains some common learning for all students (see Chapter 2). Moreover, this form of accreditation has played a role in raising levels of participation and achievement, and has proved itself adaptable enough to embrace both academic and vocational learning. In instances where there is a vocational route for attaining a baccalaureate, there is an expectation that the majority of the cohort will attain this level of study. In the French case, for example, the *Baccalauréat* with its three main variants (general, technical and professional) has been designed to enable at least 80 per cent of the age group to achieve advanced level (see Chapter 4).

In this country, however, a baccalaureate approach to qualifications has been seen as a continental European or international approach and has not, to date, been part of the English tradition. The English approach to advanced level qualifications since the 1950s has been based on single-subject A levels, with the emphasis on study in depth in a small number of subjects – typically three – and often on specialization in either the arts or the sciences. There has been no concept of common learning, and learner choice has been seen as an important feature of post-16 education.

Not surprisingly, therefore, the most well known examinations in England are A levels. As a result of their 50-year tenure, these qualifications, with their own particular features, are deeply ingrained in the popular imagination (see Chapter 1). Common perceptions of baccalaureates in this country, reinforced by the media, are based mainly on knowledge of the International Baccalaureate (see Chapter 3) and to a lesser extent the French *Baccalauréat*. Baccalaureates are seen as 'foreign'. They are largely associated with academic education and a small section of the cohort. They are also considered more demanding because of their prescribed breadth. Finally, they are seen as denying choice and specialization because of their emphasis on subject combinations.

Resistance to the introduction of a baccalaureate-style award in England has been based on these preconceptions. However, as the earlier chapters in this book demonstrate, there is more than one type of baccalaureate, and it might be better to think of the term as representing a set of curriculum principles rather than a particular qualification. In this final chapter, we take this broader definition of the term 'baccalaureate' as we reflect on the reform of post-14 education in England, and the potential role of a baccalaureate-type system within this.

For more than a decade there has been a debate within the education profession about what a British (or now English) baccalaureate system might look like. Those who argue for reform of curriculum and qualifications from 14+ have tried to apply baccalaureate principles to the English context, and in doing so, to address the preconceptions mentioned above. In particular, reformers have suggested that any future curriculum and qualifications system should tackle long-standing weaknesses in the English education and training system, but should also recognize and build on its strengths.

Since 1990 and the publication of *A British Baccalauréat* (Finegold *et al*, 1990), there have been more than 30 proposals from teacher professional associations, think tanks, researchers and political parties for the development of a unified curriculum and qualifications award framework (FEDA/IoE, 1999). We will argue in this chapter that during this period of debate, several common principles of reform for the 14–19 phase of education have been forged, and these form a strong basis of professional consensus which can now be harnessed in the next phase of reform. However, while the English curriculum and qualifications reform tradition is well known among the education profession, it has only intermittently entered wider public or political consciousness. Since the publication of the Green Paper on 14–19 education in February 2002 (DfES, 2002) and the experience of the A level crisis in the summer of the same year, however, this professional consensus for change has finally entered the political arena. As the government grapples with the future direction for 14–19 education and training in its response to the Green Paper consultation (DfES, 2003), we suggest that it needs to build on this professional consensus and knowledge if it is to achieve a long-term and sustainable approach to curriculum and qualifications reform.

English unified reform debates in the early 1990s

The English baccalaureate debates, originating in *A British Baccalauréat*, are more rooted in the experience of education and training in England (and Scotland) in the 1980s than in any particular overseas qualification models. The concept of a unified curriculum and qualifications system from 14+ was a response to the problems of the so-called 'academic/ vocational divide'. This term referred to the sharp divisions between academic and vocational education and training in the UK, symbolized by the very different approaches of education-based full-time academic A levels, on the one hand, and work-based occupationally focused part-time NVQs on the other. The academic/vocational divide was associated with low levels of participation and achievement in education and training in comparison with other countries, impoverished academic education, low-status vocational education, and inequality and inefficiency of outcomes from post-compulsory education and training (Finegold *et al*, 1990).

The 1980s was a period not only of divisions, but also of innovative curriculum developments. The unified reform tradition, in our view, owes much to the Technical and Vocational Education Initiative (TVEI) and other pre-vocational and broad vocational developments that were taking place at that time (such as the Certificate of Pre-Vocational Education (CPVE), the growth of BTEC awards, and modular developments in Scotland). Practitioner experience of these innovations led to a professional consensus for the reform of the 14–19 phase. The reform would be based on a flexible but common entitlement curriculum, core skills for all learners, process-based mechanisms for improving achievement and progression, and breadth of study at advanced level (Howieson *et al*, 1997; Hodgson and Spours, 1997).

In the wake of the Conservative government's rejection of the Higginson reform of advanced level qualifications (DES, 1988; see Chapter 1), the education profession's view of reform took an altogether more radical turn in the early 1990s. This resulted not only in the publication of *A British Baccalauréat*, but also in a wave of other proposals for a unified curriculum and qualifications system (eg Royal Society, 1991; NCE, 1995; NUT, 1995; NAHT, 1995; Jenkins and David, 1996). These can broadly be divided into two types, a 'grouped/prescriptive' approach and an 'open/framework' approach. Those who argued for the former approach wanted learners to take a combination of subjects in the 14–19 phase to ensure breadth of study, and to address the culture of dropping 'difficult' subjects such as mathematics, sciences and modern foreign languages. This approach can be seen in the proposals contained in *A British Baccalauréat* and in those from the Royal Society, National Commission on Education, the National Association of Headteachers, the Welsh Baccalaureate proposals from Jenkins and David (see Chapter 5) and in the Dearing Report (1996). On the other hand, those who argued for an open framework were in favour of a more flexible and unified curriculum and qualifications approach, but wanted to keep the elective, open and choice-based features of the English qualifications system. Proposals emerged for a unified 14+ 'framework approach' which emphasized the modular development of existing qualifications so as to provide for breadth through greater flexibility rather than through prescription (FEU, 1993; AfC *et al*, 1994; JACG, 1997).

In the mid-1990s, attempts were made to design a 'compromise' model between these two approaches, based on a core/specialization design (Young and Spours, 1996). In addition, representatives of both the 'unifiers' and the 'frameworkers' came together in 1996/97 during the debate about the Dearing 16–19 qualifications reform proposals, to agree on a set of principles for reform of education and training for 14–19-year-olds. As a result, a joint statement from the main education professional associations was produced in 1997 (AoC *et al,* 1997). It suggested that a curriculum and qualifications framework for England should:

- commence at 14 rather than 16, as learners begin to specialize in their studies;
- act as a framework for 'a curriculum entitlement' in an elective and fragmented education and training system;
- reduce the division between academic (now termed 'general') and vocational learning so that all learners could develop both theoretical and applied capacities, and so that vocational education and training could achieve parity of esteem;
- be represented by a single and easily recognizable form of certification (eg a baccalaureate or diploma) which embraced both full-time and part-time learning, and general and vocational achievement;
- be multi-level and non-age-related in order to build a ladder of achievement for all learners;
- be modular in order to support breadth, depth and more flexible approaches to study.

These fundamental principles of curriculum and qualifications reform in England have proved to be enduring, as we shall see, and underpinned much of the critique of both *Curriculum 2000* and the recent Green Paper *14–19: Extending opportunities, raising standards* (DfES, 2002).

During the 1990s there were, however, limits to both the scope and depth of the professional consensus. Most of the proposals for reform of curriculum and qualifications from 14+ were 'blueprints' and did not go into a great deal of design or operational detail. The only exception was the proposals for *A Welsh Baccalaureate* (Jenkins and David, 1996), which derived from the International Baccalaureate approach. Moreover, amid the consensus on basic principles, there were (and still are) important unresolved issues which were relatively neglected. The debates and designs focused mainly on advanced level and full-time general education, despite an appreciation in principle that a unified 14+ curriculum and qualifications framework should span different levels and embrace both full-time education and the work-based route. Little attention was devoted to the lower levels and the curriculum for 14–16-year-olds, and discussions about an approach to certificating apprenticeship remained relatively neglected, bar one attempt by a group of academics to rewrite *A British Baccalauréat* for the work-based route (Evans *et al*, 1997). Moreover, this lack of detail and scope meant that there was also relatively little discussion of the reform process itself, the architecture of the system or implementation issues.

New Labour and unified qualifications reform 1997–2001

In the period prior to the 1997 general election, the Labour Party adopted an approach to 14–19 education reform which drew upon this professional consensus in its policy document *Aiming Higher* (Labour Party, 1996). This argued for a two-stage strategy, spanning two Parliaments, to move from the existing divided curriculum and qualifications system through a framework stage to a unified diploma system. New Labour's election manifesto, however, reduced the relatively ambitious 14–19 approach in *Aiming Higher* to the more limited aims of 'broadening A Levels; upgrading vocational qualifications and introducing key skills within a rigorous framework' (Labour Party, 1997).

The election manifesto thus ended up being closer to the Dearing reform agenda for 16–19 advanced level qualifications, but without the diplomas and certificates that Dearing had proposed (Hodgson and Spours, 1999). The *Qualifying for Success* (DfEE, 1997) consultation and reforms, which became Labour Party policy in this area and eventually became known as *Curriculum 2000*, brought about a suspension of the debates on 14+ baccalaureates/frameworks, as the new government restricted its reforms to advanced level and to individual qualifications. Overarching certification proposals were effectively put on the back burner for a second Parliament (Blackstone, 1998).

The debate was also restricted by the profession itself, as discussion moved from principles of a unified curriculum and qualifications framework, and focused instead on implementation of the new advanced level qualifications, comprising the new A level made up of AS/A2 blocks, the Advanced Certificate of Vocational Education (AVCE), the Key Skills qualification and the Advanced Extension Award (AEA) (Hodgson and Spours, 2003). In private, the reformers were reassured by ministers and advisers that *Curriculum 2000* was part of a step-by-step approach to more fundamental 14–19 qualifications and curriculum reform, but without the declaration of a clear end point. In public, *Curriculum 2000* constituted the qualifications policy, and wider discussion of 14–19 reform was viewed as an issue for a second term of office.

While the late 1990s and early 2000s were dominated by the preparation for and implementation of *Curriculum 2000*, baccalaureates (or more precisely, overarching certificates) continued to be promoted in five ways.

First, in 1999, the curriculum and qualifications regulatory authorities in England, Wales and Northern Ireland commissioned research on an overarching certificate (OAC) at advanced level but within a highly constrained remit (QCA/CCEA/ACCAC, 1998). Designs had to use pre-*Curriculum 2000* qualifications, and the certificate would be for advanced level only. The research report recommended a core/specialization model (FEDA/IoE, 1999), but its proposals were not immediately acted upon.

Second, in 1999, the Social Exclusion Unit, in its report *Bridging the Gap* (SEU, 1999), recommended the development of a graduation certificate to be aimed principally at marginalized 16–19-year-olds (see Chapters 6). The SEU version of a graduation certificate was intended to motivate young people to achieve Level 2 qualifications and to recognize their wider achievements. The proposal clearly drew on some of the OAC design features, and added dimensions concerned with extracurricular activities from the English 'recording of achievement' tradition (Hodgson and Spours, 2000). In the consultation process that followed (QCA, 2000), many in the education profession let it be known that a graduation certificate should be offered at both Levels 2 and 3 to be credible over the whole ability range. Once again, educationalists could be seen to be arguing for a multi-level baccalaureate approach.

The third development took place in Wales. The Welsh Assembly in 2000 agreed to the introduction of *A Welsh Baccalaureate,* and amidst a furious debate involving the Institute of Welsh Affairs, which had first developed the concept of a Welsh baccalaureate, the tender for the pilot was won by the Welsh Joint Examinations Council (WJEC). The WJEC has designed an award broadly along the lines proposed by the constrained FEDA/IoE research of 1999, while at the same time utilizing *Curriculum 2000* qualifications components. (See Chapter 5 for the debate between the WJEC and IWA reform proposals.)

Fourth, ideas for a broader curriculum entitlement for 16–19-year-olds can be seen in the designs for an Apprenticeship Diploma (DfEE, 2000) and the Further Education Funding Council's (FEFC) decision to resource key skills, guidance and enrichment as part of the *Curriculum 2000* package in colleges (FEFC, 1999).

Finally, there were a number of local and bottom-up developments, an enduring feature of the English reform tradition, which continued to take place despite lack of clear support from national government (see Chapter 7).

During the period 1997–2001, while the debates about a 14+ unified system were deflected by *Curriculum 2000*, what we have shown here is that baccalaureate ideas and developments began to permeate parts of the 14–19 education and training system in England and Wales, but in an uncoordinated way and very much behind the scenes.

The new context for reform from 2002

Two influential events: the publication of the 14–19 Green Paper and the A level crisis

In our view, 2002 marked a critical turning point for debates on a unified 14+ curriculum and qualification system, as a result of two main events. The first was the publication of a Green Paper on 14–19 education which contained proposals for Matriculation Diplomas. The second was the A level crisis in the summer of 2002, which brought to a head concerns about the *Curriculum 2000* reforms of advanced level qualifications that had been evident from their introduction in September 2000.

Following its earlier political focus on primary education in its first term of office, the Labour government turned its attention to the modernization of secondary education in its second Parliament. As part of this new focus, in February 2002 the Government published its Green Paper *14–19: Extending opportunities, raising standards* (DfES, 2002). This document laid out proposals for a Matriculation Diploma at three levels – Intermediate, for those wishing to demonstrate employability, Advanced, for those aiming for entry to higher education and the workplace, and Higher, for those seeking access to prestigious universities or courses. At all levels, learners would be required to attain Level 2 in mathematics/ application of number, English/communications and ICT, which was described as 'common learning'. At Intermediate level, the qualification requirements would be five A*–C GCSE grades or equivalent. At Advanced level, learners would be expected to gain the equivalent of two A levels plus one AS level. A Higher Level Diploma would be available to those gaining an ABB grade profile at A level or a Level 4 NVQ. All of these diplomas would be made up of current qualifications, and achievement would be recorded on a transcript. There was a suggestion that wider activities, such as the Duke of Edinburgh Award and work experience, could form part of the Diploma, but this was subject to consultation.

These represent the first proposals and designs for a baccalaureate-style award to come from national government, and thus mark the recognition of the need for something other than individual qualifications for 14–19-year-olds. The Matriculation Diploma designs, which we see as an elitist variant of the framework approach, were short-lived. In the consultation process following the Green Paper they were rejected by the education profession on the grounds that they were not available below Intermediate level; were voluntarist and did not represent sufficient added-value over individual qualifications (eg AoC, 2002; ATL, 2002; HMC, 2002; NAHT, 2002; NATFHE, 2002; NUT, 2002). In its response to the 14–19 Green Paper, the DfES recognized that the rejection of the Matriculation Diploma proposals was a rejection of the design of the proposals and not a rejection of the principles of baccalaureate-style qualifications (DfES, 2003). An opportunity was finally presented at a national level for more radical proposals, based upon the unified reform tradition, to be considered in the period following the government response to the Green Paper.

The second event that heralded the new context was the A level crisis caused by accusations of manipulation of grading within A levels under *Curriculum 2000*. This crisis led to two reports by Mike Tomlinson in the autumn of 2002 (Tomlinson, 2002a, 2002b). The second of these proposed splitting the A level into its two component parts – AS and A2 – within the context of wider 14–19 curriculum and qualifications reform. The main significance of the 'summer crisis' was that A levels could no longer be regarded as the 'gold standard', and there were public calls from sections of the media for a baccalaureate qualification.

In addition, there may be a third factor that contributes to the new context for the development of a baccalaureate-type award in England from 2002. Both Scotland and Wales have their own curriculum and qualifications reform processes. Scotland has been able to introduce more levels into its qualifications system, and Wales is getting rid of damaging performance tables and is piloting the Welsh Baccalaureate qualification. It is highly likely, therefore, that these two neighbouring education and training systems will provide a reference point for 14–19 reforms in England.

Continuing system problems

While the policy context in England may be more conducive for baccalaureate-type reform in 2002, important historical education and training system problems persist, and new ones have arisen as a result of *Curriculum 2000*. Four major problems stand out as ones that need to be addressed in any future baccalaureate proposals: lack of a 14–19 curriculum framework, the GCSE barrier, low-status and fragmented vocational education, and the limitations of the *Curriculum 2000* reforms of advanced level qualifications.

Lack of a 14–19 curriculum framework

The current qualifications and curriculum system, divided between a compulsory and post-compulsory phase, has little explicit sense of curriculum or skill development 14–19. In Key Stage 4, 14–16-year-olds typically take up to 10 examined subjects, which means that their curriculum is content-heavy and leaves little space to develop the study or applied skills they require for progression to the next stage of education or training. Beyond the age of 16, the opposite of the 'compulsory' Key Stage 4 pertains. At this point, there are no common curriculum or skill requirements, so the content and process of education and training is decided entirely by the different type of qualifications the learner elects to take. Since the learner's choice is largely shaped by the values and priorities of either higher education providers or employers, this elective system has led most 16–19-year-olds to take a narrow and sometime incoherent set of either academic or vocational qualifications. It has also meant that there is nothing to ensure equity of experience for learners on different routeways within the English system, or to encourage learners to continue with core subjects, such as English, mathematics, sciences or a modern foreign language.

The GCSE barrier

To many, GCSE is remembered as a great educational success. The introduction of the new 'common 16+ examination' in 1987/88 led to rises in attainment at 16+ compared with the old O level, and to significant rises in post-16 staying-on rates, which then fed through to improvements in A level participation and attainment (Gray, Jesson and Tranmer, 1993). The period between 1987/88 and 1992/93 could be seen to be the 'progressive era of GCSE', associated with in-course assessment (the 100 per cent coursework in English) and more diverse approaches to teaching and learning, which was followed by rapid rises in examination attainment. The 'regressive phase' of GCSE followed in the wake of the White Paper *Education and Training for the 21st Century* (DES/ED/WO, 1991). The early 1990s saw the cutting back of internal assessment, the tiering of exam papers, and the introduction of school performance tables which accentuated the importance of A*–C grades. Rises in GCSE attainment rates slowed markedly during the late 1990s, as did post-16 staying-on rates and A level attainment.

By 2001, approximately half of all 16-year-olds in England were achieving five A*–C grades, the basic threshold for progression to advanced level study. This meant that 50 per cent were not. In the current system, those falling below this threshold feel that they are failing at Intermediate level rather than succeeding at Foundation level. Moreover, they find it difficult to progress to many school sixth forms, and many only have the option to go to further education colleges or into training schemes. Even those who do stay on in full-time education find themselves restricted to a narrow range of vocational subjects.

For those who do succeed at GCSE, the experience is not always positive. They spend their time pursuing up to 10 examination subjects, with relatively little time for skill building and personal development. In this sense, the current GCSE programme is arguably neither a rich curriculum experience nor a good preparation for advanced level study that requires learners to be able to work independently beyond the classroom. It is clear from this kind of analysis that the GCSE system is fundamentally flawed: no Foundation level, too much examination and external assessment, and little room for skill building. In addition, the current way that performance tables are compiled means that schools value those learners who attain five A*–C grades by the age of 16 more highly than others.

Fragmented and low-status vocational education and training provision

While the GCSE barrier, in its current form, is a relatively new problem for the English system, the issue of fragmented and low-status vocational provision is longstanding and deep-seated (Steedman and Green, 1997; Steedman, 2002). The way this issue manifests itself today is through a proliferation of different vocational awards, with little external recognition and public understanding. This affects the capacity of these awards to promote progression to a wide range of programmes of study. Furthermore, they have different characteristics, which makes it difficult for them to be assembled into a balanced and appropriate programme of study and experience. At one end of the spectrum, AVCEs have been 'academicized' to resemble A levels, while at the other end NVQs are competence-based and are designed to be assessed in the workplace.

The result is a complex array of certification which not only undermines public recognition and progression possibilities, but also makes it difficult to develop an equitable entitlement across different sectors and sites of learning. Furthermore, the fragmentation of certification can be seen as a reflection of the lack of employer commitment, in some sectors, to a broad and highly recognized process of qualification within apprenticeship. The Modern Apprenticeship system still only qualifies 50 per cent of its participants at Level 3 (DfES, 2001).

The limitations of the *Curriculum 2000* reforms

The fourth major problem arises from the relative successes and failures of the *Curriculum 2000* reform process to date. The majority of advanced level learners are taking more subjects in their first year of study, and are thus on fuller timetables than prior to the reforms. Many are also studying Key Skills, and a small minority is mixing general and vocational qualifications. These developments can be seen as quantitative gains over the old advanced level system. However, most learners under *Curriculum 2000* have not opted significantly to broaden their advanced level studies beyond taking a further subject. Their choice of the 'fourth' AS subject has generally been cautious, and there is little incentive for them to take contrasting subjects. Engagement with Key Skills is sporadic, particularly in schools, and there has been a decline in the uptake of extracurricular activities. In addition, the AVCE qualification has proved problematic for many learners because of its assessment regime, which has resulted in high failure rates in the first year and lower grade profiles that those in the new A level qualifications. Also concerning is the emerging research evidence suggesting that the design of the AS has encouraged a more didactic and superficial approach to teaching and learning, in order to ensure coverage of the specifications for an examination at the end of one year of advanced level study (Hodgson and Spours, 2003).

While the *Curriculum 2000* reforms, therefore, can be seen to be helpful in the development of a future baccalaureate system, because they have brought about increased volumes of study at advanced level, they have also exposed the fact that learners will not voluntarily broaden their programmes of study unless they are required to do so and are supported by higher education end-users. Furthermore, as the rushed and badly prepared *Curriculum 2000* reform process unfortunately demonstrated, any reform proposals, particularly as ambitious as the development of a baccalaureate-type system from 14+, will have to pay particular attention to the reform process itself.

The influence of system strengths

It is traditional for reformers in England to start from a position of attacking system deficits, and in the case of 14–19 qualifications and curriculum reform it is tempting still to do so. However, at this point it may be more productive to start from an assessment of strengths in the English system, because of the possibility of harnessing these in a longer and more gradual change process.

The traditional strengths of the English education system are, not surprisingly, associated with its elites. In particular, our system of higher education has low drop-out rates, given the level of participation we have in this country (NAO, 2002). Moreover the A level system, which combines subject choice with specialist study, can produce a minority of highly motivated and skilful learners for higher education. *Curriculum 2000* continued to build on these strengths in the AS/A2 qualifications, and it is this aspect of the reforms, in conjunction with newly introduced modularization and flexibility, that has been recognized as valuable by both learners and teachers (Hodgson and Spours, 2003).

As we indicated above, the English education system has developed other strengths arising out of years of reform attempts, notably in the areas of pre-vocational and vocational education. It has developed a strong tradition of process-led curriculum innovation in areas such as learner guidance and formative assessment, despite the emphasis of successive governments on external examinations. In addition teachers, pressurized and faced with constant change, have developed a capacity to mould national reforms to make them workable at the local level. Schools and colleges, within what has become a marketized system, have learnt to cope with change and to make innovative responses in order to help learners progress and achieve (Higham, Sharp and Yeomans, 2001).

A major conclusion arising from this analysis of 'system strengths' is that one should design a reform process that allows space for teacher interpretation, local development and innovation to shape the reforms. This point is actively recognized in the government's response to the Green Paper (DfES, 2003). At the same time, the reform process must also take into consideration influential system inhibitors at the national level – qualifications barriers, league tables and over-assessment – all of which have prevented this kind of local innovation from having a lasting and decisive impact in the past (Hodgson and Spours, 1997).

We have characterized the new context for 14+ reform in 2002 as one that is both politically more open, and increasingly informed by education professional opinion and expertise in this area. At the same time, this new context demands what Higham *et al* (2001) have referred to as 'policy memory' – that is, a historical understanding of what has worked in the past and what has not. In keeping with this view, we discuss below the broad principles and features of an English baccalaureate system from 14+ which seeks to build on English system strengths and what has worked, while at the same time addressing longstanding system weaknesses that have frustrated reformers in the past.

English Baccalaureate system from 14+

A policy breakthrough is now possible, but there are four immediate questions to be addressed if we are to develop a reform process that leads to real and sustainable change:

- How do we create a fully inclusive and coherent curriculum and qualifications system from 14+ upwards rather than 18+ downwards, thereby giving more attention to the design and purpose of levels leading up to advanced level?
- How do we use baccalaureate ideas to improve the experience and outputs of apprenticeships, and improve the quality and coherence of vocational education and training as well as general education?
- How do we develop a compromise baccalaureate model which avoids the disadvantages of either free choice and voluntarism or highly prescriptive approaches, and which is, therefore, capable of acceptance in the English context?
- How do we build on system strengths and address system weaknesses, including the limitations of *Curriculum 2000*, as part of a well-planned gradualist rather than 'big bang' reform approach?

If the 14+ English Baccalaureate system is to build on strengths and respond to longstanding or new system weaknesses, it will need to be founded on a number of key principles. Below we discuss these, together with some design or architectural features that might flow from them.

Promoting inclusion through a single system

One of the major criticisms of baccalaureates that has been voiced in England has been that these awards cater for a minority of learners, because they exist only at advanced level and focus primarily on general education. There are some baccalaureates or leaving certificates, for example in Sweden and France, that do include both general and vocational education at advanced level. However in the English context, which has traditionally been so divided and elitist, we believe that inclusion would need to be given a high priority within a unified award structure. The English Baccalaureate system that we describe in more detail below attempts to be inclusive in two ways: by employing a multi-level ladder of progression for all learners 14–19, and by including all types of learning, both general and vocational. In this sense, the proposed inclusiveness of the English Baccalaureate approach is based upon the premise that every learner has a place in the system.

Developing a curriculum and qualifications framework 14–19

We suggest that it would be important to lay out a framework of requirements and entitlements for each of the four levels of diploma within the English Baccalaureate system (Entry, Foundation, Intermediate and Advanced) to secure a 14–19 curriculum framework for all learners for the first time in the English education and training system. The curriculum framework accredited by the diplomas provides a means of securing both breadth and depth of achievement. For each level of diploma (we envisage that only the Advanced level would be termed a baccalaureate) curriculum demands would be specified in the form of a common core of learning and options for specialization and breadth. The English Baccalaureate diplomas would not be based upon a 'one size fits all' model, but would attempt to combine common learning with a high degree of customization and personal choice – a strong feature of the English system which deserves to be built upon. The diplomas also need to be flexible enough to be able to respond to future learning needs as the system evolves. Such a system of diplomas would, therefore, represent a compromise between the traditional free-choice nature of A levels and the highly prescriptive International Baccalaureate.

Creating a ladder of progression

At all diploma levels there would be requirements specified in terms of subjects or domains, learning processes and skills. However, the nature of these demands would differ at each level. While there would be design principles based on the concept of breadth and common learning, which would be germane to all the diplomas, the design and requirements of each level of diploma would reflect its different purposes.

The Entry Level Diploma would be the first level in the English Baccalaureate awarding structure at 14+, and would provide basic, practical and life skills alongside project work to motivate learners, including those with special learning needs or disabilities, to progress to further learning.

The role of the Foundation and Intermediate Level Diplomas would be to mark a stage of development for the majority of learners, and an exit qualification for a minority. These lower level diplomas would be designed primarily to motivate learners to progress to the next stage of education, although for some they would be used as the basis of preparation for participation in the workplace. The intention would be to provide a balance of breadth and specialist study, to create the space for learning skill development and practical activities, to reduce the examination burden associated with GCSEs, and to promote progression and genuine employability.

The main function of the Advanced Level Diplomas (the 'bacs') would be to provide broad programmes of study, with enough specialization to prepare young people for higher education or for high-skilled employment.

Involving stake-holders in the development of a single set of national awards

The use of the title 'diploma' for all post-14 awards could be seen as a form of qualifications rationalization, and would provide clarity and recognition for end-users. The diplomas (both general and specialist) within an English Baccalaureate system could provide a single set of high-trust qualifications outcomes around which the various stakeholders could collaborate and offer common recognition.

It is important to stress that these new awards would, like the International Baccalaureate, comprise specifically designed credit-bearing units and would not simply be a cluster of existing qualifications contained within an overarching certificate, such as the Matriculation Diploma designs outlined in the original *14–19* Green Paper. This would involve re-engineering current qualifications blocks and designing new ones in order to provide not only the clarity of a single system of awards, but the curriculum and learning space that current qualifications and programmes of learning lack.

Moreover, the development of an English Baccalaureate system would provide end-users with a concrete and simple point of involvement in the curriculum and qualifications reform process. While employers and higher education providers should not dictate what is taught and learnt at the previous phase, they obviously do have a stake in the outcomes of upper secondary education, not least because they need to build upon it. As a matter of principle they should, therefore, be involved in its design. Moreover, their involvement would help to secure clear progression pathways for learners taking the new diploma awards.

Securing standards and 'fitness for purpose' assessment

The existence of a grouped baccalaureate-style award would remove the need for all individual components of the qualification to be assessed externally, as is currently the case with all qualifications within the National Qualifications Framework. Standards would be secured in a number of ways. First, as now, there would need to be external assessment of some components. Second, there could be moderation and internal assessment of other areas of learning. Third, there could be an institutionally-derived grade representing the overall performance of the learner over time. This threefold approach to assessment suggests that the concept of standards is not simply found in the individual components of the award, but is ultimately secured through the diploma package as a whole and the requirement to complete all its aspects. At the same time, when these demands are made it will be important to employ a wide range of assessment tools to ensure validity, to recognize all types of learning and to promote skill development.

A new approach to the reform process based on 'strategic gradualism'

One of the most important principles underpinning the development of a new English Baccalaureate system is the need for an open, consensual and carefully planned reform process. We use the term 'strategic gradualism' to describe such a process, in which there would be a clear future goal and stages of development towards its attainment. One of the major lessons to be learnt from the *Curriculum 2000* reform process was how complex it is to implement changes to the qualifications system in this country, and how important it is to involve teachers, learners and other key stakeholders actively in this process. It will be vital to have a clearly articulated vision of the future so that teachers, learners and end-users can see what they are working towards, what changes will be necessary, and what steps they will need to take to make this vision a reality. Alongside this, there will need to be careful consideration of the intended and unintended effects of key 'levers and drivers', such as funding mechanisms, performance indicators and inspection regimes, on the reform process.

The proposed architecture of the English Baccalaureate system

Adv.2	Advanced (General)	Advanced Specialist (Domain)	Advanced Specialist (Vocational)	Advanced Specialist (Occupational)	**Advanced Diploma (the bac)**
Adv.1					
Int.	Intermediate General (pre and post 16)	Intermediate (Domain)	Intermediate (Vocational)	Intermediate (Occupational)	**Intermediate Diploma**
Found.	Foundation General (pre and post 16)		Foundation (Vocational)		**Foundation Diploma**
Entry	Entry Level Provision (pre and post 16)				**Entry Diploma**

Figure 8.1   A unified English Baccalaureate system from 14+

As can be seen from Figure 8.1, the English Baccalaureate system we propose, which is built on the principles already outlined, is a unified curriculum and qualifications system that includes all types of study from general full-time education to occupationally specific modern apprenticeship programmes. We believe that it is important to embrace all types of learning within a single framework that recognizes not only breadth but different forms of specialization, in order to raise the status of vocational education. The system also extends from compulsory secondary education for 14–16-year-olds to post-compulsory education and training, and covers five levels of study: Entry, Foundation, Intermediate, Advanced 1 and Advanced 2.

As already indicated, we currently propose that there would be four types of diploma within this unified system: General; Specialist 1 (domain-based); Specialist 2 (broad vocational); and Specialist 3 (occupational). Diplomas would be awarded at four levels: Entry, Foundation, Intermediate and Advanced, but Specialist Diplomas would only be offered post-16 and at Foundation, Intermediate and Advanced level. All diplomas would contain elements of study at more than one level (like the International Baccalaureate) in order to ensure breadth as well as depth in learner programmes.

In addition, all diplomas would have a prescribed core of learning, comprise credit-bearing qualifications units at specified levels, and be of a prescribed volume. Beyond the core, in many of the diplomas there would be a high degree of subject choice. The core would comprise three components flexibly applied to all levels of diploma: a specialist research study; underpinning taught elements (for example at Advanced level, critical thinking, theory of knowledge, people and organizations) and wider activities and experiences (such as experience of the world of work, Duke of Edinburgh Award, sport, drama and music). The core would need to be supported by individual guidance, mentoring and supervision. If the core, which would be compulsory, is to be accepted and valued by learners, it would also need to contain an element of choice and specialization. This would be achieved mainly through the choice of specialist research study and wider activities and experiences, but could also be supported through the customization of the underpinning taught components by schools, colleges and employers/training providers.

Conceived in this way, the core potentially supports six major principles within the English Baccalaureate system: breadth, progression, motivation, skill building, pedagogical innovation, and responsiveness to future demands of the education and training system.

It is important to stress that the English Baccalaureate system illustrated above does not assume that all learners would move in the same way or at the same pace. There would be the facility for both vertical and horizontal progression, and the possibility for learners working mainly within one level also to undertake units of learning at a higher level in areas in which they had particular aptitude or interest. Most learners would pass through Entry and Foundation levels as part of compulsory education, and the majority would be expected to be working towards either an Intermediate or Foundation Diploma between the ages of 14–16. However, this would vary according to ability and interest. Beyond the age of 16 there would be the freedom to continue with a more general education programme, such as that offered within the General Diploma; to specialize in a particular combination of subjects (such as the natural sciences or the humanities) by working towards a Specialist 1 Diploma; to specialize in a broad vocational area (such as business, or leisure and tourism) by working towards a Specialist Diploma 2; or to enter the workplace as a modern apprentice and work towards a Specialist Diploma 3.

We refer to the learners' individual progression paths within the unified system as their 'personal routeways'. This personal routeway represents the balance between compulsion, coherence and clarity of outcome, on the one hand, and individual flexibility and choice on the other.

Discussing principles and architecture in relation to key strengths and weaknesses of the English education and training system

In the final section of this chapter we assess to what extent the principles and architecture of the English Baccalaureate system we have outlined above are able to address the four key problems in the English education and training system highlighted earlier in the chapter. These are the lack of a 14–19 curriculum framework, the GCSE barrier, the fragmented nature and low status of vocational education and training, and the limitations of the *Curriculum 2000* reform process.

It is clear that an English Baccalaureate system from 14+ potentially provides a concept of curriculum for 14–19-year-olds that is currently lacking in the English system, and allows for the evolution of the curriculum over time in response to future needs.

The inclusion of four levels, starting at Entry level, provides a way around the GCSE barrier, not only because of the positive recognition of learning below that of the GCSE A*–C grades, but also because each of the diplomas provides the opportunity for learners to tackle their weaknesses in some areas, while playing to their strengths by pursuing their learning at a higher levels in other areas. Moreover, the idea of fitness for purpose assessment means that different styles of learning can be recognized more easily than is currently the case. Finally, the provision of more levels potentially removes the age-relatedness that is a feature of the current GCSE system, allied to performance tables.

The issue of fragmented and low-status vocational education and training can be addressed partially by vocational variants of a baccalaureate system that provide a single point of recognition for achievement of work-related learning, underpinned by relevant general education. An English Baccalaureate system that includes vocational or applied education at all levels of the award and for all learners, as well as specialist variants for those who wish to take this route, will undoubtedly help to raise the profile of vocational education. The low status of vocational education and training, however, is very deep-seated in this country and cannot be tackled by qualifications reform alone. Reform in this area will need to be allied to changes in the labour market, and the development of a more social partnership approach to education and training, which involves employers and trade unions more actively in the education and training of 14–19-year-olds.

The experience of the *Curriculum 2000* reform process shows the limitations and the costs of partial reform dictated by a political timetable. This is why we argue for thoroughgoing reform of the system which is more consensual, planned over a longer timescale, and less politicized. This longer-term reform approach is also designed to build on one of the strengths of the English system, innovative institutional involvement. As we have seen earlier in the chapter, since the mid-1980s teachers and lecturers have had to respond to constant piecemeal reform of the post-16 education and training system, and have become adept at working creatively with chaos. Moreover, schools and colleges have developed strong pastoral and guidance systems, which constitute a vital support for a baccalaureate-type system that balances curriculum demands and personal choice.

It is possible to see the English Baccalaureate system, based on the type of combined core/specialist diploma model described above, as recognizing both the importance of specialization and choice and the need to introduce more breadth, common learning and skill-building into the curriculum. It is our contention that because this system provides a clear vision for future curriculum and qualifications reform from 14+, builds on strengths and learns lessons from previous mistakes in this area, it will be capable of securing considerable consensus from the education profession.

References

Association for Colleges (AfC), Girls' School Association (GSA), Headmasters' Conference (HMC), Secondary Heads' Association (SHA), Sixth Form Colleges' Association (APVIC), and Society for Headmasters and Headmistresses in Independent Schools (SHMIS) (1994) *Post-Compulsory Education and Training: A joint statement*, AfC, London

Association of Colleges (AoC) (2002) *Response to 14–19 Green Paper*, AoC, London

AoC, ATL, GSA, HMC, NAHT, NASUWT, NATFHE, NUT, Professional Association of Teachers (PAT), SHA and SHMIS (1997) *Key Principles for Curriculum and Qualifications Reform from 14+*, Post-16 Education Centre, Institute of Education, University of London

Association of Teachers and Lecturers (ATL) (2002) *14–19: Extending opportunities, raising standards: ATL's response to the Green Paper*, ATL, London

Blackstone, T (1998) *Qualifying for Success: The response to the Qualifications and Curriculum Authority Advice* (3 April), DfES, London

Dearing, Sir R (1996) *Review of Qualifications for 16–19 Year Olds*, SCAA, London

Department for Education and Science (DES) (1988) *Advancing A Levels: Report of the committee chaired by Professor Higginson*, HMSO, London

Department for Education (DfE)/Employment Department (ED)/Welsh Office (WO) (1991) *Education and Training for the 21st Century*, HMSO, London

Department for Education and Employment (DfEE) (1997) *Qualifying for Success: A consultation paper on the future of post-16 qualifications*, DfEE, London

DfEE (2000) *Modern Apprenticeships Consultation Paper*, DfEE, London

Department for Education and Skills (DfES) (2001) *Statistical First Release 47/2001, TEC/LSC Delivered Government Supported Work-based Learning: England: Volumes and outcomes*, DfES, London

DfES (2002) *14–19: Extending opportunities, raising standards*, Stationery Office, London

DfES (2003) *14–19: Excellence and opportunity: government response to the 14–19 Green Paper*, DfES, London

Evans, K, Hodkinson, P, Keep, E, Maguire, M, Raffe, D, Rainbird, H, Senker, P and Unwin, L (1997) *Working to Learn, Issues in People Management No 18*, Institute of Personnel and Development, London

Finegold, D, Keep, E, Miliband, D, Raffe, D, Spours, K and Young, M (1990) *A British 'Baccalauréat': Ending the division between education and training*, Institute of Public Policy Research (IPPR), London

Further Education Development Agency (FEDA) and Institute of Education (IoE) (1999) *An Overarching Certificate at Advanced Level: Research for ACCAC, CCEA and QCA*, FEDA, London

Further Education Funding Council (FEFC) (1999) *Curriculum 2000: Funding for full-time 16–19 year olds, Circular 99/33*, FEFC, Coventry

Further Education Unit (FEU) (1993) *Discussing Credit: A collection of occasional papers relating to the FEU proposal for a post-16 credit accumulation and transfer framework*, FEU, London

Gray, J, Jesson, D and Tranmer, M (1993) *Boosting Post-16 Participation in Full-Time Education: A study of some key factors in England and Wales, Youth Cohort Study No 20*, Employment Department, Sheffield

Headmasters' and Headmistresses' Conference (HMC) (2002) *Response of the Headmasters' and Headmistresses' Conference to the Government's 14–19 Green Paper*, HMC, Leicester

Higham, J, Sharp, P and Yeomans, D (2002) *Changing the 14–19 School Curriculum in England: Lessons from successive reforms,* research report to the ESRC, University of Leeds

Hodgson, A and Spours, K (eds) (1997) *Dearing and Beyond: 14–19 qualifications, frameworks and systems*, Kogan Page, London

Hodgson, A and Spours, K (1999) *New Labour's Educational Agenda: Issues and policies for education and training from 14+*, Kogan Page, London

Hodgson, A and Spours, K (2000) *An Historical and Analytical Examination of the Concept of a Graduation Certificate Lifelong Learning Group*, Institute of Education, University of London

Hodgson, A and Spours, K (2003) *Beyond A Levels: Curriculum 2000 and the reform of 14–19 qualifications*, Kogan Page, London

Howieson, C, Raffe, D, Spours, K and Young, M (1997) Unifying academic and vocational learning: the state of the debate in England and Scotland, *Journal of Education and Work*, **10** (1), pp 5–35

Jenkins, C and David, J (1996) *The Welsh Baccalaureate*, Institute of Welsh Affairs, Cardiff

Joint Associations' Curriculum Group (JACG) (1997) *The Next Step Towards a New Curriculum Framework Post-16*, JACG, Wigan

Labour Party (1996) *Aiming Higher: Labour's proposals for the reform of the 14–19 curriculum*, Labour Party, London

Labour Party (1997) *Labour Party General Election Manifesto 1997: Because Britain deserves better,* Labour Party, London

National Association of Headteachers (NAHT) (1995) *Proposals on 14–19 Education*, NAHT, Haywards Heath

NAHT (2002) *14–19 Green Paper: Extending opportunities, raising standards: The proposal for a Matriculation Diploma*, NAHT, Haywards Heath

National Association of Teachers in Further and Higher Education (NATFHE) (2002) *NATFHE response to the Green Paper 14–19: Extending opportunities, raising standards*, NATFHE, London

National Audit Office (NAO) (2002) *Improving Student Achievement in English Higher Education*, NAO, London

National Commission on Education (NCE) (1995) *Learning to Succeed: The way ahead*, Report of Paul Hamlyn Foundation National Commission on Education, NCE, London

National Union of Teachers (NUT) (1995) *14–19 Strategy for the Future: The road to equality*, NUT, London

NUT (2002) *Submission from the NUT to the DfES Consultation on the Green Paper 14–19: Extending opportunities, raising standards*, NUT, London

Qualifications and Curriculum Authority (QCA) (1998) *An Overarching Certificate at Advanced Level: Research specification*, QCA, London

QCA/Council for the Curriculum, Examinations and Assessment (CCEA)/ Qualifications, Curriculum and Assessment Authority for Wales (ACCAC)(2000) *National Consultation on Proposals for a Graduation Certificate: Report summary*, QCA, London

Royal Society (1991) *Beyond GCSE: A report by a Working Group of the Royal Society's Education Committee*, Royal Society, London

Social Exclusion Unit (SEU) (1999) *Bridging the Gap: New opportunities for 16–18 year olds not in education, employment or training*, SEU, London

Steedman, H (2002) *Employers, Employment and the Labour Market,* position paper for Nuffield Foundation 14–19 Education Seminar, Nuffield Foundation, London

Steedman, H and Green, A (1997) *International Comparison of Skill Supply and Demand*, Centre for Economic Performance, London School of Economics

Tomlinson, M (2002a) *Report on Outcomes of Review of A Level Grading*, DfES, London

Tomlinson, M (2002b) *Inquiry into A Level Standards: Final report*, DfES, London

Young, M and Spours, K (1996) *Post-Compulsory Curriculum and Qualifications: Options for change*, Institute of Education, University of London and Centre for Education and Industry, University of Warwick

Index

NB: page numbers in *italics* indicate figures or tables